SHADOWS
IN THE NAVE

A Guide to the HAUNTED CHURCHES of England

Paul Adams,
Eddie Brazil & Peter Underwood

The History Press

For objective ghost hunters, everywhere.

First published 2011

The History Press
The Mill, Brimscombe Port
Stroud, Gloucestershire, GL5 2QG
www.thehistorypress.co.uk

© Paul Adams, Eddie Brazil and Peter Underwood, 2011

The right of Paul Adams, Eddie Brazil and Peter Underwood
to be identified as the Authors of this work has been asserted
in accordance with the Copyrights, Designs and Patents Act 1988.

British Library Cataloguing in Publication Data.
A catalogue record for this book is available from the British Library.

ISBN 978 0 7524 5920 2

Typesetting and origination by The History Press
Printed in Great Britain

CONTENTS

AUTHORS' NOTE

The churches and abbeys of England: nearly a thousand years of human history, drama, legend, spirituality, conflict – and ghosts; for surely if any psychic echo of these times and experiences were to survive then it would be here, permeating the stones and atmosphere of these buildings, both great and small, raised for worship and which have overseen the lives of countless human beings before ultimately receiving their mortal remains as a prelude to the great journey into the unknown that inescapably we must all face one day.

Ghosts and hauntings can be a controversial subject and the idea of a haunted church even more so. Where do these ghosts come from? How can it happen that a building specifically constructed as a sanctuary for the living can become a repository for unquiet souls after death? Are these hauntings evidence for human survival or simply imprints of the past, completely autonomous that exist due to laws of which at present organised science is in ignorance? We simply do not know the answers – at the moment. As to why these familiar and holy buildings can become associated with the supernatural and with what we are wont to call today paranormal activity, some thoughts and answers to these issues and questions are included in the Introduction.

This book contains accounts of seventy-five allegedly haunted English church buildings and we have tried to write it in a way that gives as much variety as possible, both in the choice of the buildings themselves and to their ghosts – abbeys and priories have been included as well as parish churches and chapels and these have been further selected to represent the many and varied types of supernormal phenomena reported as occurring over time – haunting apparitions, crisis ghosts, timeslips, phantasms of the living, poltergeists, as well as occultism and even devil worship.

For organisation of entries, the country has been divided into six broad areas – London and Suburbs, the South East, the South West, Eastern counties, the Midlands and the North – with the South East having the most representation as to the number of haunted buildings included in its remit. For the content of each church entry we have tried to include reference to any specific historical associations together with details of the style and architecture of the building as well as accounts of the reported hauntings. To make this a practical guide as well as a reference work, each entry includes a footnote giving an Ordnance Survey reference plus relevant directions and location information. In order to extend the scope of the work, an appendix includes brief notes on a further forty churches that for various reasons have not been included in the main text but will still be of interest to both the casual and the serious ghost hunter.

The concept of 'ghost hunting' as a division of psychical research has undergone enormous changes in the past twenty years. An increase in the general public's acceptance of ghosts and the paranormal has coincided with the development of cable and satellite broadcasting, the Internet revolution and television reality programmes to create a phenomenon which can be labelled as 'psychic entertainment', something unheard of or unprecedented in the history of paranormal research. The future of this new and at times uneasy relationship between ghost hunting and the media, one could almost say the integrity of ghost hunting as a whole, depends on many factors, one of which is how the researchers of today and tomorrow go about their investigations and act responsibly on the information included in books such as the one you are reading now.

Be that as it may, the following pages include a broad and interesting range of supernatural encounters – be prepared to meet spectral knights, ghostly horses and riders, phantom animals including revenant dogs and a supernatural rabbit as well as Civil War ghosts, apparitions of priests and organists, the shade of a Second World War bomber pilot as well as the obligatory phantom monks and nuns.

With such a rich collection of ghosts we hope that you enjoy reading this book as much as we have enjoyed compiling it.

Paul Adams, Eddie Brazil and Peter Underwood
Luton, Hazlemere and London
January 2011

HAUNTED CHURCHES
AN INTRODUCTION

In the autumn of 1968, aged thirteen, I (Eddie Brazil) moved with my family to the Camberwell district of south east London. Back in those days, before games consoles and twenty-four hour cable and satellite broadcasting had anchored a generation of youngsters in front of a flat screen television, my new found friends and I were required to find our own means of fun and amusement. This usually entailed playing outside – in all weathers – either kicking a ball around the local park or exploring further afield on our bicycles. The late 1960s, however, saw whole areas of London's crumbling Victorian housing stock being swept away to be replaced with sprawling modern estates and tower blocks. Fortunately for us in the interim between the last tenants moving out and the arrival of the demolition men these abandoned houses became our temporary playgrounds. They became our castles, battlefields, spaceships or any number of imaginary worlds that our adventures required. Yet of all the places I recall from my childhood which held the most excitement and opportunity for us to run wild, the abandoned parish church of St George stands out the most.

Located in Wells Way, Camberwell, but looking like a throw-out from ancient Athens, St George's was one of a number of places of worship known as Commissioners' Churches. Built in the early nineteenth century in the Greek or Perpendicular style, these buildings were a fearful government's response to the change in population movement brought about by the necessities of the Industrial Revolution. The exodus from the countryside had resulted in slums quickly developing in the grimy cities and the centuries-old rural communities which had been established around the village church were now scattered within the squalor of the industrialised centres. In 1818, concerned that such hardships and the break up of traditional village life would cause the populace to lose their religion, Parliament passed an Act to construct new places for worship. This was seen not only as a means to save souls but also a thanksgiving to God for rescuing England from wicked French freethinking (the memory of Napoleon and the French Revolution still lingered) and a method of halting the rising tide of dissent and preserving social cohesion.

Inevitably, by the late 1960s the world had become a different place. Population change, social mobility and a gradual decline in churchgoing had resulted in St George's echoing, galleried interior being attended infrequently by only a handful of parishioners. Eventually it fell into disrepair and in 1969 the ecclesiastical authorities decided to close the building. The parishioner's loss became, for my mates and me throughout the day, our chief place of adventure and refuge, our clubhouse where we would often escape the wagging fingers of our parents. Yet once the sun had gone down it would take on another face. The church's cavernous nave, numerous forgotten rooms, staircases, unused attics and cobwebbed lofts became areas of uninviting shadows where one did not care to be alone. A building that had once resounded to the joyous sound of uplifting hymns and thunderous sermons was transformed into a place of silent gloom.

At night the church's eeriness only increased. It became the perfect place to test one's nerve for we would challenge each other to enter the darkened building alone and climb the stairs to a room near the tower; once there we had to shine a light from the window to prove we had accomplished the task. On foggy autumn evenings, gathered on top of the high wall surrounding

The entrance to St George's Church, Camberwell, in 1974. *(Photograph by Eddie Brazil)*

the church, another challenge was to run across the graveyard, dodging the headstones to touch the far wall that separated St George's from the disused canal. It was here that the ghost of 'Old Charlie' was supposed to walk. He was a vagrant who was said to have wandered the streets of Camberwell with his coat over his head, a machete in his hand, pushing an old pram, and tradition said that he did away with himself by drowning in the canal. If one heard the squeak of a rusty pram wheel it was a sure sign that Charlie's ghost was abroad and if he caught you the cold water would be your fate. The prospect of the vagrant's macabre spectre reaching out to get us made the run across the churchyard all the more nerve-racking.

Yet perhaps the ultimate dare and test of bravery was to take up the challenge to enter the darkened crypt armed only with a torch or candle and peer into one of the many still-occupied coffins which lay stacked, wine cellar fashion, in the brick alcoves. Following the closure of the church, the local council and the Church authorities endlessly deliberated over what to do with the remains of the great and good of the neighbourhood who had been laid to rest below the church in the preceding 150 years. While the powers that be delayed a decision, the really fearless hooligans of the area broke into the crypt in the mistaken belief that the inhabitants had been laid to rest still wearing their finest jewellery. The opening forced by these modern-day graverobbers remained unrepaired and provided the way in for those tough and bold enough to venture alone into the farthest corner of the burial chamber.

One winter's night in 1970 it was my turn to prove how unafraid I was. While my pals waited secure sitting on top of the churchyard wall, I dropped down into the yard and with the feeble light of the street lamps half illuminating the way, I proceeded over to the gaping black hole that was the entrance. With a torch I had taken without permission from my father's toolbox, I made my way into the interior. I can still recall over forty years later my trepidation and anxiety as I groped my way in the musty darkness, the torch creating crazy flickering shadows on the walls, to the far end where a coffin rested with its lid half-skewed open. The test was to lift the lid and peer in at the corpse for ten seconds and then turn off the torch, the idea being that even though the crypt would be in total blackness, an image of the decayed face would implant itself on one's mind, making the frantic exit from the catacomb all the more unpleasant.

The ruinous interior of St George's Church, Camberwell during the 1960s – an atmospheric playground of the imagination now refurbished into flats. *(Photograph by Eddie Brazil)*

Yet I didn't need to turn off my torch after the required ten seconds for, on lifting the coffin lid and gazing down horrified at the occupant, I was astonished to see that the face of the corpse, far from being decayed down to a skull, was in fact still almost recognisable. The eye sockets were blackened holes but the skin, bluish in colour, was stretched taut over the features. A thin nose protruded and scanty wisps of hair lay across the forehead. However, what I recall most, and what still sends a shiver down my spine, was the mouth of the cadaver, slightly open in a sickening blackened-teeth smile with the head turned towards me in a gleeful manner, as if to say, 'You have entered this place – now we are going to get you!'

In my fright I dropped the torch, extinguishing the light, and fled. As I exited from the crypt one of my pals added to my terror by shouting words to the effect that Charlie's ghost was coming. Not surprisingly I cleared the churchyard wall in lightening fashion and ran wildly after my friends, not once turning to look back. At a safe distance from the church we all stopped breathless with fear and it was only then I realised that in my flight I had dropped my father's torch, which now lay on the floor of the crypt next to the half-open coffin. The thought of entering the church again to retrieve the torch filled me with dread and I reasoned that punishment from my father for taking his property and losing it was far more tolerable than the horrors my imagination might conjure up if I returned to the catacomb of St George's Church.

Inevitably that night I suffered nightmares in which the corpse from the crypt pursued me around the church and, not surprisingly, the church's appeal as a place for excitement and adventure wasn't the same for me after my experience. Even during the day in the company of my friends, the echoing building seemed to have become a place of menace, and if my route home after dark took me past St George's I would break into a run, not once looking over at the towering entrance or shadowy graveyard. And yet I must admit that even if I hadn't had the unsettling experience of encountering the corpse in the crypt, my attitude to this church – and any church in fact, particularly an abandoned one illuminated by a full moon and in a ruinous state surrounded by an untended graveyard – would have remained the same, an icon to feed the imagination with all manner of dark fancies.

Where (the three authors ask) does this macabre, ghostly association with churches come from? Arguably it is only churches in the western Christian tradition which seem to have acquired this sense of mystery and ghoulishness – it is hard to view or imagine a mosque, a synagogue or a Hindu temple in the same way.

We all recognise a church as a place of architectural grandness and beauty, where the mystery and majesty of religion is proclaimed in the physical properties of wood, stone and glass; a place of peace and introspection, of marriage, baptisms and religious instruction that was at one time the centre and focus of a whole community. But it is also where the dead are laid to rest, where their memorials ultimately lean and lie forgotten in unvisited graveyards; where the walls of the church interior are adorned with the iconography of death, of images of sinners dragged to hell and faces of grotesque gargoyles leer down from above. And it is a place, as Dickens observed in his short story *The Chimes*, where not many people would care to sleep at night and alone:

For the night-wind has a dismal trick of wandering round and round a building of that sort, and moaning as it goes; and of trying, with its unseen hand, the windows and the doors; and seeking out some crevices by which to enter. And when it has got in; as one not finding what it seeks, whatever that may be, it wails and howls to issue forth again: and not content with stalking through the aisles, and gliding round and round the pillars, and tempting the deep organ, soars up to the roof, and strives to rend the rafters: then flings itself despairingly upon the stones below, and passes, muttering, into the vaults. Anon, it comes up stealthily, and creeps along the walls, seeming to read, in whispers, the Inscriptions sacred to the Dead…It has an awful voice, that wind at Midnight, singing in a church!

Further reference points exist in the ghostly fiction of other writers, such as M.R. James and W.F. Harvey. James in particular was adept at using the very fabric of the church as triggers in his stories – tombs, carved choir stalls, stained-glass windows and crypts are all employed with great effect to trap those foolish enough to cross the supernatural Rubicon. Like Dickens, James understood the literary potential of an echoing church in the late winter dusk or the dead of night. Authors such as James, Dickens and Poe were in essence responding to a tradition which had emerged during the eighteenth century. It was a movement that had at its source not irrefutable cast iron evidence of the reality of the paranormal but rather a cultural, spiritual, romantic and in some ways social necessity, one which had its roots in one word – Gothic.

The word 'Gothic' was originally meant to be derogatory. It was most likely first used in the 1500s by Giorgio Vasari, an Italian historian, painter, writer and architect who looked upon the style of the Middle Ages as unrefined and barbaric, too remote from the aesthetic proportions and shapes of Classical art. Today it is hard for us to understand such a view, especially when we stand in the nave of one of our many great cathedrals and marvel in open mouthed awe at the magnificence of the architecture and boldness of the construction. At the time Vasari was writing, Italy had experienced a century of building in the Classical architectural vocabulary revived in the Renaissance, seen as the finite evidence of a new golden age of learning and refinement. The Renaissance had then overtaken Europe, overturning a system of culture that, prior to the advent of printing, was almost entirely focused on the Church and was perceived, in retrospect, as a period of ignorance and superstition

Five centuries before Vasari made his disparaging remarks, the architecture of the eleventh-century church in Europe was Romanesque. Although there are important affinities linking it with Rome, it was a compound of many influences – Roman, Viking, Celtic, and Byzantine – whose chief characteristic was its solid massiveness: thick walls, small windows, sturdy round pillars and semi-circular arches all combined to counteract the outward thrust of the vault. In twelfth-century France, however, a new style began to emerge. The pointed arch, possibly introduced by returning Crusaders from the Holy Land or more probably as a natural development of Romanesque, saw its first flowering at the Cathedral of St Denis in 1140. The new design, known as Opus Francigenum or 'French Style', soon flourished all over Europe and crossed the Channel to England with the spread of the French monastic orders. In 1174, William of Sens rebuilt the east part of Canterbury Cathedral in the Gothic style.

The chief structural benefit of Gothicism was the greater strength of the pointed arch with its opportunities for a more flexible design; a greater emphasis on lightness and refinement, moving away from the heaviness of Romanesque work. Walls became thinner, naves higher, window openings larger, allowing for adornment with stained glass and columns, capitals and mouldings were embellished with the skills of the medieval masons. The walls of cathedrals and churches were aglow with paintings and images of the Saints and the diffused glimmer of candles which bathed the interior in a soft sacred radiance. A Gothic cathedral came to symbolise in wood, stone and glass the beauty, mystery and magnificence of God on Earth. It would also become a microcosm of the hierarchal structure of medieval society. Those with the wealth and prestige to have their own chantry chapels, tombs and memorials nearest the altar would be first in line for Heaven. The chancel screen divided the educated clergy from the illiterate laity who stood in the nave and presiding over all was the King, answerable only to God. For 500 years, Gothic architecture came to dominate not only the religious but also the secular and domestic buildings in Britain.

The sixteenth century in Europe was one of great change. Martin Luther's protest in 1517 at the corruption of the Catholic Church was the spark which ignited the Reformation that soon spread across the continent. In England it was probably the greatest upheaval in the life and history of the church and was to have many lasting effects on church buildings. These effects were increased by the fact that chronologically the Reformation coincided with the arrival in England of the new ideas of the Renaissance, with its emphasis on classical study and art forms.

Henry VIII's break with Rome, the Dissolution of the Monasteries, his son, Edward VI's embracing of the teachings of Martin Luther and the establishment of Protestantism all pointed to a nation which was moving on and away from the superstition and ignorance of the medieval era. Gothic architecture served only to be a reminder and embodiment of the old practices.

By the eighteenth century, enlightenment began to sweep across Europe. It advocated that reason was the primary source for legitimacy and authority and questioned the traditional institutions, customs and morals of the day with a strong belief in rationality and science. The architecture of the Age of Reason was Neo-Classical, a style and manner which in its clearness, elegance, emotional restraint and regularity of form mirrored the ideas and beliefs of the rationalists However, just as Gothic had had its detractors in the sixteenth century, so too would the philosophy and architecture of the eighteenth in the form of the Romantics.

The Romantic Movement grew out of a revolt against the prescribed rules of classicism, a desire to return to nature and the exaltation of the senses and emotions over understanding and intellect. It was also a rejection of rationalism, the theory that only reason alone, unaided by experience, can arrive at basic truth regarding the world, emphasising emotions as horror and fear and the feelings experienced in confronting the sublimity of untamed nature. The Romantics' riposte was through art, music, poetry, architecture and literature. The Graveyard Poetry of the early 1700s, such as Robert Blair's *The Grave* (1743) and Edward Young's *Night Thoughts* (1749) dwelt upon the melancholy pleasures and fears of the tomb, of the night and of ghosts. In 1764, Horace Walpole published *The Castle of Otranto*, considered the blueprint for what would come to be known as Gothic literature. There was also Ann Radcliffe's *The Mysteries of Udolpho* (1794), Regina Maria Roche's *The Children of the Abbey* (1794) and *Clermont* (1798); novels complete with castle dungeons, ivy-clad ruins, moonlit graveyards, churches, abbeys and white-sheeted spectres.

The ghosts and phantoms of the Romantic imagination could not flourish within the conformity and logic of the architecture of classical rationalism. Their natural dwelling place was the style of the early fourteenth century – decorated Gothic, the spiritual home of not only the writers and artists of the Romantic period, but also the preferred form of the revival within the Church of England which began in 1840 and which ran parallel with interest in medievalism as a reaction against the horrors of industrialisation. To Augustus Pugin, the English-born architect and theorist, to be Christian was to be Gothic and the mystery of sublime and spiritual fulfilment could only be truly experienced among the soaring pinnacles, columns and spires of the architecture of the medievalists.

For modern investigators and the psychical researchers of today, the paranormal has become a complex presentation of imagination and reality, fact and fantasy, which is no better illustrated than in the subject of church hauntings where Romanticism and parapsychology meet head on. In 1923 Alfred Watkins, a Herefordshire brewer, put forward the now familiar theory that sites such as standing stones, tumuli, hill tops and churches were all connected by a system of 'ley' lines that could be established by dowsing. Thomas Lethbridge (1901-1971) was keeper of Anglo Saxon antiquities at Cambridge University as well as a writer and parapsychologist. He expanded Watkins' concept and held the view that Christian churches were built at a chosen location not only as a way of converting those who were still attached to the old religions but because it was recognised in these pre-scientific days that the ground itself was 'sacred'. The countless stone circles and ancient places of worship scattered throughout Britain, such as Stonehenge and the Merry Maidens, are sites where Lethbridge, who was an expert dowser, detected powerful forces very much like a mild electric current. He theorised that ancient priests had recognised this Earth force and ordered the buildings to be placed there to absorb and conduct this power.

As well as the location and physical properties of church locations as an explanation for what creates conditions conducive to experiencing paranormal phenomena, there are several other theories that have been put forward as to why people do see ghosts, not just in churches but wherever people live and congregate, and a number of these will be encountered in this book: mental imprint manifestations, atmospheric photograph ghosts, crisis apparition, ghosts of the living as well as the poltergeist enigma – the ghost organist at St John's Church Torquay, Westminster Abbey's First World War phantom soldier, the ghostly monks at Beaulieu, as well as the ghostly laughter at Stoke Dry, could be due to one or a combination of all these factors; at present we simply do not know.

We have already made mention of the master English ghost story writer Montague Rhodes (M.R.) James and perhaps, as you begin to explore our collection of haunted English churches, it is appropriate to leave the last word to him as recorded by the Irish diplomat and writer, Shane Leslie:

> Shortly before his death I asked him what he really thought on the subject, since he had written better ghost-stories than any man living. He answered: 'Depend upon it! Some of these things are so, but we do not know the rules!'

Map of England, showing the locations of the churches featured in this book.

1. ST PETER AD VINCULA, TOWER OF LONDON

The unusual dedication 'ad vincula' – meaning in chains – refers to the apostle's miraculous release from his first imprisonment in Jerusalem. Macaulay said, 'In truth there is no sadder spot on the earth' and he was probably right. The dead at Westminster Abbey and St Paul's and many other places are celebrated for their genius, their virtue, their achievement, but here one is reminded of the darkest part of human nature and human destiny; with the inconstancy, the ingratitude, the cowardice, the cruelty and the misery of fallen greatness and of blighted fame. Here are buried prematurely the bleeding relics of men and women executed nearby, many subjected to undeserved ignominy – small wonder that something of the awful and savage triumph of implacable enemies lingers here and has been witnessed in ghostly manifestations over the years.

The body of John Fisher, Bishop of Rochester, was stripped by the executioner and left naked to the common gaze until night fell, when two soldiers raised the mangled corpse with their halbards and carried it away for burial. Anne Boleyn's body was thrown into a common chest intended for arrows, and there were other shameful infamies.

Among those buried here are Sir Thomas More, Lord Chancellor and author of *Utopia*, executed on a charge of high treason in 1535; Thomas Cromwell, Earl of Essex, once enormously powerful, accused of treason and beheaded in 1540; Margaret, Countess of Salisbury, daughter of the Duke of Clarence who, at the age of seventy-one had to be forcibly carried to the scaffold in 1541; Queen Katherine Howard in 1542; Lady Jane Grey, England's 'nine day queen', beheaded with her husband in 1554; John Rotier, who designed the picture of Britannia used on our coins for 300 years, in 1703, but at least he did not die by the executioner's axe. Here also are the remains of Sir Thomas Overbury, poisoned while a prisoner in the Tower in 1613; Judge George Jeffreys, Lord High Chancellor of England, who presided over the Bloody Assizes (1685) when 300 victims were drawn and quartered and 1,000 transported as slaves; later he was responsible for committing seven bishops to the Tower, where he himself died in 1689; his remains were later removed to St Mary Aldermanbury Church in the City.

A remarkable entry in the burial register in 1587 states that one William Foxley, a Potmaker at the Mint, was buried on 4 May and remained for fourteen days and fifteen nights when he was found to be asleep and he lived for a further forty-one years. It was noted that Foxley 'could not be wakened with pricking, cramping, or otherwise burning whatsoever, till the first day of term, which was fourteen days and fifteen nights'. Physicians, learned men, even Henry VIII, looked into the matter but could find no reason for the prolonged slumber.

The persistent ghost of Anne Boleyn, apart from being seen near The Queen's House at the Tower, where she was confined for the last four days before her execution, has been reportedly seen heading a procession of departed nobility, moving down the aisle of the church. Certainly

Anne Boleyn, second wife to Henry VIII – her ghost is said to lead a spectral procession of departed nobility through the church of St Peter ad Vincula.

Anne and many of the others partaking would have known the Tower Chapel; the present building, incidentally, replaces the original which was destroyed by fire in 1512.

A long-standing story tells of a Tower guard making his rounds one evening, accompanied by a sentry, when he noticed a light showing in the chapel. He pointed this out to the sentry and asked what it meant. The sentry replied that he did not know what it meant but he had seen it often, and stranger things too. The officer procured a ladder and, placing it against the chapel wall – the chapel being locked – he climbed up and looked into the still lighted-up window and he never forgot what he saw.

Walking slowly down the aisle moved a stately procession of knights and ladies in ancient costume and in front walked an elegant female whose face and dress and bearing resembled portraits the officer had seen of Queen Anne Boleyn! After repeatedly pacing the small chapel the entire procession promptly vanished and with it the light that had first attracted his attention, and the whole place was plunged into darkness.

Other reports have told of Anne's ghost being encountered on its own, both inside and outside the chapel of St Peter ad Vincula, usually at dusk, when the haunted Tower of London comes to life. There is one well-verified account of a sentry encountering what he described as a headless woman wearing a dress similar to that worn by Anne Boleyn in famous portraits. Receiving no response to his challenge he lunged forward with his bayonet only to find it met no resistance and the figure vanished. The sentry promptly fainted on the spot and he was subsequently charged with being drunk on duty; but at the court martial he was acquitted when other sentries

The church of St Peter ad Vincula, considered to be the most haunted part of the Tower of London. *(Photograph by Eddie Brazil)*

and officers swore they had experienced similar encounters, in the open parts of the Tower and inside the quiet chapel of St Peter.

On one occasion when Peter Underwood was at the Tower making enquiries about the ghosts and ghostly activity he talked individually with several Yeoman warders (in particular Yeoman Warder Geoffrey Abbot who had many strange experiences at the Tower and wrote several books about the ghosts there). Most of the Yeoman Warders regarded St Peter ad Vincula as the most haunted part of the undeniably haunted Tower of London; probably the most ghost-ridden collection of buildings in the world. And Peter was told of two recent visitors, in broad daylight, who accosted resident Yeoman Warders to ask whether a pageant or exhibition of some kind was taking place in the chapel of St Peter as they thought they would have a look around the chapel, but when they entered they became aware of a procession of people in various costumes walking down the aisle. Thinking they were interrupting a spectacle or rehearsal or film of some kind, they had quickly left the strangely quiet chapel. The Yeoman Warders were immediately interested and hastened back with them to the chapel, which they found deserted and silent. Then the Warders told the visitors of the occasional reports of a ghostly procession in that little chapel, so full of poignant and seemingly ineffaceable memories.

 [Grid Ref: TQ 336 805] On the north bank of the River Thames adjacent to Tower Bridge (A100); nearest London Underground station is Tower Hill.

2. CHRIST CHURCH NEWGATE/GREYFRIARS CHURCHYARD, CITY OF LONDON

The inexorable march of time affects in many ways the haunted landscape of the British Isles – haunted houses and buildings are demolished; sites where ghosts are known to walk become built on or redeveloped, and roads with paranormal associations are widened or renamed. Hauntings themselves are subject to change although, as we have made mention, ghost story master M.R. James famously said, we simply do not know the rules behind them – 'psychic battery'-type ghosts appear to run down or fade out with time while other phenomena is wholly spontaneous, manifesting once or twice over a certain period, sometimes only for a day or often over a number of years, after which it is seemingly gone forever. How many people walking daily along Newgate Street in the heart of the bustling City of London realise that Greyfriars churchyard, dwarfed by vast modern buildings and now almost imperceptible amongst continuing redevelopment, is a haunted site that at one time boasted multiple ghosts?

A large medieval church was constructed here by Franciscan monks in the early fourteenth century. These were the Grey Friars and their conventual church was an immense building containing over eleven separate altars. Asset stripping in the years following the Dissolution resulted in the church loosing many of its internal features, particularly tomb marble, as monuments were dismantled and the materials sold off, but despite much damage it continued to be used as a place of worship. With the establishment of Christ's Hospital in the sixteenth century the former Friary became the principle church for the Bluecoat School and from this point on was known as Christ Church Greyfriars. Having stood for 350 years, the building was totally destroyed in early September 1666 by the Great Fire of London.

Christ Church Greyfriars was one of nearly fifty churches in the City of London, most famous of which is St Paul's Cathedral a short distance to the south, which was reconstructed by Sir Christopher Wren in the decades following the Great Fire. Wren's church was smaller than the original Franciscan building – on plan it covered the east side of the old church and the original nave became the new churchyard. The new Christ Church, including a west tower, was completed in 1687, but it was to be just over twenty-five years before the steeple that can be seen today was finally added. The church interior was noted for its elaborate carvings and the building became a focal point for music and culture in the City – both Samuel Wesley, the 'English Mozart', and Felix Mendelssohn played the organ here. A vestry house was constructed against the south side of the church in 1760 and for the next 150 years Christ Church Greyfriars continued to be used by the Bluecoat School up until the beginning of the 1900s.

On 29 December 1940, the church took a direct hit from a German incendiary during one of the most devastating nights of the London Blitz. Although the tower and walls survived, the interior was completely gutted, leaving the church a roofless shell; the only fitting recovered from the flames and known to have survived was the carved font cover rescued by a passing postman. Today the church lives on as a safe ruin although Wren's tower, now a Grade I listed building, has been converted into a private apartment; the south and east walls have been demolished, the latter for road widening in the 1960s, but the north wall with its English Baroque window arches survives and the nave and churchyard, the former resting place of four queens and over 600 people of nobility, are now a public park.

Four ghosts are associated with this remarkable building, the oldest of which would seem to be the apparition of a monk dressed in the original russet-brown cowled habit of the Franciscan order which was subsequently changed to the characteristic grey habits of their founder some time after their arrival in England. The figure has been seen during autumn time, most often in the early hours of the morning, walking in the old churchyard. Another phantom has also been seen here, but unlike the serene aura of the unknown Friar this ghost, that of Sister Elizabeth Barton, the 'Holy Maid of Kent', is said to be a wild and restless figure. A Catholic nun, she was sent to Tyburn in 1534 after opposing Henry VIII's divorce from Catherine of Aragon.

Christ Church Greyfriars in the City of London; the churchyard is reputed to be haunted by at least four ghosts. *(Photograph by Eddie Brazil)*

Barton predicted that the King would die within a few months if he went ahead with his marriage to Anne Boleyn, but these inaccurate 'divine revelations' were enough to get her charged and convicted of high treason and she was buried the day after her execution in the churchyard at Christ Church Greyfriars.

A second person executed at Tyburn who also walked again at Greyfriars is Lady Agnes Hungerford, who died in 1523 after being found guilty of 'procurement and abetting' in the murder of her former husband John Cotell. Said to have been one of the most beautiful women in Tudor England, her ghost apparently retained this beauty and was recognised one summer evening by a night-watchman, who fled in terror and resigned his post the next day. How often she has been seen since these times is unclear.

Christ Church Greyfriars is also the resting place of another unquiet spirit, that of Isabella, the 'She-Wolf of France'. The wife of Edward II, she was ultimately buried in the churchyard in her wedding dress together with a casket containing Edward's preserved heart. Neglected by Edward she had returned to France and together with her lover, Roger Mortimer, had led an army to England in 1326 which successfully deposed the King. Edward, a homosexual, was murdered by servants of Isabella and Mortimer, who it is believed ran a red-hot rod into his rectum while he was being suffocated with a mattress. After Edward III had Mortimer hanged, Isabella spent her remaining years in retirement. She died on 22 August 1358 and was interred in the old Franciscan church, the site of which, like a number of others, she is said to still frequent.

 [Grid Ref: TQ 320 813] Christ Church Greyfriars is located north-west of the junction with Newgate Street and Edward Street in the City of London.

3. ST JAMES'S CHURCH, GARLICK HILL, CITY OF LONDON

There has been a church here since at least the time of William the Conqueror and its known rectors date from 1259. It was destroyed in the Great Fire of 1666 and the present church was built by Sir Christopher Wren between 1676 and 1682 and nicknamed 'Wren's Lantern' on account of the clear glass in its arched windows and clerestoried roof.

Perhaps more than any other London church it was connected with the shipping trade, for the steep hill nearby, Dowgate Hill, was once Downe Gate, the course of the old Wall Brook, referred to by Ben Jonson as 'Dowgate torrents falling into Thames'. Directly opposite the narrow lane leads to Queenshythe Wharf, at one time the chief landing-place in London for foreign goods and London's oldest harbour. The queen in the name was Isabella, the French wife of King John. One of St James's interesting features is the structurally separate chancel; there is also the graceful spire which rises to 125 feet. St James's has in fact the tallest city centre church interior. Here may be seen ancient sword rests, a wig stand and wonderful carving.

Six of London's medieval mayors are buried here and much more recently another burial took place – of a kind. For many years this church was famous for the ancient mummified body of a young man discovered beneath the chancel before the Great Fire. There was no way of knowing who he was or how he got there but, regarded as a curiosity, the body was placed in a glass-panelled coffin and available for display in a cupboard in the vestibule.

Known as 'Old Jimmy Garlick', his spirit seemed to have resented his treatment and not infrequently his unique ghost was glimpsed inside the church. It is related that an American lady visited the church with her two sons and when the older boy looked up a staircase inside the church he saw the figure of a man, clad in a winding sheet, standing erect with his hands crossed. The figure resembled a dried-up corpse and the terrified boy ran back to his mother and dragged her out of the church. The boy had just been up the stairway and it had been deserted.

The mummified body of 'Old Jimmy Garlick', whose shrouded ghost has been seen on several occasions inside St James's Church, Garlick Hill; the cadaver is now no longer on display. *(Peter Underwood Collection)*

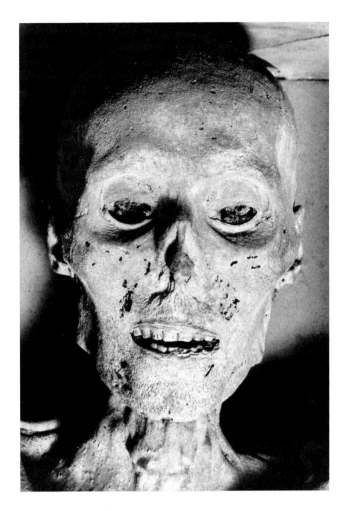

Some people think that Old Jimmy Garlick is an embalmed Roman general; others that he is the first Mayor of London; and still others that he is Belin, a legendary King of Britain. In 1942 a bomb shaved the case containing the body and penetrated into the vaults below, but failed to explode. After that the restless ghost of Old Jimmy was reportedly seen more frequently inside the church by visitors and the clergy, sometimes shrouded and sometimes un-shrouded, and new manifestations were reported such as the unexplained movement of objects and inexplicable sounds that echoed through the church, sounds that seemed to originate in one area and the next moment from an entirely different direction.

Some years ago, Peter Underwood was shown the cadaver by Prebendary D.C. Mossman, but not long afterwards it was decided to give Old Jimmy a decent burial. Once the interment rites were read over him and he was no longer the object of immodest curiosity it was felt that he would finally rest but within recent months there have been reports of a fleeting glimpse being caught of a shrouded and unexplained figure seen in the shadowy corners of St James's Church, Garlick Hill.

 [Grid Ref: TQ 324 808] Garlick Hill is due south of Cannon Street close to Mansion House Underground station.

4. ST MAGNUS THE MARTYR, CITY OF LONDON

A church has stood on this site since the early twelfth century. Its rare dedication was once thought to be to St Magnus, Bishop of Caesarea in modern day Israel, who suffered martyrdom in AD 276 under the Emperor Aurelian, although it is more probably to St Magnus, a Norse Lord of Orkney, who was not martyred in the true sense but executed in 1165 for the 'un-Viking' quality of showing mercy and compassion to his foes. The church contained many notable memorials. Master Mason to Edward III and Richard II, Henry Yevele was laid to rest here in 1400. Miles Coverdale, who was first to translate the Bible into English in 1535 and who would later become Rector of the church, was reinterred in St Magnus after removal from his original resting place in St Bartholomew's by the Exchange following its demolition in 1840.

St Magnus was the second church to be consumed by flames in the Great Fire of London in 1666. Between 1671 and 1687 it was rebuilt in the classical style by Sir Christopher Wren, with a steeple being added in 1706, and the church stood at the end of old London Bridge. The Wren building of the 1670s has had innumerable alterations. Another fire, in 1760, damaged the western end of the church and destroyed several of the houses on the bridge. Instead of repairing the buildings, the opportunity was taken to demolish them all to widen the roadway and ease traffic congestion and at the same time a new pedestrian walkway was built along the eastern side of the bridge. With the other buildings gone, St Magnus blocked the new walkway, so the western end of the church was taken down. Rather than demolish the tower its base was opened out to allow the walkway to pass through it, and the open base of the tower now forms the church porch. The church survived serious damage during the Blitz but, even so, wasn't reopened for worship until June 1951.

Just before the outbreak of the Second World War, the first incidents of paranormal phenomena were reported at St Magnus. The then rector, the Revd H.J. Fynes-Clinton, who had been inducted in 1921, received three independent reports of sightings of a cowled figure in the church and vestry. The witnesses were the wife of a former rector, a verger, and a middle-aged female parishioner. The first sighting by the former rector's wife, Mrs Gallagher, occurred in the main building. She reported seeing a silent figure in a brown habit kneeling beneath a picture of Christ near the tabernacle. Viewing the apparition in profile, Mrs Gallagher was unable to see the face because of the figure's hood. She watched for some seconds before the phantom melted away.

The second sighting took place in the vestry. It was witnessed by a long-time worker at the church, Mrs Few, who had no knowledge of Mrs Gallagher's earlier experience. Sitting alone one afternoon and concentrating on an intricate piece of embroidery, she noticed out of the corner of her eye that someone was standing close by. Observing that the person was wearing a straight cassock-like garment, she assumed that the rector had noiselessly joined her in the room. For some seconds she continued with her stitching. However, on casting a glance towards the silent figure, she saw that the upper part of the form was encased in a cowled hood – but the cowl, which was open towards her, was empty; there was no face. Mrs Few immediately dropped her work and bolted from the vestry to find the rector, who was in the church. Although she was in a state of shock he managed to calm her down and both returned to the vestry but found the room empty.

The apparition was seen on a third occasion by the verger, Mr Ridley, who again was unaware of the previous sightings by Mrs Gallagher and Mrs Few. One day he approached the Revd Fynes-Clinton in an agitated manner shortly after the conclusion of the service. Mr Ridley looked pale and seemed to be in a state of shock. The Reverend asked him what was wrong and, assuring the clergyman he was neither drunk nor of unsound mind, he told of seeing the figure of a monk standing gazing down at a tomb to the right of the altar. Before he could move or cry out the apparition vanished.

The Revd Fynes-Clinton was perplexed. He knew Mr Ridley was a former regular soldier, not given to flights of fancy or indeed easily frightened, but the man had undoubtedly witnessed

The church of St Magnus the Martyr – reports of phenomena here date back to before the outbreak of the Second World War. *(Photograph by Eddie Brazil)*

something which had unnerved him. The tomb where the verger had seen the figure was that of Miles Coverdale, his sepulchre being the only occupied vault left in the crypt. During the late nineteenth century most of the dead that had been laid to rest at St Magnus over the centuries were removed to Brookwood Cemetery in Surrey, once the largest burial ground in the world, containing up to 250,000 bodies.

During the years following the end of the war, news of the haunting of St Magnus came to the attention of paranormal investigators. The Rector made no secret of the fact that he believed the phantom monk was the ghost of Miles Coverdale. Previous experience of strange happenings had stimulated an interest in the paranormal and in July 1951 he gave permission for mediumistic sittings to be carried out at the church, perhaps to ascertain once and for all the identity of the apparition. Initial clairvoyance sessions seemed to confirm the Revd Fynes-Clinton's assumption that the ghost was that of Coverdale and that the monk was haunting the building because he wished his earthly remains to be removed from St Magnus and returned to their original resting place. Contact was also made with 'a little old lady who is very thin and infirm' and who had died five or six years previously. She was tending the tapestries on the altar and was handling the lacework lovingly. The rector immediately recognised this as the former church worker, Mrs Few, who had been startled by the ghostly monk back in the late 1930s. Further séances and automatic writing sessions were carried out at the church during the 1950s, which appeared to show that many other unquiet souls walked within St Magnus. If the ghost of the phantom monk is indeed that of Miles Coverdale, he walks the nave of St Magnus in mourning for his former resting place in vain, for St Bartholomew by the Exchange has long been demolished.

The English Bible translator Miles Coverdale (c.1488-1569), who may be the phantom monk seen inside the church of St Magnus the Martyr on a number of occasions.

On an October morning in 1951, the Revd Fynes-Clinton was preparing for the day's service. Standing by the door into the nave, he was surprised to see a black-clad figure move through the church from the direction of the altar. The form's movements were accompanied by footsteps sounding on hard stone. The shape went behind a pillar and did not reappear. The rector thought it might be the verger, but he too had heard the unaccountable footfalls before the ceremony. Both men were certain that the church was empty at the time and no explanation for the footsteps or the figure in black was found.

 [Grid Ref: TQ 329 805] On the A3211 Lower Thames Street adjacent to London Bridge; the nearest Underground station is Monument.

5. ST MICHAEL'S CHURCH, HIGHGATE, NORTH LONDON

For psychic investigators, ghost hunters and aficionados of the supernatural, the environs of Highgate in North London have had a close association with varied aspects of the paranormal and the occult for many years now. As with the Church of the Blessed Virgin Mary at Clapham on the South Downs, the Georgian church of St Michael's, where the poet Samuel Taylor Coleridge, author of *The Rime of the Ancient Mariner* (1798) and *Christabel* (1797-1800), worshipped and is buried, is not known to have a haunted history, but its immediate surroundings include several noted places with strong ghostly connections, such as Pond Square and Highgate Cemetery, so much so that some comment on this particular area would seem appropriate in a work such as the present one.

St Michael's Church, Highgate, photographed from within the precincts of Highgate Cemetery. *(Photograph by Paul Adams / Eddie Brazil)*

St Michael's was designed by the architect Lewis Vulliamy, a pioneer of the neo-Gothic style. His drawings for the church were exhibited in the Royal Academy in 1831 and it was built the following year, the construction only taking an impressive eleven months to complete. The church stands in South Grove close to The Flask public house in nearby West Hill Park, built in 1663, where it is rumoured underground tunnels were uncovered during refurbishment work in the early 1970s. Behind this building is Pond Square, whose own particular ghost, that of a seventeenth-century featherless chicken, at first seems so outrageous that sceptics of the paranormal must surely take great delight in the thought that rationally-minded people even consider the possibility of such a thing. In fact this is not the first phantom animal we will encounter during our survey of hauntings and a body of evidence does exist to support the case.

The origins of the phantom fowl seemingly date from the late winter of 1626 and involve Sir Francis Bacon, the Elizabethan philosopher, scientist and politician whose death has become associated with the story. According to the most widely reproduced account given by Bacon's friend, the antiquary and writer John Aubrey, Bacon was inspired to carry out an impromptu experiment in refrigeration while being driven through Highgate in an open carriage accompanied by the physician to King James I, Dr Witherborne. Noticing that grass buried under fallen snow still appeared fresh when uncovered by the vehicle's wheels, Bacon halted the carriage on the open green near Pond Square and instructed his coachman to buy a fresh chicken from a poulterer's shop they had passed while travelling up Highgate Hill. Once this had been procured, Sir Francis proceeded to pluck the bird by the roadside, stuff the carcass with handfuls of frozen snow and he completed his field work by surrounding the chicken with more snow inside a sack. Despite ostensibly producing what could be recognised as the world's first frozen chicken, the experiment resulted in Bacon contracting pneumonia and he died shortly afterwards on 9 April 1626.

The outcome of this experimentation has been the sighting of a spectral featherless bird in the immediate area of Pond Square, reports of which began soon after Sir Francis Bacon's death and continued with some infrequency up until the late 1960s. There were a number of encounters during the Second World War when, among others, a local family, an ARP Warden and a serviceman home on leave claimed to have seen and heard the ghost hopping and squawking about in the darkness, when approached the chicken proved its paranormality by vanishing or dematerialising through solid objects. The last reported encounters date from 1969, when a stranded motorist saw the phantom bird, and a year later, when it disturbed a courting couple in a doorway of a nearby house.

Despite the uniqueness of this particular haunting, it is Highgate Cemetery with its now heavily ingrained associations with modern vampirism which is of interest to most paranormal researchers today. The Highgate Vampire has survived what was an initial flap of press and television attention in the late 1960s to become one of London's most notorious hauntings. This longevity is due in no small part to the acrimonious relationship between the case's two major researchers, whose polarised conclusions have resulted in one of the most lengthy and bitter feuds in the history of psychical research.

Highgate is a large Victorian burying ground containing 45,000 graves, divided into two separate cemeteries by Swain's Lane, a single carriageway road which runs north-south from Highgate High Street. The older north-western cemetery, opened in 1839, is most associated with paranormal happenings and Black Magic practices. It contains the iconic Columbarium and Egyptian Avenue as well as the graves of many notables, including Australian politician Sir Charles Cowper, author John Galsworthy and the eminent Michael Faraday, who was one of the first scientists to attempt to debunk the Victorian craze for table-tipping.

Highgate's association with vampirism probably stretches back to Bram Stoker's *Dracula*, although the cemetery is not named as such and in his book Stoker may well have had nearby Hendon in mind for the location of Lucy Westenra's tomb, a place he knew well. In December 1969, David Farrant, the twenty-three year-old reported President of the British Psychic and Occult Society, claimed to have seen a tall 'ghost-like figure' with non-human eyes while investigating vandalism and ghost sightings in the cemetery during a night-time vigil. He was later joined by Sean Manchester, a young musician and researcher with a pedigree for Gothic adventure who claims to be a direct descendant of Lord Byron. Manchester quickly concluded that Farrant and others had seen a 'King Vampire' that had arrived in England from Eastern Europe in the eighteenth century and which had been recently resurrected by the activities of Satanists at work in the cemetery at night. A rivalry developed between the two protagonists, each claiming superiority in being able to rid the area of supernatural evil.

The Highgate Vampire eventually spread from the columns of local newspapers to brief inclusions in news magazines on ITV and later BBC television, generating the publicity which resulted in much vandalism and destruction to graves and mausoleums in the north-eastern part of the cemetery by sensation-seekers and freelance vampire-hunters. Corpses and bones were disturbed and on occasion removed from catacombs; a headless skeleton was found propped up in the driving seat of a parked car and one vandal later admitted watching while an accomplice danced with a body he had removed from an open coffin. In August 1973 this section of the cemetery was closed to members of the public other than those with buried relatives.

The aftermath has left the case's senior figures seriously opposed in their views as to the reality of the phenomena witnessed in the late 1960s and early '70s. David Farrant, who was found and arrested by police in the churchyard of St Michael's in August 1970, holding a crucifix and a wooden stake, and later served a prison sentence for damaging memorials in the cemetery

The iconic Circle of Lebanon in Highgate Cemetery, the haunt of vampire hunters and occult thrill-seekers during the early 1970s. *(Photograph by Paul Adams / Eddie Brazil)*

and carrying out a threat campaign using voodoo dolls, maintains that what he and others encountered there was nothing more than a 'harmless ghost', although photo shoots taken at Highgate in the Vampire heyday show him clearly enjoying a Van-Helsing-style role among the tombs. Sean Manchester's entry into the priesthood in the early 1990s, his subsequent enthronement as the Bishop of Glastonbury for the British Old Catholic Church in 1993, and his modern activities as an exorcist and vampirologist, show a clear affinity with the world and writings of Montague Summers. Manchester has claimed and published accounts of exorcising a local young woman allegedly under the influence of vampirism in early 1970, and of discovering the body of a living vampire creature in a vault at Highgate Cemetery, which he later destroyed in the cellar of an empty house nearby. Both Farrant and Manchester have written their own accounts of the Highgate case, which continue to generate interest some forty years after the main events took place.

For pure ghost hunters, the south-eastern cemetery has a more traditional haunted reputation. This has become the resting place of many noted actors, artists, writers and thinkers – Patrick Wymark, Sir Ralph Richardson, Paul Foot, Douglas Adams, Karl Marx and Anna Mahler, daughter of the great composer, are all buried here. Peter Underwood has interviewed two witnesses who claimed to have simultaneously seen from different viewpoints the fleeting apparition of an eerie long-haired old woman passing between the gravestones. A theme at times encountered with haunted churchyards is the scenario of a phantom figure perpetually searching the names incised on graves and monuments, such as the spectral airman at Clophill Old Church in Bedfordshire, and in this case the phantom form is thought to be the ghost of a mad woman seeking out the graves of her own children who she herself put to death. A second phantom reported from this part of Highgate Cemetery is a white-shrouded figure with long bony fingers which drifts in the vicinity of the imposing iron entrance gates. Sightings of both these ghosts appears now to have stopped, possibly due to the restrictive access, but the likelihood of the hauntings fading out over time could also be a possibility.

 [Grid Ref: TQ 283 872] St Michael's Church in South Grove backs onto the north-eastern section of Highgate Cemetery. The cemetery is privately owned and run by a non-profit making charity; tours of the north-west section can be arranged through the Friends of Highgate Cemetery.

6. WESTMINSTER ABBEY, CENTRAL LONDON

Standing on what was once the Isle of Thorney, nobody knows who founded the Abbey, nor the date of its foundation, but it is evident that it was built on a Roman site, for in 1866 the stone coffin of Valerius Amandinus was found here. There are persistent legends of a Temple of Apollo having once been hereabouts.

The original church may have been built (according to Bede) in the time of Sebert, King of the East Saxons, whose tomb is in the ambulation or Ethelbert, King of Kent (who flourished 560 to 616); his marriage with Bertha, daughter of Cheribert, King of the Franks, led to St Augustine's mission and by him England was converted to Christianity in 597. He destroyed pagan temples and built many churches. However, Osbert de Clare, Prior of the Abbey, in his *Life of Edward the Confessor*, ascribes the building to Sebert, nephew of Ethelbert. At all events it was consecrated by Mellitus, who had been made Bishop of London by St Augustine in 604, who called it the West Minster to distinguish it from the old St Paul's or the East Minster, built about the same time.

The existing Abbey was founded by Edward the Confessor in 1049-65. Some of the foundations discovered beneath the present structure in the Chapel of the Pyx and in the crypt have walls 17 feet thick. Henry III rebuilt the entire edifice and in 1269 the portion then completed was consecrated, including Edward the Confessor's Chapel, the choir and the transepts. Other portions were completed in 1503, and in 1695 and in 1722 by Wren. Westminster Abbey is said to be the first building in England in which window tracery was used.

A paving in the Chapter House denotes salmon and this relates to the tradition that on the eve of the consecration of the Abbey, St Peter himself appeared in disguise to a fisherman who was having no luck and asked to be ferried across the river. There Peter left the fisherman who saw a thousand golden lights and angels descend from heaven and he heard celestial singing amid the odour of incense. When Peter returned to be ferried back he told the astonished fisherman to cast his net again next day and he would catch some good salmon but he must 'give a tenth to the Abbey of Westminster'. Cynics say the story was invented by the monks to enhance the prestige of the Abbey but others point to the Abbey's red flag of St Peter with its crossed keys and regard that as symbolising a link between the saintly stranger and the fisherman of long ago. The ferry continued at the same spot until the erection of the first Westminster Bridge in 1739.

The Chapel of the Pyx was originally used as a treasure-house for the storage of jewels and money and in 1303 thieves broke into the treasure-house and escaped with millions of pounds in gold and jewels, but most of the treasure was recovered from its temporary burial in a plot of flax in the middle of the Great Cloister. The thieves were captured, convicted and skinned; their skins being tanned and used to cover both sides of a door opening into the passage from the cloisters, a doorway used by the monks to gain entrance to their dormitory, and so they were continually reminded of the theft and what happened to those who committed sacrilege. The door still exists and attendants will show a small piece of skin from one of the thieves, Richard le Pedlicote, now framed for preservation after having been on the door for centuries.

Another curiosity worth examination – some say with binoculars – is the thirteenth-century altarpiece behind a glass window; the details of its painting and jewels and enamels benefit greatly from magnification. This wonder of medieval art has recently been meticulously restored. One of the pictures shows Christ holding an orb or globe represented with a boat on the waves, the barque of St Peter perhaps, while the serene face of Christ may have been present at the dedication of the East end of the church in 1269, on the feast of Edward the Confessor. The whole wooden panel is much damaged as well it might be, for in the eighteenth century it was used as the top of a cabinet or press in which old wax effigies of past monarchs were bundled; these were known as the 'Ragged Regiment' and used to be exhibited to visitors. One of the 'jewels' was stolen in 1972 but it was not real; the gems are made of glass and even the 'enamel' is a painted imitation.

The alleged ghosts at Westminster Abbey are numerous and varied. One autumn night a policeman on duty saw a man in ecclesiastical robes hurrying towards the Abbey entrance, where he disappeared through a closed door! As the officer approached to investigate, he felt a tap on his shoulder and, turning, saw a procession of black-clad figures approaching the Abbey, walking two by two, heads bowed, hands clasped in front of them but their feet making no sound on the stone-paved Sanctuary. They passed close to the astonished policeman and, like the figure that had proceeded them, they too disappeared through closed doors, this time the western doors of the great Abbey. After a moment the officer approached the doorway and heard 'sweet and plaintive' music from within the closed and unlit building. As he stood and listened he was distracted by the sound of someone passing nearby and, when he turned back to resume listening, all was quiet within and without the historic Abbey.

Westminster Abbey used to possess a haunted clock or at least a clock with a haunted reputation. Back in the seventeenth century, James I appointed David Ramsey, a keen student of magic, alchemy and astrology, to be Keeper of the King's Clocks; he was the first President of the Clockmakers' Company. By means of his divining rod he thought he had located the whereabouts of the unrecovered treasure long thought to be hidden somewhere within the Abbey precincts and he set about seeking its recovery, but he was interrupted by supernatural appearances, which he described as 'demons', and he was so frightened that he fled and never resumed his search. Ramsey was familiar with the widespread belief that 'Tom', the great clock at Westminster, was reputed to be haunted and to exhibit its preternatural powers by striking out of order whenever an important member of the royal family was about to die. The belief persisted and was apparently perpetuated by many instances even after the clock was removed to St Paul's, which has many strange stories of its own – and a few ghosts.

Perhaps the best-known ghost at Westminster Abbey is 'Father Benedictus', a monk said to have been murdered when thieves robbed the Abbey in 1303, although there do not appear to be any records of the killing. Those who have seen the apparition, and there have been many over the years, variously describe the figure as tall and thin, with a prominent forehead, sallow skin, a hooked nose and deep-set eyes. He has most often been seen walking through the cloisters between five and six o'clock in the evening and disappearing into a solid stone wall. One witness estimated that she had watched him for about twenty minutes.

Two young women reported seeing such a form when they attended evensong. They both noticed a monk – they thought a Benedictine – standing silently in the south transept, seemingly watching them. His hands were concealed in the sleeves of his habit and his cowl was thrown back to reveal a domed head. His leisured gaze swept over the assembled congregation and then he slowly walked backwards, pausing occasionally to look somewhat contemptuously at the assembled flock. At length he disappeared into a solid wall.

On another occasion the figure was seen by three visitors, who stated that the cowled figure approached to within a few feet of where they stood and they noticed that his feet appeared to be an inch or so above the stone flooring; this puzzled them until they were told that the floor of the cloisters had been worn down over the centuries since Father Benedictus had walked there in reality.

Mrs Cicely M. Botley told us that the night before a royal marriage, she and two friends had seen a brown-robed monk who disappeared mysteriously. Electricians and other sane and sensible workmen have refused to work inside the Abbey after dark because the atmosphere was so creepy with unexplained and unaccountable rustling and sounds of objects or bodies being dragged over the stone floor.

Another well-known Abbey ghost is a khaki-clad and muddy soldier of the First World War, whose occasional appearance near the tomb of the Unknown Warrior (buried here on 11 November 1920, the second anniversary of the Armistice) is sometimes seen with outstretched arms, and is invariably accompanied by a feeling of sadness. One witness told Peter Underwood that the figure seemed to be trying to say something but no sound of any description accompanied the appearance, which lasted only a few seconds in the dying sunlight of a winter's day.

The Islip Rooms are named after the last of the great abbots, who saw the completion of the nave and the West window being fitted with glass in 1517, and so the completion of Westminster Abbey. John Bradshaw, President of the High Court of Justice, occupied these rooms and it is thought to be his footsteps often heard on the deserted stairs and in the empty passages at dead of night. It was here that Bradshaw, having put aside all legal objections to the court, refused to allow Charles I to speak in his own defence and having pronounced the death sentence on the King, finally signed the warrant authorizing the execution. Bradshaw's ghost has also been seen here on occasions. Long after his death and burial his body was disinterred at the Reformation in 1660, dragged to Tyburn and there hanged and decapitated, with the head being exhibited on Westminster Hall.

More than thirty royal personages are buried in the Abbey, together with more than a dozen members of the nobility and many notable actors, admirals, architects, divines, explorers, historians, novelists, painters, poets, scientists, soldiers and statesmen; with connections and associations such as these is it to be wondered that the place is haunted if anywhere is and the evidence for paranormal activity of one sort and another at Westminster Abbey is overwhelming.

From Dr Edward Moody of Lawrence University, who experienced curious and unexplained happenings during filming in the crypt, to a couple on their first visit to London who were surprised to see a cavalier as they entered the Abbey, a royalist in full seventeenth-century

Westminster Abbey, whose ghosts include a cowled monk and the figure of a First World War soldier. *(Photograph by Eddie Brazil)*

costume who disappeared within seconds, one never knows when they may encounter one of the Abbey ghosts. Incidentally, Elliott O'Donnell traced an eighteenth-century eyewitness account of an apparitional cavalier in Westminster, a ghostly form witnessed by no less than nine people, and we have often wondered whether the figure of a cavalier occasionally encountered in the vicinity of Dean's Yard has any connection with the Abbey; just one of its assorted ghosts.

Many visitors have commented on the deep silence and lovely tranquillity of Westminster Abbey, the very silence of the mighty church seeming to whisper of past deeds and the history of the English people – and their many reported ghosts.

 [Grid Ref: TQ 301 794] The Abbey is close to the House of Commons, Parliament Square and the A302 Victoria Street; nearest Underground station is Westminster.

7. ST DUNSTON'S CHURCH, EAST ACTON, WEST LONDON

A Victorian church in Friar's Place Lane, an appellation that has its origin in the stately mansion that once stood close to the church called Friar's Place. During the Middle Ages a chapter of St Bartholomew's the Great at Smithfield – itself the haunt of a phantom monk – existed here and in those days monks, singly and in procession, must have walked where St Dunston's now stands; a remarkable circumstance in view of what has taken place subsequently.

This church has been the locale of repeated sightings of ghostly monks for many years, as Peter Underwood first learned from the past vicar, the Revd Hugh Anton-Stephens, who had formerly been an army chaplain and who had no doubt about the authenticity of the sightings of ghosts repeatedly seen and reported in his church.

Long before he arrived at St Dunston's in 1944, there had been numerous accounts of the church being haunted and when a well-respected curate in the 1930s, the Revd Phillip Boustead, himself 'saw things' in the church, it soon came to his knowledge that other people had seen identical figures and he began to suspect that the ghost monks seen in the church may have been the spectres of monks who once lived and worshipped in the vicinity, and he wondered whether they were attracted to the nearest existing consecrated building in their domain. The Revd Philip Boustead insisted that he had seen the ghost monks on numerous occasions, 'on many evenings up to a dozen can be seen here,' he said. Most of them wore golden-brown habits but one, he noticed, kept apart from the others and he wore a violet-coloured habit and hood.

Alleged sightings of ghost monks at St Dunston's go back to the 1920s, and there seems to be some justification for believing that the manifestations take several years to build up and then occur in four-year cycles. It has been suggested that there is a steady accumulation of psychic energy within the church, with occasional visitations of ghostly forms leading to the cumulative effect of the build-up: a procession of hooded figures; before whatever is necessary for the appearances dissipates and the whole four-year cycle begins again.

Once when the vicar, his secretary (who was also interviewed by Peter Underwood) and a visiting parishioner, opened the vestry door, all three were met by a group of ghostly monks who faded and disappeared as they watched! Another parishioner then came to see the vicar to report that several times, while in the church in the early evening, he had witnessed a ghostly procession of monks moving through the church towards the chancel. He claimed he had seen the silent column on several, perhaps four, occasions. He was a devout, sincere and much respected member of the congregation of St Dunston's.

The vicar revealed that one of the most memorable sightings was reported by a visitor, Kenneth Mason, a no-nonsense former lieutenant in the Royal Navy, a sober and serious person who visited St Dunston's on a cold and damp November evening, having heard that ghosts had been seen there. He found the large red-brick church in the middle of semi-detached houses and noted, as he approached the church door, the stained-glass windows showed no lights within the building. Inside it was quite dark and utterly silent. He was rain-soaked, cold and alone – or so he thought.

He settled himself into a pew on the left-hand side of the nave and prepared to sit there for a while to see whether he would experience or feel anything not of this world. After a while he dozed but then suddenly found himself wide awake – and of this he was absolutely certain – and there, walking slowly towards him, he saw a procession of six or eight hooded figures, their heads bowed, moving silently up the aisle in the direction of the altar.

According to Jack Hallam, Kenneth Mason asserted: 'Slowly and without a sound, they approached. I took my courage in both hands and, getting up from the pew, I faced them and barred their way'. The next moment he had to turn and look at their backs – they had passed right through him! As he watched, Mason became conscious of a voice speaking quietly to him, one of the hooded monks perhaps, he thought afterwards, the one who seemed apart from the others and wore a violet-coloured habit; and the voice said: 'Near here, five hundred years ago, stood a monastery and we were the occupants. This is our past. This is our future.' When they reached the altar the monks knelt and at that moment a light snapped on from the back of the church; a human voice asked who was there and the spell was broken. From the tower a bell tolled for worship and when Mason looked again the monks had vanished. He looked at his watch and discovered the time was 7.15 p.m. He left the church, uncomfortable, wide-awake and wondering what on earth had happened to him. He mumbled some greeting to the parishioner who had arrived and switched on the lights. 'I cannot explain it,' Kenneth Mason said later, 'but I saw those things that night.'

The next day Mason returned to the church, taking with him a professional photographer and hoping to get pictures of the phenomenon. They saw nothing. There were a number of people in the church, some no doubt hoping to catch a glimpse of the ghosts, and some children scrambling about, and Mason felt all this upset the necessary atmosphere. He returned to St Dunston's on several later occasions, alone and accompanied, but he never saw the ghosts again.

Mrs Alma Baker, who used to assist in arranging the church flowers for special occasions, has revealed that sometimes, usually when she was alone in the church, she had an overwhelming impression that she was being watched, although she never saw anything. She said the feeling was so strong that sometimes she had to leave what she was doing and go outside for a few moments. She never had a similar feeling anywhere else. Another parishioner told Peter Underwood that discussion groups held in the vestry were made aware of the fact that a ghostly procession of monks sometimes moved through the church towards the chancel and indeed the parishioner relating this revealed that he had himself witnessed the singular event on no less than four occasions. He was put in touch with a churchwarden who for years scoffed at the story but everything changed when, one evening, he too saw the spectral monks.

The phantom procession at St Dunston's seems to have been quiescent of late but there are still those who talk about the ghostly monks and who know what might occur to those who are in the right place at the right time in this haunted church.

 [Grid Ref: TQ 210 807] St Dunston's Church and Friar's Place Lane is close to the A40 Western Avenue; nearest Underground station is Acton Central.

8. ST GILES CHURCH, CAMBERWELL, SOUTH EAST LONDON

At first glance, St Giles appears to be a typical medieval church of the early fourteenth century. The elaborately curved tracery of its windows, tall spire and finely carved stonework would date it to the decorated period between 1300 and 1350. In fact this church was built in 1844 by Sir

George Gilbert Scott following the Victorian's renewed interest in all things medieval during the mid-nineteenth-century Gothic revival. Although a place of worship has stood on this site since Saxon times, in 1154 the pre-Conquest building was demolished and a new church erected. This lasted until it was destroyed by fire in 1841, although memorials and the fourteenth-century sedilia from the medieval church survived and were incorporated in Gibert Scott's new design

With the coming of the railways in the 1800s the urban sprawl of London swallowed Camberwell, which had for years continued as a sleepy Surrey village famous for the healing properties of its wells and springs. Henry V passed through here on his return from the victory over the French at Agincourt in 1415. For many years Camberwell was much regarded as a place of peace and tranquilly for those wishing to escape the smoke and grime of London. John Ruskin and Robert Browning were residents. Today it has become a noisy and congested part of the metropolis. However, places such as Camberwell Grove, a thoroughfare of Georgian and early Victorian houses, and the grandeur of St Giles Church and its churchyard, remind us of its former splendour.

It is the graveyard of St Giles where sightings of ghosts have been reported. The spectral figure associated with the church does not appear within the building but in the churchyard passage, a pathway which skirts the west end of St Giles before crossing an old burial ground. In the early 1930s the ghost of an elderly priest was seen walking along the passage, believed to be a former vicar who would have used it to return to the clergy house which had been demolished long ago. His appearance was reported by two people in 1970 and was noted in the parish magazine, with the result that other people came forward to report that they had also seen the apparition.

Eddie Brazil was raised not far from St Giles. As a child he can recall that the churchyard passage always had a sinister reputation and was a walkway not many people frequented after dark. Solitary sodium lamps feebly illuminated its length through the headstones and a particularly intimidating section, closed in by the skirting garden fences and high surrounding walls of the houses in Camberwell Grove, created an instantly spooky location where an active imagination could furnish all manner of ghostly figures. Indeed on many occasions during the late 1970s and early '80s, on cold winter evenings, the then vicar of St Giles would often walk along the churchyard passage attired not only in his clerical garb but also a long black cloak. His appearance to those who had knowledge of the church's ghostly reputation caused many a fright when they viewed the cloaked figure coming towards them in the dark. He became known locally as the 'Reverend Dracula' and Eddie Brazil twice had the unnerving experience of meeting the shadowy clergyman in the walkway at night.

Of course the vision of the cloaked vicar might well explain some of the sightings of the ghost at St Giles. However, in July 1984 a young man who had spent the night socialising in the Grove House Tavern public house, which stands in Camberwell Grove, decided to take a short cut home through the churchyard passage. Halfway along the walkway he turned to see a figure in black walking some distance behind him. Mindful of south east London's reputation for street crime he increased his walking speed. However, before he could reach the end of the passage he heard the alarming sound of footsteps closing from behind. Expecting any moment to here the words 'Give us your wallet!' he turned around and was astonished to find no one there – the passageway was deserted. Even through it was a warm summer's night the young man felt a chill run through him and hastily made his way out of the passage to the relative security of busy Camberwell Church Street. He later recounted that there was no way that anyone making the footsteps could have got out of sight so quickly.

The spectre of the ghostly vicar has not been seen for many years, although that is not to say that St Giles isn't still a haunted place. Its eerie churchyard passage may well continue to be the site of a ghostly figure in black or the unnerving sound of disembodied footsteps.

■ [Grid Ref: TQ 330 766] St Giles Church is located on the A202 Camberwell Church Street, 450 yards from the junction with the A215 Denmark Hill.

The church of St Giles at Camberwell in South London, where the ghost of an elderly priest was seen as late as the 1970s. *(Photograph by Eddie Brazil)*

9. CHAPEL OF ST PETER ON THE WALL, BRADWELL-ON-SEA, ESSEX

To the untrained eye the chapel of St Peter on the Wall, Bradwell-on-Sea, would at first sight appear to be nothing more than a farmer's age-old weather-beaten barn. In fact, when the chapel was abandoned in the seventeenth century it was used for that very purpose, and remained so until it was handed back to the Diocese in 1920. However, this remote and lonely structure, which has stood for centuries upon the bleak windswept marshes of south Essex, is one of the most architecturally important buildings in England.

When the Roman legions departed from Britain in the fifth century they abandoned the fort of Othona on this site, which would become the centre of a small village or city known as Ythancestir. It was to this community in AD 653 that St Cedd came with a group of Christians to spread his gospel to the East Saxons at the invitation of King Sigbert. St Cedd built his chapel on the foundations of the old fort and across its enclosing wall, and it is from this that the chapel derives its name. St Cedd died of the plague in AD 664 yet St Peter's continued to be used as a place of worship for the next 650 years. Today it is still a place of pilgrimage and prayer.

The traveller to this lonely spot seeking not only the paranormal but also a sense and experience of the dim and distant past will be well rewarded. During the bleak winter months when visitors are rare and the only accompanying sounds are the far off cries of sea birds and the rise and fall of the moaning wind hissing through the marsh grass, it is easy to feel that the stresses and frustrations of the modern world are far away. Beyond the chapel the marshes merge into mud flats and then out into the waters of the River Blackwater to join the sea. As one might expect from such an ancient and evocative site, Bradwell is not without its ghosts.

On the pathway leading to the chapel from the car park, the sounds of a horse in full gallop accompanied by the noise of Roman weaponry and armour have been heard. Such is the realistic nature of the phenomena that people have mistaken the sounds for a runaway horse, and it is only when the hoof beats go past them that they realise there is no visible cause. The figure of a Legionary has also been seen marching along the old Roman road in the direction of the former fort and the chapel. It is often remarked that during daylight hours St Peter's exudes an air of tranquillity and calm. Only after dark does this atmosphere change and the place becomes unsettling. Perhaps this is to be expected of remote coastal areas which are often shrouded in sea mist within the gathering dusk and where all manner of shapes and forms might be mistaken for something more sinister or unnatural. Yet nearby villagers have often reported seeing figures moving about within the chapel itself and strange lights have been observed late at night shining from the widows. On investigation there has been nothing to account for them and the place has been deserted.

To the sceptic the origin of these ghost stories have their foundation in one word – smuggling. From 1700 to the middle of the nineteenth century this area was rife with smugglers and the many creeks, inlets and deserted beaches along the coast were perfect sites for the clandestine landing of contraband. To keep away the prying eyes and ears of the God-fearing locals, tales of ghostly horsemen, phantom lights and long dead seamen risen from the deep were told and retold in the taverns and inns of the area and it cannot be denied that shadowy figures seen in the distance, lights quickly extinguished when someone is heard approaching and the sound of muffled hoof beats would all have been practices associated with the transportation and hiding of contraband. Their tales would have been handed down over the years and eventually become local ghost folklore.

Perhaps the most infamous of eighteenth-century smugglers who employed scare tactics to frighten inquisitive locals or impressionable revenue men was Dr Christopher Syn. By day a respectable clergyman who provided spiritual guidance to the people of Dymchurch in Kent, at night he and his gang would masquerade as phantom scarecrows as they plied their illegal trade across the dark and wild expanse of Romney Marsh.

Nevertheless, to the villagers of Bradwell, the ghostly lights, spectral horses and shadowy figures which continue to be reported at this ancient site are real enough. As one longstanding resident magnanimously observed to Peter Underwood during a visit to St Peters, 'Perhaps the smugglers did invent ghosts to frighten off those who would run to the revenue men, but what about the phantom Legionary who is said to walk on the path to the chapel. Who ever heard of an eighteenth-century smuggler trying to scare off the locals by pretending to be the ghost of a Roman soldier?'

 [Grid Ref: TM 031 082] Bradwell-on-Sea on the Dengie peninsular is difficult to get to without a car. The nearest station, Southminster, is five miles distant. By car the village can be found off the B1021. Proceed through the village and follow directions along East End Road to St Peter's. The last half mile has to be made on foot along a grass track.

The enigmatic chapel of St Peter on the Wall at Bradwell-on-Sea in Essex – ghostly lights and the figure of a Roman soldier have been seen here. *(Photograph by Eddie Brazil)*

10. ST NICHOLAS CHURCH, CANEWDON, ESSEX

On a grey rainy day in July 1987, Mrs Sybil Webster arrived at Canewdon church. It was the church's Open Day and hundreds of visitors were expected. Being early, Mrs Webster found the building empty. As she waited for the festivities to get under way she sat in the choir stalls near the chancel. After some time, and without any warning, she suddenly saw out of the corner of her eye a garment of bright, shiny blue material. She later described it as a large dress or wide pantaloon. The sudden sight of the vision made her jump with shock and the apparition immediately vanished. Mrs Webster says she saw only the bottom half of the figure which appeared close to a bricked-up door that once opened into a chapel used by the De Chanceaux family, who owned the manor of Canewdon. The chapel was demolished during the eighteenth century.

The experience of Sybil Webster is typical of many recorded ghost sightings. The majority of reported apparitions, far from being full-on lengthy observations of floating wraiths or spectral ladies posing for the camera, are more often described as a fleeting glimpse out of the corner of the eye – there one moment, the next gone in a flash. Had Mrs Webster briefly glimpsed the ghost of one of the De Chanceaux family, perhaps one of the ladies in elegant attire? Or is it possible she witnessed something more sinister?

The fourteenth-century church of St Nicholas stands high on a hill above the marshes of the River Crouch. The name Canewdon is derived from the Saxon name 'Caningadon', roughly translated as 'hill of the Can people'. However, Canewdon is claimed to be also the site of an ancient camp used by Canute (he who tried to hold back the sea) in battle during his invasion of Essex in 1013. Christianity came to Canewdon at an early date, probably in Roman times.

Interior of Canewdon church, where Mrs Sybil Webster saw the apparition of a lady in blue. *(Photograph by Eddie Brazil)*

The church of St Nicholas at Canewdon in Essex. *(Photograph by Eddie Brazil)*

Some 200 years after the Romans, during St Cedd's mission from Lindisfarne to Essex in about AD 653 and after he had established ministers at Bradwell-on-Sea and Tilbury, the gospel was then carried from Bradwell to Canewdon. Although this place has been a centre of Christian worship for nearly 2,000 years, Canewdon church is said to be also the site of a far older belief – witchcraft.

One legend has it that while the church tower stands, there will always remain six witches in Canewdon. Another states that if you walk around the church seven times (anticlockwise) on Halloween you will see a witch, while thirteen circuits will make you disappear. Indeed the ghost of a witch, believed to have been executed in the seventeenth century, is said to haunt the churchyard. The apparition is reported to rise from her grave, wander slowly to the west gate, stop there for a while and then move quickly down the lane to the river, where she vanishes. Anyone who encounters her is lifted up and deposited in the nearest ditch. Other accounts describe the spectre as being headless and dressed in a crinoline, and the ghost has also been reported within the church.

It would seem that these tales of ghosts, witches and the old religion have their origin in the folklore of not only Canewdon but also of Essex. This is the county of Witch Finder General, Mathew Hopkins, and throughout East Anglia between 1582 and 1660, over 700 people were put on trial for witchcraft. Three of the accused were Canewdon women.

Canewdon was also the home of George Pickingill. He was born in 1816 and died in 1909. Known throughout the village as a 'cunning man', he was said to be able to bewitch machinery

Occultist George Pickingill (1816-1909), who is associated with witchcraft ceremonies in the churchyard at Canewdon.

and magically find lost property. It was also claimed that he was the 'master' of a supposed group of witches traditionally associated with Canewdon who performed their rituals within the churchyard of St Nicholas. George Pickingill is also thought to have been a major influence on the order of the Golden Dawn, a magical society which practised occultism and Wicca, a form of modern witchcraft, although they eventually broke with Pickingill over his increasing reputation for Satanism and Black Magic. The famous magician Aleister Crowley was supposed to have been a Pickingill initiate.

Unfortunately for the people of Canewdon, its reputation for ghosts and association with witches sees the village plagued by sensations seekers eager to experience the headless witch or to dance naked through the churchyard. In recent years, on Halloween night, the local police have been required to cordon off the church and certainly the many people who noisily invade St Nicholas's Church every 31 October are hardly likely to encounter the ghost of the headless witch. Yet that is not to say the church is not haunted. As has been said before, people often experience paranormal phenomena when they least expect it. When Sybil Webster sat in the empty choir stalls on that rainy day in 1987, ghosts were the last thing on her mind, but it seems highly likely that she did witness something supernatural. Whether it was the ghost of one of the De Chanceaux family or that of the headless witch, we shall never know.

 [Grid Ref: TQ 897 945] Canewdon is three miles north-east of Rochford where there is a mainline station; the village has to be reached by country lanes.

11. ST GEORGE'S CHURCH, ANSTEY, NEAR BUNTINGFORD, HERTFORDSHIRE

Much haunted, Hertfordshire is a county that the three authors know well and whose ghostly history has provided an impressive quota of eight churches for our survey. The first of these is the church of St George in Anstey, a Domesday village located in the north-east of the county, close to the Essex border. The name is derived from the Saxon 'Heanstige', meaning 'high pathway', and it was Count Eustace of Bologne who built the first castle here. When the manor was given to Geoffrey De Mandeville (*d*.1144), described as 'one of the most villainous men Hertfordshire has ever had the misfortune to know' and whose ghost is said to haunt the East Barnet to South Minns Road at Christmas time, he constructed a new stone castle which was later enlarged by Nicholas De Anestie. Today only the mounds of the motte and bailey remain and this has become linked in an extraordinary way with the haunting that concerns us here.

St George's Church dates from the twelfth century, totally replacing an earlier and original Saxon building. Parts of the nave and the tower are the oldest parts of the structure; the

The twelfth-century church of St George at Anstey in Hertfordshire. *(Photograph by Richard Flagg / Eddie Brazil)*

trancepts and chancel were reconstructed in the 1400s and by the end of the fifteenth century, clerestory windows and a south porch had been added. The church saw two nineteenth-century restorations, the first in 1831 and the second in 1872 by William Butterfield, who removed the west gallery, rebuilt the south end of the south transept and refitted the building. Externally, St George's tower boasts a Hertfordshire spike, a common county feature, while the Norman font is one of only two known in the country to have a carved design of four mermen creating the effect of a boat with their split tails. Like another haunted Hertfordshire church included in this book, St Mary's at Ashwell, examples of medieval graffiti can be seen at St George's; the chancel walls are marked with the signature of the Revd John Creyk, incumbent in 1342, as well as Thomas Montford, rector in 1584, together with a drawing of a man in Elizabethan clothes.

Three quarters of a mile to the north-east of Anstey is the former RAF Nuthampstead airbase, finally closed in the early 1960s, when concrete from its runway was used in the construction of the new M1 motorway. During the Second World War this was used as a centre of operations by the United States Army Air Force's 398th Bomber Group, which now has a unique physical and seemingly supernatural connection with the Norman church of St George. At the west end of the south aisle is a stained-glass window dedicated to those members of the 398th who lost their lives during the 1939-45 conflict. This window was unveiled during a special ceremony by HRH the Duke of Gloucester on 11 June 2000.

In October 1944, an American Flying Fortress taking off on a bombing raid from Nuthampstead experienced sudden engine failure and crashed into the motte and bailey mound of Anstey Castle, immediately adjacent to St George's Church. The aircraft burst into flames, killing all members of the crew; amazingly the full payload of bombs failed to explode. This incident in particular has given rise to reports of phantom airmen being seen, both at the old Nuthampstead airbase and in the vicinity of the church of St George.

There are a number of airfields and former Second World War airbases that have ghostly associations, such as the haunted Avro Lincoln bomber at the Aerospace Museum at RAF Cosford, Shropshire – investigated by Peter Underwood during a Ghost Club visit – and Bircham Newton near Kings Lynn in Norfolk, known for its haunted squash court, where the apparition of a man in flying kit has been seen and also where broadcaster Denny Densham made a recording of seemingly paranormal sounds, including voices and the flypast of a wartime aeroplane. Nuthampstead, known as Station 131, was vacated by the 398th Bomber Group in June 1945 and handed over to the Royal Air Force, who used it as an area-wide collection site for bombs and ammunition which were ultimately disposed of in the North Sea. During this time parts of the airfield gained notoriety among the RAF personnel present on the base as being haunted, particularly the old hospital morgue, where the figure of a man dressed in full flying gear was said to have been seen; as well as 'B' Hangar, where former RAF airman Vic Jenkins later recalled (in 1995) hearing on one occasion during a night-time patrol a snatch of music, this being a building where American band leader Glen Miller is known to have performed. In 1984, Adam Gurney, an aviation enthusiast, claimed to have encountered a spectral horse and rider while driving his car along part of the old airfield runway.

It seems that as well as the site of the old airfield, paranormal echoes of Anstey's unique wartime associations have been both seen and heard in and around the vicinity of St George's Church. Paul Adams has collected accounts of two separate sightings of a figure, described as being that of a man wearing old-fashioned flying clothes dating from the Second World War, seen walking in the churchyard. Both these, albeit second-hand reports, took place within a few weeks of each other in 2004, within a few years of the dedication and publicity of the dedication of the 398th stained-glass window in the church. Whether this fact influenced the experiences of the two witnesses to see a phantom airman is debateable, as is the idea that this may be a much later sighting of the same apparition reported in the old airbase hospital in the months following the end of the war.

A memorial window to the USAF 398th Bomber Group in Anstey church – in recent years there have been reports of a ghostly airman walking in the churchyard. *(Photograph by Richard Flagg / Eddie Brazil)*

More difficult to date but certainly no less interesting is a report of a church service at St George's being stopped due to the sound of a heavy wartime plane overflying the church. This was said to have taken place in the 1950s, by which time military traffic at RAF Nuthampstead had ceased, leading to the conclusion that the sounds were paranormal in origin. We have found similar difficulties in obtaining confirmation locally of another incident where a church service was curtailed due to seemingly paranormal activity, namely at Borley Church in Essex, where a Sunday service was stopped by the vicar due to one of the altar candles bending by itself in full view of the assembled congregation – an account of this incident was given to Paul Adams by medium Rita Goold, who currently possesses the candle involved in the incident.

 [Grid Ref: TL 404 328] Anstey lies close to the B1368 between Barley and Great Hormead.

12. ST LAWRENCE CHURCH, ABBOTS LANGLEY, HERTFORDSHIRE

The old village of Abbots Langley is the birthplace of Nicholas Breakspear, the only Englishman to become Pope. After an exceptional ecclesiastical career he became a cardinal and then Pope Adrian IV in 1154.

In the graveyard of St Lawrence's ancient church lie the unquiet remains of Mary Anne Treble, a housekeeper or servant at the nearby vicarage soon after the First World War. Local folklore has it that the vicar's wife treated her badly and poor Anne was either murdered or committed suicide in her bedroom.

The church of St Lawrence at Abbots Langley, haunted by the unhappy ghost of Mary Anne Treble. *(Photograph by Eddie Brazil)*

Her ghost is said to have been seen not infrequently in no less than three places: walking or wafting her way between the vicarage and the church; in her old bedroom at the vicarage – where the daughter of a former clergyman occupant became used to waking up and seeing the back of the ghostly Anne, seemingly looking out of the window towards the church; and inside the church, kneeling or at mass, especially on All Souls' Day. Interestingly enough, when Peter Underwood investigated the story, he talked with the occupant of a cottage just across the road who had also seen and recognised the phantom form of Mary Anne.

A former clergyman of the parish related that the ghost was very active when he first moved into the vicarage. When he made structural alterations to the rambling Queen Anne building a local builder remarked, in the 'haunted' room, that there was no point in replacing the old fireplace, which stood out from the wall, as it 'would be out again within six months'. It was replaced, several times, but, as predicted, within a few months it was out again. It was believed that Mary Anne Treble died a horrible death in the room 'and the place will never be free of her'. For some years the room was locked and unused on account of 'unaccountable noises'. At the time of one investigative visit the daughter of the then vicar revealed somewhat proudly that she slept undisturbed in the 'haunted' room!

Over the years visitors, clergymen, laymen and women, local people and strangers have all reported unexplained footsteps inside the church, especially at the west end, or have felt 'something' touching them, or have seen the form of a young girl who mysteriously disappears – and there are other tales of 'disturbances' inside St Lawrence's Church.

 [Grid Ref: TL 094 023] Abbots Langley and its mainline railway station is close to the A41 junction (No. 20) on the M25 motorway. Follow Gallows Hill Lane into the village and St Lawrence Church is in the High Street.

13. MINSDEN CHAPEL, NEAR HITCHIN, HERTFORDSHIRE

The chapel of St Nicholas, a flint and rubble ruin now fast disappearing, located two and a half miles south-east of Hitchin in Hertfordshire, has had a haunted reputation stretching back many years. When this first became established is unclear, although its ghostly status throughout the twentieth century and beyond was and is helped no end by an undoubtedly fraudulent 'ghost' photograph taken by a local photographer T.W. Latchmore in 1910. This shows a hooded and sheeted figure framed in one of the building's crumbling archways and had become an iconic paranormal image appearing in numerous ghost books and now latterly on many websites in our fast expanding digital age.

Minsden Chapel was built according to most accounts some time in the early fourteenth century but fell into disuse around 1675, although marriages were still occasionally carried out there for another sixty years. Four hundred pounds of lead was stolen from the roof in 1690 and the chapel's three bells suffered a similar fate in 1725. The last recorded wedding took place on 11 July 1738, when Enoch West and Mary Horn exchanged vows in the roofless building. It was on this occasion that a piece of falling masonry knocked the prayer book from the parson's hand, a near miss that resulted in the Bishop of Lincoln closing the chapel for good, consigning Minsden to decades of neglect and decay.

The three authors have visited the site on a number of occasions. The first was in the late 1940s, when Peter Underwood held an all-night vigil on All Hallow's Eve in the ruins accompanied by his brother John and Tom Brown, another enthusiastic ghost hunter from nearby Weston. In the early hours of the morning the three men saw what appeared to be a luminous Latin cross glowing on the stonework on one of the bare chancel walls, an effect which continued for several minutes. A few days previously the ghost hunters had visited Minsden by daylight and had had an unusual experience when both Peter and Tom heard what they were convinced was a snatch

The famous Minsden
Chapel 'ghost',
photographed in
the ruins by T.W.
Latchmore in 1910.
*(Tony Broughall
Collection)*

of music floating through the lonely and isolated ruins. John Underwood, two steps behind his
brother, heard nothing. However, during their nocturnal stay all three members of the group felt
that at times a presence could be detected under one of the archways.

Elliott O'Donnell (*c.*1872-1965) was another psychical researcher who spent time at Minsden,
sometimes accompanied and on other occasions alone. He also reported feeling a presence in
parts of the ruin and on one visit (also on All Hallow's Eve) claimed to have heard strains of
music and to have glimpsed a white robed figure beneath one the the arches.

One person who was clearly affected by the stillness and atmosphere of Minsden Chapel more
than anyone else was Reginald Hine, born in 1883, a solicitor and writer from Hitchen. Hine,
author of a two-volume history of Hitchin, written so he claimed by candlelight in order to
imbue the writing with a sense of the past, was a gentle and sensitive man for whom a harsh and
materialistic world ultimately proved too much to bear. Plagued with nervous breakdowns he
found solace in the ruins of Minsden, leasing them from the church authorities for the duration

Lonely and isolated Minsden Chapel, where one of the authors heard seemingly paranormal music during a visit in the 1940s. *(Photograph by Paul Adams / Eddie Brazil)*

Hertfordshire historian Reginald Hine (1883-1949), whose troubled spirit may still walk at Minsden.

of his life, which ended dramatically on 19 April 1949 when he calmly walked off the platform at Hitchin railway station and into the path of a London-bound locomotive. Hine's ashes were interred appropriately at Minsden, beneath a stone slab which can be seen by visitors today close to the north side of the chapel, a place he vowed to haunt from beyond the grave.

Ghost hunters who make the effort to visit this lonely spot today should note that the building is now in an advanced state of disrepair. A large section of the arched north wall, a familiar sight in contemporary photographs, collapsed in 2009 and other parts of the structure are equally unstable. Despite this, Minsden remains a unique and intriguing site that all those interested in the history of the paranormal should visit at some time.

 [Grid Ref: TL 198 246] The nearest access point for Minsden is on foot off the B656 road between Hitchin and Welwyn. Take the appropriately named Chapelfoot Way public footpath to the left of The Royal Oak pub. After a quarter of a mile look out for the chapel ruins in the trees just off the public path.

14. THUNDRIDGE OLD CHURCH, NEAR WARE, HERTFORDSHIRE

The old church of St Mary and All Saints at Thundridge Bury in the valley of the River Rib, two and a half miles north of Ware in Hertfordshire, shares much common ground with that of ruined St Mary's at Clophill, over the county border in Bedfordshire. Both are former fifteenth-century buildings whose redundancy by the church authorities in the middle of the 1800s was the beginning of decades of neglect which have become interwoven in time with stories of alleged hauntings and the all more real and disturbing reality of modern devil worship and black magic rituals.

At Thundridge only the heavily buttressed three-stage west tower, imposing in its eerie dereliction, now remains, although this shows evidence that a stone church occupied the site for at least 300 years before major building work took place in the 1400s; the tower has a twelfth-century doorway and following the demolition of the nave and chancel in 1853, a fourteenth-century window was rebuilt into the masonry, closing off the opening on the east side of the structure. A large amount of the stonework salvaged from St Mary and All Saints was used in the Victorian refurbishment of Sacombe church, three miles to the north-west. The surviving structure was given Grade II listed status by the Department of the Environment in the mid-1960s and at present resides on English Heritage's 'Heritage at Risk' register of nationally important buildings under threat.

Unlike the former churchyard at Clophill, here at Thundridge many of the old gravestones still remain *in situ*, with the result that the overgrown and weed-strewn burying ground possesses a

The derelict tower and abandoned churchyard of St Mary and All Saints at Thundridge Bury, said to be haunted by strange noises and a procession of phantom figures; the pensive face has been created by graffiti. *(Photograph by Eddie Brazil)*

gloomy and decidedly charged atmosphere ideal for the development of haunting tales. Reports of Satanic ceremonies appear to be quite common locally, but have not reached the notoriety of those which made national headlines at old St Mary's at Clophill in 1963. Despite this, the interior of the tower is completely sealed although the churchyard remains open to the public.

As for reports of paranormal phenomena at Thundridge, these, like a number of the buildings contained in our survey, are very much anecdotal in nature. The churchyard is said to be haunted by a sinister growling or moaning noise although the most startling account is that dating from 1978, when a female visitor wrote to a local newspaper claiming to have witnessed an army of phantom figures marching out of the church tower and through the churchyard when she was a young girl several years previously. Nothing therefore can be substantiated with any certainty and this is one site for which a detailed investigation remains outstanding. However, the derelict nature of the surviving tower and the problems inherent with any kind of paranormal vigil carried out in an outside location, where the possibility of mistaking natural sounds such as the weather, passing vehicles and particularly animals for supernormal ones are high, make it highly likely that the alleged haunting of Thundridge Old Church will remain just that.

 [Grid Ref: TL 367 174] Turn off the B158 main road through Thundridge onto Old Church Lane. A third of a mile past the A10 flyover the churchyard and tower are located in the trees on the left-hand side close to the roadway.

15. ST NICHOLAS CHURCH, STEVENAGE, HERTFORDSHIRE

Hertfordshire is a county with a generous quota of phantom animals, of which spectral dogs and horses are not surprisingly the most commonly encountered. Tony Broughall, who made a systematic survey of haunted locations in both Hertfordshire and neighbouring Bedfordshire during the 1970s, recorded a number of cases involving phantom hounds, two of which are associated with churches in the county.

St Nicholas Church, Stevenage, where one of several Hertfordshire ghost hounds is said to haunt the churchyard. *(Photograph by Eddie Brazil)*

The first of these is the church of St Nicholas in Rectory Lane, Stevenage, which dates from the twelfth century although the tower is the only part of the building which remains from this period today, the nave, aisles, chapels and vestry having been altered and rebuilt several times over the years. The church occupies the site of a Saxon village when the original church building would have been a wooden one, but it is in fact the churchyard which concerns us here as it is reputedly guarded by the apparition of an enormous black dog. As with many of these haunting stories, modern experiences or even detailed encounters from the past are hard to come by. Tony Broughall notes that the animal was sighted at various times during the 1800s but nothing has been reported here for well over a hundred years how.

However, despite the inactivity at St Nicholas there is another location in Stevenage which may – with some stretch of the imagination – be in some way connected with this particular case or a continuation of the haunting. A mile and a half to the south is a complex of ancient Roman burial mounds known as the Six Hills, which are regarded as one of the finest surviving examples of this type of barrow formation. A local legend has it that the mounds are the work of the Devil, who passed the time by hewing half a dozen huge clods of earth from the ground from nearby Whomerley Wood and throwing them at unfortunate passers-by; according to the story a seventh shot went astray and struck the tower of St Mary's Church at Graveley. Interestingly enough, the Six Hills also have the reputation of being haunted by another ghostly black dog, which in this case is reported to have been seen as late as the 1960s.

 [Grid Ref: TL 241 263] St Nicholas Church is located at the junction of Rectory Lane and Weston Road close to the flyover across the A1072; the Six Hills are on the west side of the B197 London Road at the junction with the A1070 Six Hills Way.

16. ST MARY'S CHURCH, ASHWELL, HERTFORDSHIRE

One of Hertfordshire's most notable churches lies in the remote and rural setting of Ashwell, a delightful Domesday village five miles north-east of Letchworth. St Mary's was built in the fourteenth century from locally quarried 'clunch' or chalk stone, which gives the building a distinctively pale, one could say almost 'ghostly', appearance. There is a pillared five-bay nave with north and south porches, both dating from the fifteenth century, and chancel. However, the church's most impressive feature is its massive four-stage west tower which was extended and practically doubled in height, so it is believed, after the Battle of Agincourt in 1415. The later addition of a leaded spike some time during the early 1500s made the tower the tallest in Hertfordshire, rising to an impressive 175 feet.

Ashwell flourished and developed into a thriving medieval market town but in 1350, during the time that St Mary's Church was being built, the plague swept through the town, decimating the population who struggled with the pestilence in their midst for eleven long years. This has given rise to the church's other well-known feature, the Black Death graffiti, which exists as incised inscriptions in Latin and early English on the pillars and most prominently on the north wall of the tower. Like a tormented cry calling out through the centuries, the translated words give some idea of the anguish of its medieval writer and the despair of living in that plague-ridden world, together with the violent gales which interestingly coincided with its departure from Ashwell:

> There was a plague
> 1000, three times 100, five times 10,
> a pitiable, fierce violent
> [plague departed]; a wretched populace survives to witness and in the end
> a mighty wind, Maurus, thunders in this year in the world, 1361.

The church of St Mary at Ashwell, whose haunting dates from the middle of the nineteenth century. *(Photograph by Eddie Brazil)*

Ashwell church's famous Black Death graffiti. *(Photograph by Eddie Brazil)*

The church was completed some twenty years later but the end of this decade of the plague was the beginning of a gradual decline in the fortunes of the town. Its market was gone by the beginning of the 1800s, which forced a later reliance on agriculture – and during the nineteenth century other local industries such as straw plaiting for the Luton hat makers and brewing – which now have ceased entirely.

The alleged haunting of St Mary's appears to stem from a single incident which Luton-based ghost hunter William King has dated as occurring in 1850 when a local woman, Georgina Covington, went to attend a Friday evening choir rehearsal being held inside the church. As she walked through the churchyard she became aware of another person approaching from the direction of the nearby rectory, and as this individual passed through a shaft of moonlight it was revealed to be a black-draped and headless figure. The apparition came closer before finally fading away as it reached the church door. The horrified woman was able to reach the interior of the building before collapsing in a faint in front of the already assembled choristers. To our knowledge this experience has never been repeated and as such its origins remain unknown.

 [Grid Ref: TL 266 398] Ashwell is a remote village three and a half miles north-east of Baldock; nearest railway station is Ashwell at nearby Odsey and closest main road is the A505 between Baldock and Royston.

17. ST LAWRENCE'S CHURCH, BOVINGDON, NEAR HEMEL HEMPSTEAD, HERTFORDSHIRE

Another Hertfordshire church which has its own particular canine ghost is St Lawrence's at Bovingdon, three miles south-west of Hemel Hempstead. The church is Victorian and dates from 1845 but as with St Nicholas in Stevenage, it is the churchyard, which at over four and a half acres is the largest open burial ground in the county, that is reputed to be haunted by a ghost dog – this time with fiery eyes, something along the lines of the legendary 'Black Shuck'. Tony Broughall interviewed several local people who related to him that a story commonly held in

The haunted churchyard of St Lawrence at Bovingdon, near Hemel Hempstead, Hertfordshire. *(Photograph by Eddie Brazil)*

Bovingdon village in the past told of the first person to be buried in the churchyard being charged to guard the church and its environs against all evil-doers until the end of time. In order to assist with this, the sexton placed the body of a large black dog on top of the coffin as it was lowered into the grave and the animal's ghost has been seen over the years patrolling along the top of the churchyard wall on the lookout for graverobbers and similar troublemakers. Unfortunately, Broughall was unable to find any record of the animal being seen in recent times and as such the haunting of St Lawrence's Church remains a colourful and interesting supernatural tradition rather than a well attested case of genuine paranormal phenomena. Rather more substantial is the double row of Irish Yew trees which line the main path to the church, a well-known feature of the churchyard. A 'gleaming presence' has long been seen running along a wall in nearby Box Lane according to Hertfordshire historian W.B. Gerish, and an account of an insubstantial white figure in the same road was given to Paul Adams in 2002.

 [Grid Ref: TL 017 037] Turn into Bovingdon High Street off the B4505 Hempstead Road; after a quarter of a mile go left into Church Lane by The Bell public house and the churchyard entrance is 50 yards down on the left.

18. CHURCH OF ST PETER AND ST PAUL, TRING, HERTFORDSHIRE

When Sheila Richards addressed the Ghost Club some years ago, the title of her lecture was 'The Most Haunted Town in Hertfordshire – Tring' and it does seem that this small market town situated in the Chiltern Hills some thirty miles north-west of London, where Lawrence Washington, the great-grandfather of the First President of the United States of America, lived in the early seventeenth century, can in fact live up to this reputation.

Tring has many reported ghosts and haunted places – the Tring Park School for the Performing Arts building – the former Tring Mansion designed by Sir Christopher Wren in 1685 – is haunted by the apparition of a beautiful lady; as late as 1976 in Langdon Street another female ghost, that of a lady in a flowing dress wearing a picture hat, was seen floating along the driveway of a house and also walking in the road; headless men and women have been observed proceeding in both directions from time to time along the ancient Icknield Way on the outskirts of the town; Station Road, between Tring and Aldbury, is haunted by a spectral horse and rider, and there are many others. It should be of no surprise therefore to learn that the church of St Peter and St Paul, located close to the main High Street in the centre of the town, is a haunted building.

The first recorded rector of St Peter and St Paul's was Nicholas de Evesham in 1214 and an unbroken list of rectors, perpetual curates and vicars can be traced from this time to the present day. The aisled nave and chancel date from the thirteenth century and the church itself has seen much alteration work over the years. A south porch was added in the fourteenth century, at which time construction work began on the heavily buttressed three-stage west tower, which was completed by the end of the fifteenth. The chancel and north aisle were partly rebuilt in the 1700s and the church saw two Victorian restorations, one in the early 1860s and a second twenty years later. A number of tombs and monuments can be seen inside and there are three churchyards, two adjoining the church to the south and north and a third,separate burial ground also to the north, adjacent to the grounds of the former vicarage which was built in 1825 and is now a private house.

Former Luton-based ghost hunter Tony Broughall has collected the account of phenomena in St Peter's and St Paul's, a single occurrence which may be unique in the history of haunted English churches, being an encounter with the ghost of one of the church builders (but see also the entry for Winchester Cathedral). In his *Two Haunted Counties* (2010), Broughall recounts the experience of a lady visitor who attended a morning service in the church in the early 1960s. As the woman sat listening to the sermon, she suddenly became aware of an old man standing in the space between the end of her pew and the side wall of the church. Of ruddy complexion with tousled hair, he wore an old-fashioned smock and held in his right hand some kind of tool

The church at Tring, Hertfordshire, where psychical researcher Tony Broughall collected an account of a ghostly mason. *(Photograph by Eddie Brazil)*

which the witness took to be a hammer. As their eyes met he gave a brief nod of recognition and then with immense pride said, 'I built this wall,' and, reaching out, placed a hand on the stonework. Amazed, the un-named woman glanced around, thinking his voice must have interrupted the vicar's sermon, but nobody had apparently noticed anything amiss. Looking back she was astounded to find that the man had completely disappeared.

After the service had finished she told the vicar, the Revd Therold Lowdell, of her strange experience but found him quite unsympathetic and was curtly told that she must have fallen asleep and dreamt the whole episode. Broughall's informant was quite adamant that this was not the case and as such the incident remains an interesting one. To our knowledge, the spectral builder has not made any appearances to other parishioners since this particular time over forty years ago.

 [Grid Ref: SP 924 115] St Peter's and St Paul's Church is located on the north side of the B4635 High Street in Tring town centre.

19. ST MICHAEL AND ALL ANGELS, ASTON SANDFORD, BUCKINGHAMSHIRE

Aston Sandford, east of Haddenham and some six miles south-west of Aylesbury, is a peaceful cul-de-sac hamlet in the meadows of the Thame Valley. Its tiny church, with a chancel, nave and bell turret, seems to have been rebuilt in the thirteenth century. However, the building has undergone extensive restoration over the centuries and now it is difficult to clearly date the fabric.

Thomas Scott, grandfather of architect Giles Gilbert Scott, who designed the Albert Memorial in London, was Rector of Aston Sandford between 1803 and 1821 and it is his ghost which has been seen in the church at various times. The apparition is said to appear at the altar behind the incumbent as he conducts the service and then slowly fade away. The last recorded sighting took place some years ago, although a lady informant at the church could not give a precise date. On this occasion one of the church helpers entered the building one day to carry out cleaning and was shocked to see the figure of a clergyman standing at the altar. She reported that the apparition remained in view for just a few seconds before vanishing.

It is believed that the Revd Scott so loved Aston Sandford that his ghost returns to keep a kindly, guiding eye on the present incumbents, although many of the villagers have their doubts about the authenticity of the haunting of the church, and put the apparition down to nothing more than a trick of the light. At certain times of the day it has been suggested that the sun shining through the south windows into the chancel casts odd shadows onto the east wall of the church behind the altar. To the more imaginatively minded this mixture of light and shade creates the illusion of a figure on the rear wall; when the sun becomes shaded by clouds the impression of the figure naturally fades from view.

It was believed the ghost of Revd Scott was seen only within the church. However, during our research at Aston we were contacted by a previous resident of the village, who informed us of a curious series of sightings she experienced in November 1996. Although the young woman has a deep interest in the paranormal, even more so since her experience, she requested to remain anonymous for the purposes of this book.

Miss A is a commercial artist and between October 1996 and March 1997 she took a short let on a cottage in the village whilst working on a temporary contract for a company in the nearby town of Thame. At the time of her tenancy, Miss A, aged thirty-six and single, kept herself to herself and rarely had contact with the rest of the villagers. Her normal daily routine saw her travel the few miles to her place of work in Thame and return in the evening, and, on the basis of this, her stay in Aston Sandford should have been a rather uneventful six months.

St Michael and All Angels at Aston Sandford, Buckinghamshire, haunted by the ghost of the Revd Thomas Scott. *(Photograph by Eddie Brazil)*

There were days when she was afforded the luxury of working from home. Following a day spent at the easel she would find time to get some fresh air and it was her practice to take a half hour stroll through the village up to the junction with the main road to Haddenham and then return the same way. Her route took her past the church of St Michael and All Angels, which she always found to be locked. On a cold afternoon in late November 1996, just as dusk was turning into evening, she was passing the church and, looking over to the south door, saw a person whom she assumed was the vicar about to enter the building. She describes the figure as dressed in typical clerical garb. Thinking no more of it she continued on her walk. On her return she noticed that no lights shone from the church and that the interior was in darkness. Assuming that the vicar had quickly concluded his business and left the building she returned home.

Some days later she was taking her late afternoon stroll past the church and again noticed the clergyman at the south door. She made a mental note that if she saw the vicar on her return she would go and introduce herself and see if it would be possible to have a look around inside. The late November afternoon had grown almost into early evening gloom and once again on her way back she found the church in darkness and assumed that, being so familiar with the church layout, either the vicar didn't need to turn on the lights in the church or was conducting his business in a side vestry.

After two weeks of hectic coming and going from Thame on business she again had the pleasure of working from home and as before, after a hard day at the easel, took her leisurely stroll down through the village. As she passed the church she once again looked across to the south door and in the half-light there stood the clergyman about to enter the building. Miss A thought it might be a good time to go over and introduce herself and see if the vicar might give her a brief tour of the church. As she entered the churchyard she momentarily looked away from where the vicar was standing and on looking back towards the building she was surprised to see that the cleric was no longer there. He could not have gone inside the church; she would have surely heard the opening and closing of the door and, looking around, she saw that the graveyard was deserted. Now more than a little puzzled, she walked to the south door and tried its handle. The church was securely locked and in darkness. It was at this moment that Miss A said she became icy cold and a little unnerved. It began to dawn on her that there was no clergyman in the church or for that matter in the churchyard and what she had thought was the vicar on previous days was not a real person.

It is hard for us to imagine what our own actions would be if we found ourselves alone in a darkened graveyard and became aware we were witnessing a genuine paranormal incident. For Miss A there was only one thing to do – she turned and hurriedly left the churchyard; yet as she did so she says she had the horrible feeling that someone was walking quickly behind her. When she reached home she rather dramatically, as she now concedes, locked the door and turned on all the lights.

Following her experience, Miss A curtailed her late afternoon stroll through the village past the church in favour of a midday walk in the November sunshine, or more likely the grey of an overcast day. Although she admits this was an overreaction to a curious episode which she cannot explain she is convinced that she saw a ghost, but who or what the apparition was remains a mystery. Eventually, before leaving Aston Sandford, she got to view the interior of St Michael and All Angels and from the villagers learnt of the story of the ghost of the Revd Thomas Scott. She refrained, however, from sharing her strange experience with the residents of Aston and only contacted the present authors about her strange episode when made aware of the preparation of this book.

 [Grid Ref: SP 756 079] Off the A4129 between Thame and Longwick.

The interior of Aston Sandford church. (*Photograph by Eddie Brazil*)

20. CHURCH OF ST PETER AND ST PAUL, ELLESBOROUGH, BUCKINGHAMSHIRE

Ellesborough church stands proudly on a steep knoll halfway between the towns of Wendover and Princes Risborough in South Buckinghamshire. As one looks south from the churchyard, the beech-covered landscape rises and dips across to the dominating Beacon Hill with its grassy mound and lone tree, iconic amongst the Chiltern hills when viewed from within the Aylesbury Vale. It is also the site of Cymbeline's Mount, referred to in Shakespeare's play *Cymbeline*. In reality, the reference is to the British King Cunobelinus who, alongside his sons, battled at this site against the Roman invasion of the British Isles. This is rambler's countryside and many ancient tracks and pathways criss-cross the area. Looking north, the churchyard slopes precariously down through the trees and tumbling gravestones to give views out over the wide, flat vale of Aylesbury.

Although built in the late fourteenth century, the building is very much a Victorian restoration. The Hawtry family, once owners of the Prime Ministers' country home Chequers, are laid to rest here. St Peter and St Paul is often referred to as the 'Prime Ministers' church' as many incumbent premiers have attended Sunday morning worship here when in residence at nearby Chequers. Margaret Thatcher was famously known to have prayed at Ellesborough church, finding comfort there during the 1982 Falklands War.

There are several apparitions associated with the church although it would seem these are not in fact long deceased Members of Parliament. Over the years the ghost of a tall man in medieval garb has been seen to glide towards the memorial tablets commemorating the Hawtry family and disappear within, although it is unclear whether or not the apparition is that of Sir Thomas

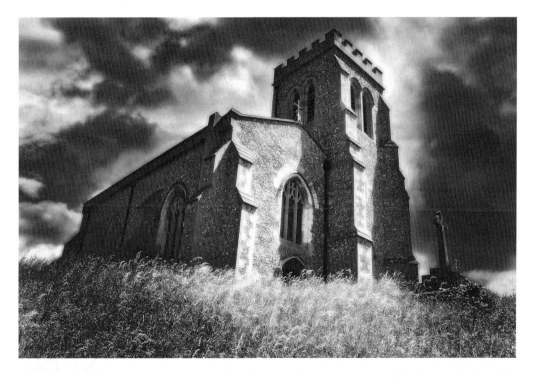

The church of St Peter and St Paul at Ellesborough, Buckinghamshire – a number of different apparitions have been reported here over the years. *(Photograph by Eddie Brazil)*

Hawtry, who restored Chequers in the late sixteenth century. On many occasions the spectral figures of two women have been observed sitting in the pews nearest the altar. Their identities remain unknown.

Ellesborough church is not without its own White Lady ghost. She is said to be the revenant of the unrequited lover of the Revd Robert Wallis, who was rector in the early seventeenth century. He is said to have remained in his post for only two years before resigning, perhaps leaving with his conscience troubled after their forbidden tryst was discovered. Why his lover's spirit should choose to haunt the church is a mystery. The ghost of Wallis himself has been seen on the footpath leading to the south door of the church, the rector of Ellesborough during the 1980s having apparently witnessed the apparition on many occasions.

As can be seen from these brief accounts of paranormal activity at Ellesborough, the phantoms which haunt the church are not easily identified. The spectres witnessed may well be the ghosts of Sir Thomas Hawtry or the Revd Wallis, but until a thorough investigation of the sightings is undertaken we can only speculate as to who or what the apparitions are. Critics would argue that the sighting of the alleged ghosts may well entail a certain amount of psychological suggestion. If the church has a reputation for being haunted then an individual in possession of that prior knowledge is more disposed or primed to witness something strange. Yet at Ellesborough it would appear that on many occasions, people who have no prior knowledge of the church's ghostly reputation have witnessed apparitions, in particular a tall man dressed in medieval attire. The infrequency of the sightings, however, would suggest that the paranormal 'energy' of the area is diminishing and one could regularly visit Ellesborough and not experience anything out of the ordinary. It remains one of the many allegedly haunted sites where a chance encounter with the unseen may still be possible for the dedicated psychical researcher who, as so often happens in ghost hunting, is in the right place at the right time.

 [Grid Ref: SP 836 067] Ellesborough is a mile east of Little Kimble on the A4010 which has a railway station.

21. HOLY TRINITY CHURCH, PENN, BUCKINGHAMSHIRE

The village of Penn sits high in the Chilterns on the B474 between High Wycombe and Beaconsfield, some thirty miles north-west of London, and the picturesque beech-covered hills and wooded valleys of the surrounding area belie its close proximity to the sprawling capital. Building of the church was begun in the twelfth century with a tower being added in the late 1300s. In 1725, the north side of the chancel was remodelled. Sir William Penn, founder of the city of Philadelphia and after whom the state of Pennsylvania takes its name, claimed Penn as his ancestral village and his five sons and their families lie in the vaults beneath the church. However, Sir William, his wife and their children are buried in the churchyard at Jordans, seven miles to the south-east where, so tradition says, the seventeenth-century Quaker meeting house was constructed out of timbers taken from the *Mayflower*. Despite their close association with the area it seems that the Penn family do not feature in the paranormal activity reported at Holy Trinity Church.

In the eighteenth century, an unfortunate farmhand by the name of Clarke was killed when he was thrown from his horse, and for many years afterwards it was his restless spirit which was said to bring terror to anyone passing through Penn after dark. The ghost was said to be particularly troublesome in 1880. Four farmers, perhaps fortified by strong ale, decided on a spot of ghost hunting. As they rode along the moonlit village lanes they suddenly saw the phantom rider as he appeared through a hedge and galloped off ahead of them, the spectral horse's hooves making no sound on the frosty road. They set off in pursuit but on reaching Penn church the apparition entered the churchyard, whereupon it turned and laughed at the pursuers before vanishing in a grey mist. The next day the farmers returned to the spot where the ghostly rider had disappeared and were alarmed to find that there were only the hoof prints of four horses, not five.

This account has all the hallmarks of a traditional ghostly legend told endlessly around the Penn village fireside, impossible to substantiate by the ghost hunter and just another old wives' tale for the sceptic. Is it possible to prise some grain of authenticity from such a typical anecdotal tale? Folk stories are rarely conjured out of thin air and even the most outlandish have at their root some grain of truth. We can reasonably accept that at some period in the eighteenth century a farmhand by the name of Clark was killed when he fell from his horse, thereafter the locals believing it was his restless spirit which haunted Penn churchyard and the village. What is curious is the year 1880 – over a hundred years after the farmhand was killed – is singled out as a period when the ghost was being particularly troublesome. This would seem to suggest that the tale of the ghostly rider, far from being just another piece of local superstition retold in a traditional manner, was in fact some kind of genuine paranormal phenomenon which was experienced and substantial enough to be remembered and the year noted. Whether or not it was the restless spirit of Clark we shall never know, but it could well be a case of folklore flesh being grafted onto the bones of an actual paranormal incident.

A relatively recent report of paranormal phenomena at Holy Trinity Church may well have its own bones eventually clothed in local folklore, if only for the need to identify the apparition. In the late 1980s a figure in white was said to walk through the churchyard at night, passing through the east gate and descending Paul's Hill. The figure was described as a woman in pale, flowing garments or perhaps wearing a white nightdress. When approached, the figure vanished and the identity of the apparition is unknown. However the local pub, the seventeenth-century Crown Inn which stands just across the road from the church, is also said to be haunted by an unknown woman in white. Could the spectre from the Crown also be the figure which walks in the churchyard? In recent years it has been suggested that the lady in white could well be the ghost of the last woman to be hanged in Britain.

The ill-fated Ruth Ellis and her equally doomed lover David Blakeley, a resident of Penn, often frequented the Crown during their tempestuous relationship. They would have also visited Penn

Holy Trinity Church at Penn with its haunted churchyard. *(Photograph by Eddie Brazil)*

church and walked in the churchyard. In April 1955, Ruth Ellis murdered Blakeley outside a London pub and three months later she was executed by Albert Pierrepoint and Royston Rickard at Holloway Prison. Blakeley was brought back to Penn and laid to rest in All Saints. Before her death Ellis wrote to Blakeley's parents, saying, 'I have always loved your son, and will die still loving him'. Is it possible that the troubled spirit of Ruth Ellis still walks in Penn churchyard? Ghost hunters should be wary of assigning identities to traditional 'white lady' spectres in order to substantiate incidents of paranormal activity, or give it some kind of solid foundation. If Ruth Ellis was to haunt any churchyard it might be thought it would be St Mary's, Amersham, five miles north-west of Penn, where she was laid to rest after being disinterred from Holloway in the early 1970s. However, if there is any validity in Carl Jung's view that ghosts of Women in White are archetypal personifications of outraged feminine feelings, then an identification with Ellis would, to many, be plausible.

 [Grid Ref: SU 916 933] Penn lies on the B474 between Beaconsfield and Hazlemere.

22. ST LAWRENCE CHURCH, WEST WYCOMBE, BUCKINGHAMSHIRE

The criteria for the churches, abbeys and cathedrals included in this book is of course that they have been, at sometime during their history, the site of reported paranormal phenomena. However, there are one or two locations, even though they may appear to be outside the remit of our survey and in the strictest sense cannot claim to be haunted, which are nonetheless places which have stories, histories and peculiarities we feel will appeal to the paranormal researcher, the historian and those fascinated by the macabre and the bizarre. The church of St Lawrence, West Wycombe is one such location. Although as far as we can ascertain no paranormal activity has ever been reported within the building, ghosts, murder, Satanic rites, pagan worship, debauchery and the eccentricities of England's eighteenth-century titled gentry are all inextricably linked with this church, which stands proudly on top of West Wycombe Hill.

Of all the church locations described, St Lawrence readily deserves the word 'spectacular'. Standing within the ramparts of an Iron Age hill fort, the church looks out over the grand sweep and roll of the Chiltern Hills. The site has been continuously occupied for centuries. A Bronze Age settlement is widely believed to have first existed on the hill and research has shown that a pagan temple was constructed in a similar style to Stonehenge. The Romans also built their own settlement and religious temple here. During the Saxon period the site became the village of Haeferingdune, the 'hill of Haefer's people', a name which later evolved into Haveringdon. The hill retained its religious importance and the first Christian church was erected in 635. Haveringdon was greatly reduced by the Black Death in the fourteenth century and by the early 1700s, the village had relocated to the valley along the Oxford road and was subsequently renamed, due to its position 'west' of the town of High Wycombe, with the villagers retaining St Lawrence as their parish church. Today no trace of Haveringdon village on the hill survives.

In 1724, Sir Francis Dashwood (1708-1781), 2nd Baronet, and later fifteenth Baron le Despencer, succeeded to the West Wycombe estate and set about remodelling the house. Like many titled gentlemen of his day, he embarked on the grand tour of Europe and returned to England with his own grandiose plans for West Wycombe. In 1763, the fourteenth-century church of St Lawrence disappeared within Dashwood's rebuilding of the interior, copied on the third-century temple of the sun at Palmyra in Damascus. Only the medieval tower was retained, which itself was considerably heightened and topped by a great golden ball fitted with benches and was large enough to contain six people. In 1764, the vast hexagonal Dashwood mausoleum was built east of the church. Its design was derived from the Constantine Arch in Rome and it was where the Dashwood memorials would later be erected.

The hilltop church of St Lawrence at West Wycombe. *(Photograph by Eddie Brazil)*

Of all Sir Francis' grand schemes for West Wycombe perhaps the most ambitious was undertaken between 1748 and 1752, with the extension of a series of ancient chalk tunnels under West Wycombe Hill into an elaborate labyrinth of caves and chambers. In order to provide work for the unemployed following a succession of harvest failures, Dashwood paid each labourer a shilling per day to excavate the passageways, which extended a third of a mile into the hill. Although it was a generous show of altruism, the Baronet had other motives. The caves' design were much inspired by Dashwood's travels in the Mediterranean. The descent through the passageways and underground chambers concluded by crossing a subterranean river named the Styx and entering into the inner temple, which is said to lie directly 300 feet below the church of St Lawrence. According to Greek mythology, the River Styx separated the mortal world from the immortal world and the subterranean position of the Inner Temple directly beneath St Lawrence Church was supposed to signify both Heaven and Hell.

Between 1750 and 1766 the Knights of St Francis, better known today as 'The Hellfire Club', held their nefarious meetings here. Their number included artist William Hogarth, the political activist John Wilkes, John Montague, 4th Earl of Sandwich, poet Paul Whitehead and possibly at times the American, Benjamin Franklin. It is uncertain what exactly the Hell Fire Club members got up to during their twice monthly meetings. They greeted each other as 'Brother' and dressed as monks while their accompanying ladies were attired as virginal nuns. Possibly some form of Satanic or pagan ritual mimicry took place but more likely they indulged in drinking, gambling and whoring. The Club disbanded in recrimination in 1766 following a practical jape played on the Earl of Sandwich during one of their drunken ceremonies and his subsequent ridicule for believing that the materialisation of a monkey, jokingly released from a box by a fellow member, was the physical manifestation of the Devil.

Following Dashwood's death in 1781 the caves fell out of use and became derelict. It was in the early nineteenth century that the subterranean passageways and West Wycombe Hill became the site of reported ghostly phenomena. Paul Whitehead, a steward and secretary of the Hell Fire Club and close friend to Sir Francis Dashwood, had his heart placed in an elegant marble urn in the mausoleum although his body was buried at St Mary's Church in Teddington (haunted by the ghost of Alexander Pope, 1688-1744) just outside London. In 1829 the body was allegedly stolen by an Australian soldier and it is believed that the ghost of Whitehead haunts West Wycombe caves and the hill, searching for his heart. Numerous visitors and staff have reported seeing a man in old-fashioned clothing wandering in the passageways. When faced he is said to vanish into thin air. The apparition of a man in eighteenth-century clothing has also been reported roaming the ramparts of the Iron Age hill fort which surrounds the mausoleum.

Perhaps the most well known and frequently sighted ghost to walk the caves is that of Suki, an attractive sixteen-year-old barmaid employed at the George and Dragon pub during the late eighteenth century. It is said that she fell for the charms of a gentleman who was passing through the village, much to the annoyance of three local lads who also had their eye on the pretty serving girl. A message, purporting to be from the handsome visitor, was sent to Suki at the tavern instructing her to meet him in the caves at night. Dressed in her finest white dress she entered the caves only to find that the message had been a hoax planned by the three jealous boys. In anger she threw rocks at the laughing lads but when the boys responded by throwing a rock back Suki was knocked unconscious. She was secretly brought back to her room at the inn but next morning was found dead. Her ghost is said to walk the corridors of the George and has also been reported to glide across the garden there.

The Dashwood family mausoleum, constructed between 1763 and 1764; the design is based on the Constantine Arch in Rome. *(Photograph by Eddie Brazil)*

The atmosphere of the past hangs heavy over West Wycombe Hill with the fingerprints of all who have left their mark: Bronze and Iron Age, Roman, Saxon, Norman, and perhaps most conspicuous of all, eighteenth-century excess. Sixty-five years before Sir Francis Dashwood was born, Roundhead soldiers of the Parliamentary army marching through West Wycombe would have defaced and destroyed any images, statues or iconography they found in St Lawrence Church as superstitious and un-Christian idolatry. In 1765, the Baronet remodelled a Christian building in the guise of a pagan temple and below created his own playground Hades, a breeding ground for the paranormal perhaps.

 [Grid Ref: SU 827 949] St Lawrence Church is 330 yards north of the A40 West Wycombe High Street; from the junction with Chorley Road follow West Wycombe Hill Road to a car parking area just north of the church and the Dashwood mausoleum.

23. PRIORY CHURCH OF ST MARY THE VIRGIN, HURLEY, BERKSHIRE

Hurley sits peacefully beside the River Thames near the town of Maidenhead in the county of Berkshire. The village lies within a valley amid an amphitheatre of green and wooded hills. St Birinus is said to have inspired the building of the parish church here around the year AD 700 during his mission to convert the Peoples of Mercia. In AD 894, the marauding Danes forded the Thames at Hurley when marching from Essex to Gloucester and may have destroyed this early building. It was rebuilt as Hurley Priory by Benedictine monks in the mid-eleventh century as a memorial to Athelaise, the first wife of Geoffrey De Mandeville, who was Lord of the Manor. The priory was dissolved in 1536 during the reign of Henry VIII. However the nave of the building became the parish church and in that capacity it remains today. Throughout the village one can still see the remnants of the priory's outbuildings such as the fourteenth-century barn, a pigeon house and the Bell Inn, thought to have been the Priory guesthouse established in 1135.

It is the site of the priory cloisters where paranormal activity has been experienced. The garden between the cloisters and the church was once the monks' burial ground. What was once the refectory of the Priory of St Mary has been converted into residential accommodation and it is here that the vision of a ghostly blue face has been seen floating across the ceiling of one of the apartments, although the identity of the image is unknown. One night the seven-year-old daughter of one of the residents had the terrifying experience of witnessing the apparition as it drifted above her as she lay in bed. Other phenomena include a door which frequently unlocked itself despite the efforts of a locksmith to prevent this, the apparition of a girl, aged about thirteen, who has been seen walking within the flats and across the cloister garden, and an invisible presence which has often been felt brushing against people walking down the apartment complex staircase.

As is often the case with paranormal occurrences, it is difficult for the researcher to pin down the causes and reasons for reported phenomena as the incidents can appear to be random and unconnected. We may reasonably assume that the presence which has been experienced on the stairs is that of the ghost of the young girl who has been observed in the garden, or that the unlocking of the door within the complex is some form of poltergeist prank that a ghost child might commit. However, clues to the phenomena of the eerie blue face, along with an explanation for other reported ghosts at Hurley, may well lie within the house which stands just across from the church.

Ladye Place was built in 1834 on the site of a Tudor mansion, which itself had been constructed on part of the priory site. When St Mary's was dissolved in the sixteenth century the land was purchased by the Lovelace family. In 1600, Richard Lovelace, first Baron Hurley, built his great Elizabethan mansion, converting the monks' refectory into stables with a hayloft for his horses.

It was in the cellars of Ladye Place that the Whig conspirators met in 1688 to plot the overthrow of James II. The house stood for over 200 years until falling into such disrepair that it was eventually demolished.

In 1924, a retired Colonel of the Royal Engineers, Charles Rivers-Moore, bought Ladye Place. Knowing something of the history of the house and priory and being a keen archaeologist, he was eager to begin excavations, in particular to try and discover the location of the grave of Editha, sister to Edward the Confessor, who was believed to have been interred at Hurley. It was her ghost, the Grey Lady, so the locals said, who was supposed to haunt the house. Although not a complete sceptic on the paranormal, Colonel Moore viewed such stories with amusement, preferring to concentrate on archaeology.

The Colonel's first tentative excavations were unsuccessful as the ground around the priory and the floor of the building had been raised in the past some 3 feet due to flood trouble. Yet in the spring of 1930, the Colonel's brother-in-law came to stay and related an extraordinary dream in which a monk had told him to sweep away the fireplace in the dining room, for behind it lay a semi-circular hearth with a great oak beam. Feeling he had nothing to loose from such a preposterous idea, Moore did so and was astonished to find an older fireplace behind the modern one exactly as described in the dream. Feeling there might be more to psychic phenomena than he initially thought, the Colonel, his wife and a few friends conducted a number of séances at Ladye Place. What the sitters learned from these, together with table-tipping sessions, was that during the Middle Ages a monk from Hurley priory had practised Black Magic and ever since had tried to keep his persecutors out of the house. Through a medium, the monk was assured that he had been forgiven by the Father Prior, whereupon he promised not to cause further difficulty in the house.

The cloisters of Hurley Priory, where a monk-like figure was seen on several occasions throughout the 1930s. (Photograph by Eddie Brazil)

Later sittings seem to establish contact with a spirit entity that had lived 400 years previously and which gave information about a secret passage which had led from the moat to the cellar of the house, and which had been constructed over the monks' burial place. The entity was angry that skeletons had been dug from the floor. Throughout the 1930s, many friends and guests of Colonel Moore and his wife continued to report sightings of spectral monks. Visitors walking on the site of the cloisters in the early evening would see a man dressed in monkish robes with his arms crossed. The figure would walk past the onlookers and to their astonishment suddenly vanish completely.

During his later years at Ladye Place, Colonel Moore compiled a dossier of all the strange events which had occurred and also obtained signed statements from various witnesses. These included doctors, archaeologists, solicitors and members of the armed forces. Although he continued to carry out excavations at the house and was successful in tracing the outline of the Lovelace mansion and parts of the old priory, he never did find the last resting place of Editha. In 1947, Ladye Place was put up for auction but failed to reach its list price. It was sold off in lots in much the same way as the priory had been in 1536. Colonel Moore eventually moved from Berkshire and settled in Scotland, where he was interviewed by Peter Underwood and where he died in 1965.

We may wonder why the ghostly monks of Hurley haunted the locality and possibly still do. Undeniably the seizure of the priory had robbed them of the peace and contentment of their monastic life. Yet it would seem, even in death, following the building of the Lovelace mansion and the despoliation of their burial grounds, they are fated never to rest in peace.

 [Grid Ref: SU 825 841] On the A4130 between the A404 and Henley-on-Thames; the church and priory ruins are at the north end of the High Street.

24. CHURCH OF ST MARY AND ST NICHOLAS, LEATHERHEAD, SURREY

Unlike a number of churches included in our survey, the haunting of the church of St Mary and St Nicholas in the town of Leatherhead, close to the busy M25 motorway in north-east Surrey, is not wholly anecdotal in nature. Good first-hand accounts collected on a number of occasions during the twentieth century reveal this attractive parish church has a persistent and ultimately mysterious resident phantom.

Dating from the eleventh century, the church has undergone much alteration work down through the passage of many years. The original Norman building was renovated in the early 1200s when aisles were added and, around 1320, the chancel was extended. An interesting feature of the church was uncovered during archaeological excavations carried out in 1906 and may possibly date from this period. This is a small cell-like room which at one time formed part of the chancel and of which now only the buried foundations and a bricked-up doorway in the north-east wall remain. The origins of this are obscure and there have been a number of proposals to explain its presence. One theory suggests it was a vestry constructed during the time the chancel was extended, while another possibility is that the chamber was an original anchorite's cell that was converted into a sacristy or vestry at some point after the Reformation. Whatever the explanation, this ancient room has a connection with the phenomena reported here.

The church's three-stage west tower was added in the late 1400s but the spire, also constructed at this time, was blown down during a gale in 1703. Internal alterations took place during the eighteenth century and as with many English churches, Victorian renovation was carried out, in this instance in the 1870s. Inside are two interesting memorials, the first a wall monument to Robert Gardiner, Sergeant of the Wine Cellar to Elizabeth I, and the second a sarcophagus dedicated to Richard Dalton, who held the same position to King Charles II.

The bricked-up doorway in the north-east wall of Leatherhead church, associated with an apparition seen by a parishioner in the building during the 1950s. *(Photograph by Eddie Brazil)*

The ghost of St Mary and St Nicholas is an unidentified apparition that witnesses have been unable to determine as being male or female. During the early 1900s the figure was seen by the Revd Coleridge (whose famous descendant we have already briefly encountered), who at the time kept his experience to himself so as not to alarm his parishioners.

In the 1950s, Mr F.B. Benger, an officer of the Leatherhead and District Local History Society, had occasion to visit the church to assist the verger in hanging a picture donated by a member of the congregation. While waiting alone inside the building for the verger to return from a shopping expedition to buy suitable fixings, Mr Benger happened to be looking down the length of the nave when something caught his attention. Several years later (1983) he recalled the incident: 'I suddenly became aware of what appeared to be a human figure moving from the north wall of the chancel towards the altar, where it vanished...It appeared to be clothed in a long gown of rough material like hessian...My first thought was that it must have been a shadow from a passing cloud coming through a window, but then I recollected that it was a November day and very misty with no sunlight to create shadows'. The point where the apparition appeared, so Mr Benger subsequently established, was a point that coincided exactly with the blocked-up doorway visible on the outside wall of the chancel.

In 1984, Christopher Slater, then organist and Director of Music at St Mary and St Nicholas, saw the ghost while conducting a choir rehearsal inside the church. He subsequently gave an account of his experience to writer Graham McEwan and described seeing a hooded figure, which he presumed was female, enter the church from the direction of the north door and move in the direction of the tower before passing out of sight behind a pillar. Assuming this was a chorister arriving late, Mr Slater went to investigate but found the outer door locked and that part of the church deserted.

As with many of the church buildings described here, the church of St Mary and St Nicholas may well reward the serious psychic researcher who is prepared to carry out a sensitive and discrete investigation at this interesting location.

 [Grid Ref: TQ 167 563] St Mary and St Nicholas is located south of the main town centre at the junction of the B2033 Church Road and the B2450 Dorking Road.

25. ST ANDREW'S PARISH CHURCH, FARNHAM, SURREY

Here, in the edifice built on the site of the original Saxon church and dating from the 1200s, there have been a number of well-authenticated ghostly happenings including the sound of chanting, phantoms and visions, or time-span illusions of the alteration of the interior of the church to how it would have been in pre-Reformation days.

A fire-watcher on duty during the 1939-1945 war heard Latin prayers being recited and saw a procession of candle flames form a double-line and move towards a closed door where they disappeared.

Dorothea St Hill Bourne, a local historian, talked with a witness of the pre-Reformation mass that is occasionally reported. She had been kneeling in prayer, alone at the back of the church, when she raised her eyes and saw a gold-clad celebrant and his assistants in bright vestments performing mass amid a cloud of incense. The whole church seemed to be crowded with shadowy, silent figures, some motionless but others moving up and down the aisle. She listened carefully but heard no sound of any kind. The vision lasted perhaps a few moments and was then abruptly shattered by the entrance into the church of the vicar and his churchwarden, coming to empty the alms boxes.

St Andrew's parish church at Farnham in Surrey. *(Photograph by Eddie Brazil)*

The interior of Farnham church, where historian Dorothea St Hill Bourne experienced a vision of a pre-Reformation mass. *(Photograph by Eddie Brazil)*

Dorothea told Peter Underwood that she was herself often conscious of unseen presences in Farnham church and once, while attending a service there, she was astonished to see, in the middle of the service, what appeared to be a semi-transparent veil or curtain descend, cutting off the chancel and altar, through which she could see, indistinctly, figures and lights moving. After a short while, probably only seconds, the curtain lifted and everything was normal again. She later discovered that a former curate of the church had witnessed something very similar. In addition he and a fellow curate sometimes saw an elderly lady enter the church ahead of them as the bell was ringing for evensong, but when they entered the church themselves the woman they had both observed quite distinctly was nowhere to be seen. One of these curates confirmed the experience, saying the figure they saw appeared to be 'absolutely real' and adding that the same figure had been seen many times within the previous twelve months.

Another ghostly phenomenon at St Andrew's is the unmistakable sound of horses champing and pawing the ground that has been heard apparently coming from the back of the church. It cannot but be interesting to know that at one time Cromwell used the church as stables. St Andrew's, with its fine stained-glass windows and historic tombs and monuments, is often regarded as one of the most haunted churches in England.

 [Grid Ref: SU 838 466] St Andrew's is located in Middle Church Lane off the A287 Downing Street in the centre of Farnham close to its junction with the A325 West Street.

26. BAYHAM ABBEY, NEAR TUNBRIDGE WELLS, KENT

These wonderful and picturesque ruins are haunted visually, audibly and mentally. Founded in 1200, these ruinous remains once housed a community of Premonstratersian Canons, a strict, reformed sect of the Augustinians. The English branches of the Order were called White Canons after the thick, woollen cloaks they wore of un-dyed material. They must have presented a splendid sight in the silent abbey in medieval days, and today, amid the enduring silence, these isolated ruins are still 'a place of absolute peace', as a poet and novelist has described them. Gentle Richard Church CBE says it is not surprising that legends survive of a procession of white-clad and torsured figures seen at certain times passing down the nave of the abbey, an abbey dedicated to the Virgin Mary.

Visitors cannot but be impressed and it is not difficult to visualize something of the grandeur that must have been Bayham Abbey in its heyday – and something of those times and its inhabitants possibly remain in the paranormal activity reported from time to time. Spectral monks repeatedly walk here as they walked 800 years ago and a procession of white-clad monks have been seen on innumerable occasions, among these hallowed remnants of a once thriving religious community. Solitary monks are also sometimes seen, just for a moment; a silent, white-robed figure disappearing behind an ancient wall. Most often, it seems, the ghost monks walk when there is moonlight, wandering among the ancient masonry and vanishing almost as soon as they are seen into the shadows of this evocative place.

Here too, as we mortals walk among the old stonework and admire the lasting work of past centuries, an overwhelming smell of incense sometimes invades the nostrils, although none has been burned here since 1536. At other times visitors have suddenly become aware of an irresistible feeling of peace and tranquillity, of calm and order in a busy world, and the impression of being not alone but in the middle of a crowd of quiet and holy men. When Peter Underwood was there in 1971 a friend, looking from the choir towards the nave and west entrance, became convinced that she was in the middle of a crowd of monks whose Latin chanting filled the air – and then as suddenly as it had arrived the vivid impression vanished. Other reported experiences in different parts of the ruins include the sound of sweet music, voices chanting in unison, the faint sound of bells tolling and, more puzzling perhaps, the sound of revelry.

There again in 2008, Peter Underwood was accompanied by a Polish friend and they were both admiring the remains of a holy water stoup and, in the niche, the forlorn remnant of a tomb, when both felt something of the mysterious attraction and overwhelming sense of religious devotion and quiet peace that pervades these beautiful and haunted ruins; a sense of solitude, isolation and serenity that is rarely found anywhere these boisterous and busy days.

 [Grid Ref: TQ 652 365] Bayham Abbey is located four and a quarter miles south-east of Royal Tunbridge Wells on the B2169 between Bells Yew Green and Lamberhurst.

27. ST NICHOLAS CHURCH, PLUCKLEY, KENT

Pluckley, magnificently situated on the side of the North Downs with grand views of the enchanting beauty of the Weald of Kent, is a candidate for 'most haunted village in England' and certainly the number and variety of alleged ghosts is impressive. Ghosts reported here over the last few years have included a screaming man; a gypsy watercress lady; a coach-and-pair; a Victorian girl; an elderly lady; a brown-habited monk; a Tudor lady; a highwayman; a schoolmaster; a miller; a soldier – known as The Colonel; a lady in white; a lady in red, a woman in modern dress and a cavalier, not to mention mysterious lights, disembodied voices and other aural hauntings and poltergeist-like phenomena!

St Nicholas Church at Pluckley, Kent, part of the 'most haunted village in England'. *(Photograph by Eddie Brazil)*

The noble church of St Nicholas, where many members of the Dering family, who were granted an estate at Pluckley by Charles II for their loyalty in the Civil War, lie buried, is haunted by several ghosts and various ghostly activity. There may be the ghost of a John Dering, who died in 1425, and there were Derings here until the Great War of 1914-1918. Unfortunately, according to Arthur Mee, Sir Edward Dering (1599-1644) who 'restored many of the family brasses in the thirteenth-century church, may have falsified names and dates since he was not above a little forgery for the aggrandisement of his family'. Be that as it may one Lady Dering, who died while still young and beautiful, was so venerated, so loved and so missed that her husband, wishing to preserve her loveliness, had her dressed in rich apparel and laid a red rose at her breast, and she was placed in an air-tight lead coffin which was in turn encased in a second coffin and then a third, also of lead. The three coffins were then encased in an oaken one and the quadruple casket buried in the family vault, beneath the Dering Chapel. In spite of all these precautions and encumbrances, Lady Dering's ghost has been seen in the church and churchyard many times, resplendent in her finery and holding a red rose (the last gift from her husband) at her breast. This story was a long-guarded family secret and there are suggestions that she may have been as wicked as she was beautiful.

Unexplained and mysterious lights have been reported in the stained-glass windows of the Dering Chapel where eerie knockings, echoing thuds and the sound of a woman's voice have been heard. One investigator, inside the church, heard sounds he could not explain and saw 'splashes of flaming yellow-green light' blazing in the upper half of the stained glass. This light was also witnessed by a companion. Twelve months later a disembodied woman's voice was heard in the churchyard.

This phenomenon of a woman's voice, calling in a far-away and pathetic manner, has been heard on many occasions. Sometimes too the figure of a woman wearing red, known as the Red Lady, has been seen among the gravestones. It has been suggested that she is another member of the Dering family searching for the baby she lost. Some students who camped here reported seeing a huge white and silent phantom hound in the churchyard; unaware that there had long been reports of such a spectral animal in the vicinity. According to a report published in 1995, a phantom white dog was encountered inside the church.

A phantom woman in modern dress has also been glimpsed from time to time inside the church but no one knows who she is or why she walks. Greystones, part of Rose Farm close by, is reportedly occasionally visited by a phantom brown-habited monk who has also been seen inside St Nicholas's. The local rector, when one of us was last there, the Revd John Pittock, was by no means sceptical of all the ghostly activity reported in and around his church.

 [Grid Ref: TQ 926 454] Pluckley is two miles due south of the M20 motorway and four and a half miles north-west of Ashford; the nearest town on a main road is Hothfield on the A20. The village and church has to be reached by country lanes.

28. CHURCH OF THE BLESSED VIRGIN MARY, CLAPHAM, NEAR WORTHING, WEST SUSSEX

Despite our knowledge of there being no reported paranormal phenomena having taken place inside the Church of the Blessed Virgin Mary at Clapham, its prime location and collateral involvement in the notorious Clapham Wood and Chanctonbury Ring mysteries over the past forty years makes it an ideal subject for discussion in the present work. The fact that the death of a former vicar of the parish has become linked with Satanic activities in this part of West Sussex and the church building itself exhibits physical evidence of having been adapted to repel local witchcraft and occult practices strengthens our decision to include it here.

Clapham is a small village comprising a single street located close to the South Downs, three and a quarter miles north-west of the centre of the coastal town of Worthing. Mentioned in Domesday Book, a continuous line of parish rectors can be traced back to William de Radenore in 1257, although the church itself dates in part from the eleventh century. The church is of a simple design comprising a north-west tower, nave and chancel; on plan the nave is at a noticeable angle bearing northwards from the entrance at the west door, an irregular shape which has been put down to the builders trying to make a representation of the angle of Jesus' head on the Cross. The dedication to the Blessed Virgin Mary took place in 1406 although the church's three historic bells, named Jacobus, Caterina and Caterina Margarita, date from nearly a hundred years earlier and are notable as being the earliest ring of three in the country.

As with many churches throughout England during Victorian times, Clapham church underwent substantial restoration, in this particular case during the early 1870s by noted architect Sir George Gilbert Scott. The connection of the north side of ecclesiastical buildings and churchyards with the burials of murderers and suicides and by association the presence of an unseen world of darkness and evil is well known. At Clapham this is evident in the old fifteenth-century doorway in the north wall of the church, being at some unknown point blocked up so that today only the outline of the original opening remains, an act that may be explained as an attempt on the part of an earlier generation of Clapham parishioners and clergy to prevent an ingress of imagined evil, possibly associated with local witchcraft, into the church. Given the reputation that Clapham Wood, which borders the north and west sides of the churchyard, has acquired in recent years for paranormal happenings and covert occult practices, this ancient alteration seems now strangely relevant to our modern world.

The blocked north door of Clapham church, a noted sign of past efforts to repel evil forces and the effects of witchcraft. *(Photograph by Paul Adams / Eddie Brazil)*

Accounts of unusual happenings in the Clapham area, particularly sightings of UFOs over or near Chanctonbury Ring, the site of an old hill-fort on the South Downs four and a half miles north-east of Clapham village, were reported with some regularity in the local press from the mid-1960s onwards. However, it was not until the beginning of the 1980s and the publication of a series of articles by journalist Toyne Newton in *The Unexplained* part-work magazine that these and other mysterious events associated with the region achieved a wider public. As well as strange lights and shapes seen in the night sky over Clapham Wood, Newton reported other unusual and disturbing incidents – a mysterious black mass seen amongst the trees and the impressions of strangely shaped footprints, both reported by a local ghost hunter; a crater-like site in the centre of the woods where higher than normal levels of radiation were picked up by a Geiger counter; a powerful debilitating force which on occasion appeared to temporarily take control of animals and people walking through a section of Clapham Wood known as The Chestnuts, and the regular disappearance from the area of domestic animals including several dogs and on one occasion a horse.

Newton's research brought him into contact with Charles Walker, a paranormal investigator from nearby Worthing. Initially interested in UFO sightings, Walker had subsequently carried out investigative visits to both Chanctonbury Ring and Clapham, where he and fellow researchers had several strange and, on occasions, frightening experiences. During a night-time vigil to Chanctonbury in August 1974, a member of Walker's party, William Lincoln, was apparently levitated five feet into the air before being thrown to the ground. Five years later in the same location Charles Walker was again present when another researcher, Dave Willis, was knocked off his feet by a powerful unseen force.

Throughout the 1970s, Charles Walker's investigations led him to believe that the woodland around the church of St Mary's at Clapham was being used for the practice of occult and Satanic rituals. In the autumn of 1978 this was confirmed when Walker met and was threatened by an anonymous informant, who claimed both Clapham Wood and Chanctonbury were being used by

The Church of the Blessed Virgin Mary at Clapham on the South Downs, geographical centre of the Clapham Wood enigma. *(Photograph by Paul Adams/Eddie Brazil)*

a Satanic coven called the Friends of Hecate, who carried out animal sacrifices at their regular meetings.

Both Charles Walker and Toyne Newton discovered evidence of occult practices in the area. At Clapham, Walker photographed a Satanic mural painted on the wall of a farm building close to St Mary's church and at Chanctonbury Newton likewise found makeshift Satanic altars constructed from stones and pieces of wood. Shortly before the Great Storm of 1987, which destroyed many of the trees at Chanctonbury Ring, Paul Adams also found the remains of what appeared to be an occult altar at the same site.

The two researchers also had reason to believe that the disappearance of a number of local people in the Clapham area during the 1970s could be linked to the activities of Satanists and their followers. In 1972 the body of a police constable from Steyning who had been reported missing six months earlier was found near Chanctonbury Ring. A second missing person, sixty-year-old Leon Foster, was found dead in Clapham Wood in August 1975. Three years later, the Revd Neil Snelling, vicar of St Mary's church between 1960 and 1974, disappeared while walking home over the Downs in the direction of Clapham Wood; it was to be 1981 before his skeleton was recovered in woodland at nearby Wiston. In all three cases the coroner's verdict was inconclusive as to the cause of death.

In his book *The Demonic Connection* (1987), Toyne Newton expanded on his investigation into the Clapham case, considering it part of a larger occult conspiracy involving Black Magic and Satanic practices. According to Charles Walker, the publicity generated throughout the 1980s resulted in the Friends of Hecate abandoning this part of the South Downs as a centre of activity, although the area's reputation for the strange and mysterious continues to attract the attention of both serious researchers and sensation seekers, both to Clapham Wood and the church of St Mary's.

 [Grid Ref: TQ 095 066] Clapham lies on the A280 Long Furlong Road just under half a mile from its junction with the A27; 340 yards down The Street take the single-track roadway on the left to the church.

29. NETLEY ABBEY, NEAR SOUTHAMPTON, HAMPSHIRE

The evocative ruins of Netley Abbey are located close to Southampton Water, three miles to the south-east of the main city centre. The Abbey complex is the most complete surviving Cistercian monastery in the south of England, being founded in 1238 by the Bishop of Winchester, Peter des Roches, who also provided land for the creation of Titchfield Abbey on the outskirts of Fareham. Despite his patronage, des Roches died at the age of sixty-three on 9 June – the same year as building work began at Netley – without seeing a single stone laid. In 1239 a founding colony of monks from Beaulieu settled at Netley and after the construction was complete the Abbey enjoyed the later patronage of Henry III.

The Dissolution of the Monasteries caused great change at Netley. In August 1536, Henry VIII gave the Abbey to Sir William Paulet (1475-1572), Marquis of Winchester, who carried out major alterations, including the demolition of the former monks' refectory, to transform the monastery into a large Tudor courtyard house. Later owners included William Seymour, 1st Marquis of Hertford and Theophilus Hastings, 7th Earl of Huntingdon. The mansion was occupied up until the beginning of the 1700s when the then owner, Sir Berkeley Lucy, began demolition work with the intention of selling the salvaged stonework and timber for building materials. However, the death of one of the demolition contractor Walter Taylor's labourers, who was killed by a section of falling masonry, was seen as a bad omen and the work was halted temporarily before Sir Berkeley ultimately abandoned the project.

As the years progressed, much of William Paulet's Tudor alterations were gradually removed and the fabric of the Abbey was stripped back to its original medieval structure. Thomas

The haunted ruins of Netley Abbey near Southampton Water. *(Photograph by Eddie Brazil)*

Dummer (1739-1781), an English MP, dismantled the former north transept in the mid-1700s and rebuilt it as a folly in the grounds of Cranbury Park, near Winchester, but the remaining abbey quickly fell into ruin. By the nineteenth century it had become a popular Victorian tourist attraction, which excited many of the Romantics of the day – John Constable painted at Netley, Jane Austen found inspiration for *Northanger Abbey* (1817) in the ruins, while poet Thomas Gray was captivated following a visit in 1764. According to vampire hunter David Farrant, Gray was introduced to the supernatural side of Netley Abbey by the boatman, who, when ferrying him across Southampton Water, spoke of the buried treasure said to reside in the ruins and the 'things seen near it' at times, guarding the hoard.

Stories of buried treasure have long been associated with Netley and have given rise to the Abbey's principle haunting – that of the apparition of a hooded monk, said to have been seen on many occasions in the vicinity of the original sacristy. In his book *Dark Journey* (2005), David Farrant states that the ghost has also been known to manifest as a 'hostile presence' and gives examples of encounters with this invisible manifestation. In 1981, two visitors camping out on the Abbey site were awakened by their dog barking fiercely at an unseen presence, which lowered the temperature drastically in the vicinity of their tent, while around the same time – the early 1980s – two nuns had a similar experience while passing the site of the sacristy, a localised and unnatural chill accompanied by a feeling of being watched by a malevolent but unseen personality.

A decade earlier in 1970, a Mrs Neal of Netley village claimed to have seen a beckoning monk-like figure clad in a dark brown robe with a large loose-fitting hood while dowsing with a divining rod in the grounds of the Abbey House, a private nursing home adjacent to the Abbey ruins. A friend who accompanied her was unable to see the apparition but picked up an unnatural atmosphere in the location indicated by Mrs Neal. In recent years the sound of chanting has also been reported as well as the sighting of a figure in white. Whether or not this is the shade of the monk fading as the years pass by, a possibility if one buys into the 'stone tape' theory of ghost manifestations, remains to be seen.

Another story which has been passed down over the years concerns a secret underground room somewhere beneath the Abbey ruins akin to the hidden chamber at Glamis Castle, which contains, in the words of ghost writer Antony Hippisley Coxe, 'so awful a secret that a man called Slown literally died of fright'. Archaeological work over the years has failed to locate this particular aspect of Netley Abbey's association with the supernatural. It should be mentioned that close to the ruins is the site of the former Royal Victoria Military Hospital of which, following demolition in the mid-1960s, only the chapel now remains. It was here that the ghost of Florence Nightingale was reported to have been seen several times, particularly during the period when the hospital building was being demolished.

 [Grid Ref: SU 453 090] Netley Abbey is now in the care of English Heritage. Look out for a parking area where Victoria Road runs into Abbey Hill on the route out from Netley village adjacent to Southampton Water.

30. BEAULIEU ABBEY, NEAR LYNDHURST, HAMPSHIRE

'There is no place known to me in which you would be more likely to see a ghost in daylight than the ruins of Beaulieu Abbey – it is a quiet place, full of ghosts'. So said H.V. Morton, arguably Britain's most popular travel writer. As Lord Montagu, whose home is Beaulieu, said to Peter Underwood: 'You will find that ghosts are an accepted part of the scene here.' And so they are.

Monks first came to Beaulieu in 1204 when King John, frightened by a dream, released some Cistercian abbots he had imprisoned and provided money for them to build an abbey. Today, amid the ruins of that abbey, there are ghostly monks, strange lights, the fragrance of incense, celestial singing and the sound of chanting at dead of night.

No monks have lived at Beaulieu since 1538 when the Abbey was dissolved, yet for many years there have been numerous reports of ghost monks being seen in the vicinity, especially about the Cloisters. In view of the fact that some reports appear to conflict with others, it is important to remember that the Cistercian abbots wore white, the choir monks also wore white but, when working, they covered their robes with a black scapula, while the lay brothers wore brown. The Revd Robert Frazer Powles spent some sixty years as curate and then vicar at Beaulieu and to him the ghost monks were as genuine and as natural as any mortal, and he quietly accepted them as part of his daily life, speaking of them with reverence and complete conviction.

Evidence is not only abundant but varied in description and comes from many different witnesses and informants. Officers during the Second World War drove past a group of monks in the abbey grounds; a nurse saw a monk, seated beside a magnolia tree, reading a small scroll – he disappeared after a few moments; a lady known to H.E.R. Widnell, steward to the Montagu family for more than thirty years, was so troubled by the appearance of a phantom monk that she arranged for Sir Arthur Conan Doyle and Lady Doyle to visit, which they did, and thereafter the disturbances began to decrease. Clairvoyant Tom Corbett and authoress Diana Norman told Peter Underwood they 'had never encountered such a mass of evidence from one stately home as they encountered at Beaulieu'. Michael Sedgwick, when he was curator of the Montagu Motor Museum, occupied a cottage on the east side of the Abbey Church and he said he had twice heard the unmistakable and quite inexplicable sound of chanting there. One of Beaulieu's manageresses also said she had heard similar chanting, describing it as 'quite beautiful and something to be remembered for always'.

Paul Sangster from Bognor Regis and two friends spent a night in the Cloisters area and saw several spots of light moving across the centre of the Cloisters, north to south, and at 2.15 in the morning a photograph was taken which appears to show two groups of three lights followed by a single one. They could discover nothing to account for these lights. They also saw the shadowy form of a monk in the gateway on the west side of the Cloisters, directly facing them; the figure turned and took two or three steps before suddenly disappearing. The investigators immediately walked over to the spot where the figure had appeared and disappeared and found the temperature to be ten degrees colder than the other side of the Cloisters.

That Beaulieu has ghosts cannot be disputed, but as Lord Montagu says, 'The ghosts here have never been evil, in fact I don't think they have ever been anything but extremely friendly, but they have been seen and heard by countless people…'

 [Grid Ref: SU 388 027] Beaulieu is six and a quarter miles south-east of Lyndhurst on the B3054 between Lymington and Hythe.

31. ST LAWRENCE PARISH CHURCH, ALTON, HAMPSHIRE

Alton is a country market town once known to Edmund Spenser (1552-1599), the prince of poets whose friend Sir Walter Raleigh presented him to Elizabeth I, and whose immortal *Faerie Queene* he dedicated to the Queen. Spenser's house still stands in Amery Street – and it may well be his ghost that is seen occasionally in the vicinity.

The parish church of St Lawrence is full of interest with its carvings of a dragon, a dove, an ass, hyena and cockerel executed by men who could have fought at the Battle of Hastings. Six hundred years later the staunch Royalist Colonel Boles made his last stand here against Sir William Waller and his Cromwellian troops – and there still exist musket holes and marks of the affray which can be found on pillars inside the church, in the doorways and on the great church

St Lawrence's parish church at Alton, Hampshire, known for its psychic impressions of fighting soldiers.
(Photograph by Eddie Brazil)

door itself. It all brings to life as little else can, the harsh and cruel Civil War; indeed visitors to this church have become so immersed in the atmosphere of this stirring episode in history that they have become convinced that the apparently deserted church is filled with struggling and fighting men and they have reported hearing the frightening sounds of battle that would have filled the building more than 350 years ago.

Witnesses to paranormal activity here include a family consisting of husband and wife and their two children who, while quietly reading something of the history of the church, suddenly all found themselves in the middle of a melee of invisible struggling men with all the sounds of fierce and violent fighting. These alarming sounds, which each reacted to independently, caused them all to make a hurried exit from the haunted church. Once outside the parents wanted to return to see whether the phenomenon persisted but the children were terrified and only wanted to get away. In the event the mother stayed with the children outside on the open ground and well-tended grass while the father returned gingerly back into the church, but inside found all was quiet and calm and all the sounds and impressions of battle had completely disappeared – for the time being.

Dorothea St Hill Bourne, the historian, located one Alton resident who had personal knowledge of at least half-a-dozen people who had experienced similar psychic activity and once Dorothea herself, visiting the church alone, had the overwhelming impression that the church was full of grim fighting men but she heard no sound on that occasion, which was in fact when she was attending an evening church service.

A far more tranquil influence from some forgotten episode from the past is perhaps duplicated by the overwhelming smell of lilies-of-the-valley that has been reported occasionally in the porch of the church, usually completely out of season. In August 1971 the strong but delightful smell was experienced by a party of five people visiting St Lawrence's one morning. Dr W.S. Scott, the authority on Joan of Arc, was among the party and he searched diligently and persistently for a natural cause for the overwhelming scent but was completely baffled, as were the other members of the group. At the time no one, including Dr Scott, were aware that this scent had been reported in this spot by other visitors over the years.

 [Grid Ref: SU 717 396] From the A31 dual-carriageway take the B3004 into Ansty Road; after this becomes Normandy Street look out for Church Road and St Lawrence's Church on the right.

32. ST MARY'S CHURCH, BRAMSHOTT, NEAR LIPHOOK, HAMPSHIRE

There are those who consider Bramshott a meritorious candidate for England's most haunted village and it has to be accepted that there are many interesting ghosts here.

The old manor house, nestling among fields at the end of a short lane, has long had the reputation of harbouring a ghostly White Lady who is generally thought to be Lady Hole, a former much respected and benevolent owner who, it seems, shares the haunting of this fine old house with two other ghosts, a priest from Elizabethan days and a Quaker. There is a still, quiet atmosphere here that may be conducive to ghosts, as there is in the lush and tranquil meadows beside a slow flowing stream where the ghost of a suicide walks. Mistress Elizabeth Butler, it is said, became so unhappy that she drowned herself here in 1745 and, ever since, her ghost walks occasionally beside the water and nearby church.

Amid watchful yew trees of indeterminate age, this delightful church boasts a beautiful thirteenth-century chancel and seventeenth-century silver church plate, an early pewter flagon and wonderful portrait medallions – and a ghostly girl.

The unidentified figure of a young girl in a poke bonnet, seemingly rather large for such a small girl, has repeatedly been seen wandering through the churchyard before disappearing through the churchyard wall. One inhabitant, who lives nearby, has stated that the girl has been seen many times from the window of his house, usually in daylight and more often in the summertime than at other seasons of the year.

There are stories that she became lost, many years ago, when visiting Bramshott with her parents and although they searched the lanes and byways and the fields guarded by high hedges, she was not found but eventually she made her way back to the church and lay down to rest among the gravestones. And there she died, whether through being attacked or from natural causes is unknown, but it seems her phantom form still walks forlornly among the graves and perhaps her ghost cannot leave the scene of her death, for she never seems to have seen seen beyond the churchyard wall.

Other ghosts at Bramshott include a Grey Lady, who is seen lingering beside a well where she is thought to have jumped to her death; a pot-boy who hurries hither and thither with pints of ale as he did in the days when coaches stopped and the passengers called for refreshments; a host of ghosts in Tudor costume haunt one of the leafy lanes, and there are at least half-a-dozen other ghosts in this spectre-ridden village, including the unmistakable ghost of horror actor Boris Karloff, who spent some of his last days at one of the original and lovely cottages here.

 [Grid Ref: SU 843 329] Bramshott is just north of the A3 at Liphook; from the junction with the dual-carriageway St Mary's is 300 yards north along Church Road.

33. ALL SAINTS' CHURCH, CRONDALL, HAMPSHIRE

Hampshire was the centre of prolonged resistance to the Parliamentarian forces led by Oliver Cromwell and during that time nearby Basing House became a stronghold for the Royalist cause. In 1643, in preparation for an attack on the stubborn garrison, Sir William Waller, a general of the highest skill (known as William the Conqueror!), posted his troops at Crondall, itself the scene of several skirmishes, where he fortified the churchyard and he and his troops probably used the church itself, so perhaps it is not surprising that over the years there have been persistent reports of ghostly Roundhead soldiers haunting the immediate neighbourhood of the church.

There is also reliable evidence that on some moonlit nights a uniformed and mounted trooper is seen to emerge from a private drive opposite the church and ride through a wall and then up the avenue of lime trees, vanishing into the church through a closed door. He is said to be the ghost of one of Waller's men, who was killed while this house of God was being attacked.

One of these seventeenth-century ghosts is said to have disturbed a wedding ceremony within living memory when the sound of unexplained horses' hooves were heard by the wedding party and guests, seemingly tramping across the roof of the building being used for the celebrations.

The fine late-Norman church with its seventeenth-century tower does seem to be haunted by ghostly Cromwellian soldiers and the historian Dorothea St Hill Bourne has furnished us with a first-hand account which is quoted verbatim:

Last night, Wednesday 2 November, being a very fine moonlit night, a friend suggested that we should enjoy an hour's cycle ride so we set off to Crondall. The time was 10.15 p.m. when we reached the church. We had left our cycles against the wall of the churchyard and were about to go up the lime avenue to the church when we noticed a misty object coming, it seemed to us, from a carriage drive opposite the wall. We stood perfectly still and waited to see what it really was when, to our amazement, we saw it was a rider on horseback, dressed in what looked like the armour of Cromwellian days. Whatever it was rode right through the churchyard wall, up the avenue, and disappeared, it seemed to us, into the church. We waited about half-an-hour, hoping it would return, but we did not see it again.

The church path at Crondall in Hampshire, haunted by the apparition of a spectral horse and rider. *(Photograph by Eddie Brazil)*

This took place during the Second World War.

The late Mrs Edgecombe of Shalford near Guildford was present at a wedding in Crondall church. Before the wedding there had been talk of a ghost having been seen in the vicinity of the church and during the wedding service, while the congregation were standing, heavy footsteps were heard clumping from end to end of the building. Several of the gathering were visibly upset and no explanation was ever discovered for the loud and disturbing noises.

In 1971, Colonel Cromwell interviewed a local man who had seen the Cromwellian ghost. It was at Christmas time and he was walking past Crondall church when he saw a mounted figure in armour appear from a house opposite the church and ride through the wall, up the avenue of trees, and hammer on the church door. He never forgot the reverberating knocks but at the time he became frightened and hurried away and never again went that way at night-time. When Colonel Cromwell spoke to this witness, he was told the incident had happened about thirty years previously.

It could well be that this ghostly soldier was among those involved in a skirmish at Crondall on 27 January 1645, when six Roundheads were put to death.

 [Grid Ref: SU 795 485] All Saints' Church is located at the junction of Church Street and and Croft lane in the centre of Crondall village opposite the village hall.

34. ST PETER AND HOLY CROSS, WHERWELL, NEAR ANDOVER, HAMPSHIRE

Legend has it that the picture postcard village of Wherwell, on the road between Winchester and Andover, was once the scene of a fierce battle involving a cockatrice – a fearful winged monster that had four legs, the wings of a fowl, the tail of a dragon that ended in a hook, thorny pinions and the head of a cockerel. This peculiar aberration is supposed to have appeared in the cellar of Saxon Wherwell Priory and terrorised the locality until a certain local man named Green produced a mirror of highly polished steel, which he lowered into the cockatrice's lair whereupon the creature did its best to battle with its reflection, which it took to be an enemy, until it collapsed from exhaustion, whereupon Green descended into the dungeon and killed the creature with his spear. A plot of land to this day is named after the plucky Green and traces of the priory can be found.

In Andover Museum a relic of the cockatrice battle can be seen: a metal cockatrice that once adorned the steeple of the church at Wherwell. Ghostly nuns are reputed to haunt the site of Wherwell Priory, carrying candles, and sometimes the place where the nuns were buried is lit up by supernormal light.

The church contains thirteenth-century sculpture and the sleeping figure of a nun, possibly the Prioress; there are also the remains of a seventeenth-century stone wall that was once part of the Priory destroyed on the orders of Henry VIII. The Priory was originally founded by Queen Elfreida, who arranged the murder of her stepson at Corfe Castle so that her own son could become king. Later she retired from the world to Wherwell, where, in an effort to atone for what she had done, she 'clothed her body in hair cloth, slept at night upon the ground and mortified her flesh with every kind of penance'.

Is it her ghost and that of her followers who are seen from time to time hereabouts, usually at dusk in late autumn? These ghost nuns have been reportedly seen in the churchyard and among the fragmentary ruins of their lost Priory.

 [Grid Ref: SU 392 408] Wherwell is three miles south-east of Andover at the junction of the B3420 and the B3048.

35. WINCHESTER CATHEDRAL, HAMPSHIRE

Inside this magnificent cathedral, standing proudly in this fine, historical city – the capital of England before London – lie buried the remains of Izaak Walton and Jane Austen among other notables. Here, in bygone days, were crowned William the Conqueror and Richard I and here too Queen Mary married Philip of Spain – Mary's chair is still in the cathedral. St Swithun (the cathedral's first bishop) is said to have expressed the wish to be buried outside the place of worship he knew so well; in his humility he wished for the feet of passers-by to tread on his grave and for the rain and sun to fall directly upon it, and there his body lay for more than a century and a chapel was erected over the site of the grave – faint traces can still be seen in the north-east corner of the cathedral, where ghostly chanting has been heard. The skull of St Swithun is said to have been removed to Canterbury in the eleventh century and the arm of this patron saint of Winchester was long a treasured possession at Peterborough.

The cathedral is certainly haunted and well it might be, for there are numerous historical associations with numerous historical personages and reports of phantom monks walking in procession both inside the cathedral and nearby, supposedly on the site of a former convent or religious establishment of some kind. A limping monk is frequently seen in the garden of one of the houses in the Close, witnesses including a canon's wife; she said the figure glided through a wall into the cathedral. Interestingly enough, at least three skeletons have been discovered hereabouts, probably members of a religious monastic order.

An occupant of a house near the cathedral was visited by a ghost monk when she was a child. Miss Clare de Hamel was about ten years of age when she found herself awake one night and she saw a figure in brown (she thought at the time it was a man in a brown dressing-gown), later she realized it was a Cistercian monk who walked through her bedroom and disappeared in the direction of a window. She never had any similar experiences but once met someone who lived near the cathedral who had several times seen a ghost monk pass through her bedroom.

By the eighteenth century the crypt floor of the cathedral had become covered with several feet of earth and when this was removed during alterations a lead coffin was found, thought to be that of Bishop Courtenay who died in 1492. Other coffins have been discovered in the cathedral walls and flooring and might well have connection with the various ghostly monks seen here, sometimes solitary, sometimes in pairs, and sometimes in procession.

Among the ghost sightings here is the not infrequent one of a phantom monk seen walking up the aisle and seemingly mounting invisible steps, while phantom figures have been seen and photographed within the precincts of the cathedral. Alasdair Alpin MacGregor once exhibited a photograph to Peter Underwood, taken in 1957 by an electrical engineer, Thomas L. Taylor. He took two photographs, one after the other, of the high altar and the carved stone screen. The first photograph was completely normal but the second photograph showed what appeared to be a number of human male figures in medieval costume. The cathedral clergy sought to explain the thirteen figures in terms of reflection or a freak combination of light and shade, but photographic experts disagreed and there the matter rested until the late Hans Holzer, the American parapsychologist, became intrigued by the fact that a photograph showed a procession of monks walking where no monks had walked since the sixteenth century.

Holzer learned that there had long been a suggestion that people standing at a certain spot in the nave sometimes saw transparent monks pass along the nave. He decided to try to photograph the phantom monks and, using no artifical light, no flash or floodlights and ascertaining that the cathedral was completely deserted in that area, his resulting photograph 'quite clearly showed three transparent hooded monks, seen from the rear, walking on what appeared to be a floor just below the present level of the floor (as a result, they were only visible from the knees up)'. Only later did he discover that the floor in that particular area used to be much lower.

The ghost monks at Winchester Cathedral are not only visible on occasions to people in the right place at the right time but it seems they can be photographed and have been, at least twice.

 [Grid Ref: SU 483 293] The cathedral is a landmark building close to the west bank of the River Itchen and the B3404 ring road.

36. FORMER CHURCH OF ST BARNABAS, BLACKWATER, NEAR NEWPORT, ISLE OF WIGHT

The following story of an encounter with the paranormal at the old Church of St Barnabas at Blackwater was collected by Isle of Wight ghost hunter and author Gay Baldwin and is so startling in its implications that first impressions for any reader must surely be that it reads like a work of supernatural fiction. We include it here as an example of the kind of narrative that anyone known to be involved with psychical research or paranormal investigation may at times be presented with and have to assess as to its authenticity or genuineness.

Blackwater is a small village two miles south of Newport and for several years the community was served by an equally small church dedicated to St Barnabas. This was a simple rectangular 'scout hut'-type building with a pitched and gabled roof constructed at some time during the twentieth century and faced with red-painted corrugated iron sheets; there was a simple bell arrangement over one of the end gables, a small entrance porch, and a seating capacity for a congregation of around eighty people.

In 1980, two Isle of Wight builders, Reg Blake together with another un-named workman, spent time at the little church carrying out repairs to the roof. This involved removing sections of the corrugated sheets and re-insulating the cavities between the rafters with sawdust. As the two men worked they became aware of an elderly lady dressed 'in old-fashioned clothes' who,

The former Church of St Barnabas at Blackwater on the Isle of Wight, scene of an amazing paranormal encounter during the early 1980s. *(Photograph by Gay Baldwin)*

unnoticed, had entered the church until she called out to them from below the scaffolding. She said she lived close by, gave an address and announced she had brought the men some tea. This was in an old aluminium flask, which she left on the church altar with a request that they drop it off to her when they had finished work.

After the lady had left, Blake and his partner took advantage of the impromptu tea break and, climbing down from the scaffold, retrieved the flask. However, the contents were completely cold and undrinkable and had to be thrown away. At the end of the day, when Reg Blake's mate went to return the flask to its owner, he was mystified to find that where the old lady had said she lived there was no house, only an empty patch of ground which showed signs of where a former building – now demolished – had once stood. The following day the two men questioned the churchwarden, who had called in at the church to see how the roofing work was progressing. It will be no surprise to anyone familiar with tales of the paranormal that after being given a description of the lady visitor and the address to where she said she lived, Reg Blake and his friend were told that the woman was in fact dead; in this case it was the churchwarden's predecessor, who had died in 1977. What became of the aluminium flask does not seen to have been recorded.

It is easy to dismiss this kind of encounter out of hand as being either too fanciful or too good to be true. When looked at objectively it is clear that accounts such as this contain specific paranormal elements that, when considered in isolation, have not only been reported by credible witnesses but documented by experienced researchers. For example, an impressive instance of an apparition interacting with a living person was collected by broadcaster and former *Tomorrow's World* presenter William Woollard for his television documentary series *Ghost Hunters*. Woollard interviewed a commercial airline pilot who recounted meeting another pilot whom he knew while walking through the concourse of Glasgow Airport. The two men stopped and exchanged a few words. Woollard's informant recollected the other man looked unwell and had been disinclined to shake his hand, but otherwise appeared as a normal solid person who spoke and responded to his questions. He thought nothing more of the incident until the following day, when he learnt, to his total astonishment, that at the time of their meeting the pilot had in fact been dead for two weeks.

Materialised objects such as the tea flask handled by the workmen at St Barnabas's church, sometimes termed 'apports' by researchers, are a familiar aspect of Spiritualist séances and have been reported throughout the entire history of organised psychical research, although it must be admitted that adequate control conditions in many recorded instances have been lacking. The series of physical mediumship séances held in Norfolk during the 1990s – known collectively as the Scole Experiment – recorded the appearance of many apported objects into a closed room during organised sittings; these included coins, jewellery and, on one occasion, a wartime newspaper dating from February 1944. Several highly respected members of the Society for Psychical Research, including Montague Keen and Professor David Fontana (acting in private capacities), visited Scole and were inclined to believe that the phenomena they experienced was genuine. Although apports were not received during the sittings the men attended, the unprecedented nature of the proceedings at Scole makes it unwise to reject the testimony that on several occasions solid physical objects materialised there in a way that modern science cannot either accept or understand.

There appear to be no further reports of the phantom lady of St Barnabas's church. The building was later considered to be surplus to requirements by the Church of England and, following de-consecration, was sold off in the early 1990s. At the time that Gay Baldwin included the case in her *Most Haunted Island* (2004), it had been used as a fruit and vegetable shop for some years.

■ [Grid Ref: SZ 507 864] The former church of St Barnabas is located on the A3020 Blackwater Hollow road close to the junction with the A3056.

37. ST OLAVE'S CHURCH, GATCOMBE, ISLE OF WIGHT

Narrow country lanes bring visitors, be they tourists or ghost hunters, to Gatcombe, a small village located centrally on the Isle of Wight, two and a half miles south of Newport. Despite its seemingly ordinary rural scene, Gatcombe has an affinity with the world of ghosts and the unseen. A White Lady is said to walk through the valley from Garstons Down in the direction of New Barn Farm, and an apparition wearing a long coat and a hat haunts the old wooden bus shelter close by on the main road to Newport. But it is the thirteenth-century church of St Olave, built as a manorial chapel by the Estur family, descendants of the Norman knight William Fitz-Stur, that concerns us here, mixing as it does supernatural fact and fiction in equal measure.

St Olave's is a small church comprising nave, south porch, a chancel that was rebuilt in the mid-1860s, and a fine three-stage west tower with a crenulated parapet; there is also a vestry on the south-west side. The renovated porch roof contains timbers which are said to have been salvaged from HMS *Thunderer*, a warship that fought in the Battle of Trafalgar.

The Esturs traded surnames, sometimes calling themselves l'Isle or Lisle, on other occasions d'Estur. In 1306, Edward I bestowed a knighthood on John Lisle, but his son John died without issue and the Manor of Gatcombe passed to the female line, of whom Edmund Estur, a Crusader who returned to England in 1365 with amnesia following a head wound received in battle, is of particular interest. Inside the church, close to the south wall, is a fourteenth-century carved oak figure representing Edmund. He is portrayed recumbent with crossed legs, a sign of his pilgrimage to the Holy Land, and has a small dog crouching at his feet and an angel by his pillow. Engravings from the 1700s show that at one time the figure held in its right hand a misericord

An oaken effigy of Sir Edmund Estur in Gatcombe church – the strange story of Lucy Lightfoot was carefully written around it during the 1960s. *(Photograph by Gay Baldwin)*

– a short-bladed weapon used to despatch fallen enemies quickly and cleanly in order to reduce their suffering – and it is around this and the enigmatic effigy of Edmund Estur that a certain amount of mystique has grown in recent years.

In the late 1960s the Revd James Evans, rector of Gatcombe between 1965 and 1973, created something of a paranormal enigma. He set down an account of happenings over 100 years before involving a young woman named Lucy Lightfoot, the daughter of a farming family from nearby Bowcombe, who, as a teenager, became a regular worshipper at the small church of St Olave's. Lucy was a beautiful girl, 'dark-haired, passionate, a fine horsewoman full of fiery spirit', for whom life in a small rural community clearly would never be enough to satisfy a deep longing for adventure. She became fascinated with the wooden effigy of Edmund Estur, visiting the church for hours on end to stand silently gazing down at his carved wooden face, her thoughts lost in dreams of accompanying the Crusader on his journeys to foreign lands.

At around half past ten on the morning of Monday, 13 June 1831, Lucy Lightfoot visited St Olave's and was seen to tether her horse by the iron churchyard gate and slip into the church. While she was inside there occurred a total eclipse of the sun, which plunged the landscape into an eerie premature darkness that lasted for half an hour. This was followed by a violent thunderstorm – torrential rain flattened crops and flooded fields, and a number of houses were struck by lightning. Several hours later a passing farmer from Chale noticed the frightened horse still tied up outside the entrance to St Olave's church and, recognising it as Lucy's, he hurried inside the building. Lucy Lightfoot was not there and in fact was never seen again. Despite extensive searching in the weeks that followed, she had, for all intents and purposes, vanished off the face of the earth along with, mysteriously, the jewel, a mounting of chrysoberyl in lodestone, from the hilt of the steel misericord held in the wooden hand of the effigy of Edmund Estur, a dagger which was found by the rector broken into pieces on the floor of the church.

As if this was not strange enough, several years later according to James Evans, in 1866, the Revd Samuel Trelawney, a Methodist minister from the Scilly Isles, while researching the history of the crusades, uncovered a manuscript collated by Phillipe de Mezières, Chancellor to Peter I of Cyprus, who had overrun Alexandria in the year 1365. This contained reference to several knights recruited by the Cypriot king in London in 1363, one of whom was Edmund Estur, who was accompanied by a young and beautiful woman from the Isle of Wight, whose name was Lucy Lightfoot. Trelawney discovered that Lucy had travelled with Edmund to Cyprus, where he had left her to sail on to Alexandria. There, wounded and with a weak mind unable to remember his youthful companion, he was brought back to England, where he died at Gatcombe, never recovering his memory for Lucy, who, after waiting for three years for her lover to return, ultimately married a Corsican fisherman and was heard of no more.

Such was the clarity and detail of the Revd Evans' narrative that his recounting of the story of Lucy Lightfoot, rooted as it was in the real world of the crusading Edmund Estur and the history of the little church at Gatcombe, had a convincing tone that seemed to transcend the bounds of local legend. Could this have been some form of timeslip or paranormal transportation – a side-step in time somehow created by the intense electrical storm that enabled the young girl to cross into a medieval world with which she had a clear attraction and affinity? Some people have thought so. Commenting on the case in the early 1980s, researcher Brian Innes wrote:

> Whether or not the 14th-century Lucy Lightfoot existed, there is no doubt that something very strange happened in Gatcombe church on that June morning in 1831; and it seems in some way to have been connected with the remarkable geological nature of the Isle of Wight, and with Gatcombe's position at its very centre.

James Evans' story is in fact simply that, an imaginative mystery cleverly blending fact with fantasy. The Trelawney manuscript is a fabrication, albeit with a convincing air of scholarly reality to it, existing only in the Welsh cleric's lively mind, who in later years was seemingly much bemused by the interest shown in his ultimately far-reaching tale. Evans was also responsible for another local legend attached to St Olave's which concerns the small dog resting at Edmund Estur's feet. Christened Flacon Caprice, this dog is said to come to life every 100 years on a moonlit Midsummer night and dance and tell stories with the little people from the hidden hollows under Chillerton Downs until morning.

With all these colourful tales, is it possible to believe any account of unusual happenings in this remote corner of the Isle of Wight? Writer and ghost hunter Gay Baldwin believes so and has collected two reports that suggest the churchyard at St Olave's is in fact haunted by the ghost of a little girl. On 31 October 1995, a group of Halloween ghost hunters carried out a light-hearted night-time visit to Gatcombe, not expecting to see or hear anything unusual. As they moved around the outside of the church with torches, they all suddenly became aware of the small figure of a female child with blonde bobbed hair and wearing a pale dress close to one of the churchyard walls. The girl skipped towards them before moving away and disappearing into the darkness. Unnerved the group left, but returned the following day and examined the churchyard in full light. The gravestone behind which the apparition had appeared was that of a child who had died in October a few years before. This may be the same grave that another separate correspondent reported being drawn towards by an 'unseen force' during a subsequent visit to St Olave's some time after the first encounter.

 [Grid Ref: SZ 492 851] St Olave's church is located on a bend in Gatcombe Road on the eastern outskirts of the village; access is off the road between Carisbrooke Castle and Chillerton.

38. KNOWLTON CHURCH, NEAR WIMBORNE MINSTER, DORSET

Christianity and paganism sit cheek by jowl at Knowlton in deepest Dorset. The ruins of a twelfth-century church stand within the ramparts of a Neolithic henge, both of which are now diminished through the ravages of time. When the Romans arrived in Britain in AD 55, monuments such as Knowlton, Avebury and Stonehenge were just as mysterious and enigmatic to them as they are to us today. No doubt such sites were used as some form of religious centre or possibly as astronomical observatories. Yet theories such as these are difficult to confirm either scientifically or archaeologically. In the first century AD, Britain had its own set of religious icons; pagan gods of the earth and Roman gods of the sky. It was into this land of contrasting beliefs that Christianity made its first tentative steps as one cult amongst many spread throughout the country by Roman artisans and traders alongside stories of their own pagan deities.

By the third century, British Christianity was being referred to and bishops from Lincoln, York and London attended a council at Arles in France, capital of the Roman province to which Britain was attached. With the departure of the legions in AD 450, Christianity retreated to the western fringes of Britain in the face of incursions by warriors and later settlers from across the North Sea. These Anglo Saxons had their own form of paganism which focused around the worship of deities. In 597, St Augustine landed on the south coast of England and embarked on his mission to convert the heathen English with a mandate from Pope Gregory that assimilated pagan festivals and practises into the Christian calendar and also to re-appropriate heathen places of worship to Christian churches, so as to ease the transition to Christianity. The change was a gradual one and was symbolised by the continued use of pre-Christian sacred places.

The church sited within Knowlton henge is Norman and underwent several alterations up to the fourteenth century. The village, like so many in England, suffered during the Black Death and was abandoned, although the church continued to be used up to the middle of the 1700s, when it too was abandoned and left to the elements, isolated and alone.

Not surprisingly, such an ancient site is not without its legends and myths, the most famous being the fate of Knowlton's church bell. Local folklore says that the bell was stolen by the bell ringers of Sturminster Newton who, fearful of being detected, reversed the shoes of their horses so as to baffle pursuers. Two of the party went ahead to White Mill Bridge to make sure the coast was clear, but they failed to return. The thieves, knowing the game was up, threw the bell into White Mill Hole on the River Stour. All attempts by the Knowlton villagers to retrieve it failed and there perhaps the bell lies to this day. Other tales tell of the Devil stealing the bell and throwing it into the River Allen. Attempts by the villagers to retrieve it were thwarted by the Devil; the bell sank to the bottom of the river and was never seen again.

However, despite the romantic folklore of Knowlton, the site is said to be one of Dorset's most haunted locations, with many sightings of unexplained phenomena being reported. The most recent report concerns a mother and her two children who were walking round the site during the day when they saw a shape dressed all in black cross their path right in front of them. The figure appeared to have come from nowhere and then disappeared as it reached the henge. The incident left the woman and her son and daughter shaken. There have also been sightings of phantom Roman soldiers, figures kneeling outside the church, the sound of fighting, disembodied voices sounding within the ruined nave, ghostly faces which appear at the windows in the tower, and men on horseback who ride through the church as if it wasn't there.

In the Introduction we encountered T.C. Lethbridge, the Cambridge Don, archaeologist and writer on the paranormal who died in 1971. He held the view that ancient stone circles and henges such as Knowlton and Stonehenge, together with Christian churches, were constructed at their chosen sites because it was recognised that they were places of energy, possibly some kind of transformer of powerful earth magnetism which could be used by the holy men or priests of the community, who may well have been psychic and possessed mediumistic abilities as a means to communicate with the dead, or what they thought were the spirits of those who had passed on. Lethbridge also theorised that this earth magnetism could in some way act as a psychic recorder of emotional vibrations of events which have taken place. They could be negative or positive vibrations and on occasions so strong that they can be picked up by 'sensitive' people who visit a particular site and who experience psychic phenomena, seemingly sounds and images of incidents which occurred many centuries before.

The lonely shell of Knowlton Church, where visitors have encountered ghostly Roman soldiers. The apparitions of horsemen are said to ride through the ruins. *(Photograph by Eddie Brazil)*

The varied paranormal incidents reported at Knowlton would suggest that there is some weight to Lethbridge's theory, in particular the phantom Roman soldiers and men on horseback could be recorded vibrations of people who were at Knowlton long before the church was ever built.

 [Grid Ref: SU 024 103] Knowlton Church lies on the B3078 between Cranborne and Wimborne Minster.

39. FORDE ABBEY, NEAR CHARD, DORSET

Two and a half miles due south from a point midway on the A30 road between Chard and Crewkerne, where the ghostly hoof-beats of a phantom highwayman's horse are said to travel along lonely Windwhistle Hill, is the former twelfth-century Cistercian monastery of Forde Abbey. Constructed between 1141 and 1148 close to the bank of the River Axe, the community was founded by Richard de Brioniis and originally carried a dedication to the Virgin Mary. By the time of the Dissolution of the Monasteries in 1539 the Abbey estate encompassed over 30,000 acres of land, which Henry VIII leased to a succession of absentee landlords, the first of whom was Richard Pollard.

In 1649, Forde Abbey was bought by Sir Edmund Pridaeux, a solicitor and MP for nearby Lyme Regis, who began alterations to turn the former monastery into a private house. However, Pridaeux became caught up in James Scott's West Country Rebellion of 1685 and, accused of being a Protestant sympathiser, was arrested and incarcerated for a period in the Tower of London before being ultimately released; he continued to live at Forde and died there in 1702,

Forde Abbey, where the ghost of the last Abbott, Thomas Chard, lingers in the Great Hall. *(Photograph by Eddie Brazil)*

following which a lengthy succession of private owners have eventually brought the beautiful house and its grounds into the twenty-first century. Today Forde Abbey is a popular tourist attraction and a soft fruit farm has been established on the estate.

The haunting of Forde Abbey is mainly centred on the Great Hall, where the apparition of a man has been seen from time to time, thought to be that of Thomas Chard, who was the last Abbott at the monastery at the time of the Dissolution and became the rector of St Mary's Church at nearby Thorncombe until his death in 1543. In his *Haunted Houses You May Visit* (1982), Marc Alexander describes the figure as wearing a 'pensive expression as he gazes around the place he loved so much during his lifetime'. How many times Chard, if it is indeed the old Abbott, has been encountered is unclear, although his ghost is reputed to haunt the 'Monk' Walk in the Refectory. The haunting is also associated with the Cloisters, an area of the building where Thomas Chard carried out alteration work that was left unfinished at the time the monastery was handed over to the Crown; here a monk-like figure is reported to walk on occasions.

Another ghostly connection with Forde Abbey concerns Jeremy Bentham, the philosopher and social reformer who rented the estate for a brief period beginning in 1815. On his death in 1832, Bentham's body was dissected and his head and skeleton were preserved and later acquired by University College London. Dressed in Bentham's original clothes, it can be seen on display in a glass case located in the South Cloisters. Bentham's ghost is said to walk the University corridors accompanied by the sound of his tapping cane, which resides in the cabinet with him.

 [Grid Ref: ST 359 052] Forde Abbey is four miles south-east of Chard; on the B3162 at Winsham take Western Way and follow the tourist signs to the Abbey.

40. CHURCH OF ST NICHOLAS CHURCH, SANDFORD ORCAS, DORSET

For psychic investigators active in the 1970s, accounts of ghostly phenomena in and around the sixteenth-century manor house at Sandford Orcas, three miles north of Sherborne in Dorset, kept alive the notion of a 'most haunted house in England' in a post-Borley Rectory world. Boasting an incredible total of twenty-two ghosts, it was an obligatory stop-off point for paranormal enthusiasts and this fine gabled Tudor building remains an enigmatic and interesting case. Sandford Orcas is a small village with records dating back to the eleventh century. The Manor House was built around 1550 by the Knoyle family who lived there until 1737, when it was sold and subsequently leased to a succession of tenant farmers for the next 120 years. In 1918 it passed to the Revd Sir Hubert Medlycott; his son lived there until 1964 and the Medlycott family continue to own it to this day.

In the churchyard of St Nicholas, directly opposite the manor's imposing gatehouse, lies the person who put this notable haunting firmly and squarely on the paranormal map – Colonel Francis Wilson Claridge, whose stirring family motto 'Fear Nought But God' is inscribed on his gravestone. Claridge took on a full repairing lease in the early 1960s, unaware that he was moving into a haunted building. Opening the house to the public for the first time he also began describing its impressive list of resident phantoms, some of which have been seen in the vicinity of St Nicholas's Church. This building dates from the fourteenth century but has been substantially altered – the chancel is original but the nave and south chapel were rebuilt in the 1600s and the three-stage west tower, embattled with gargoyles, and south porch are also fifteenth century. A north aisle was added during a Victorian renovation in 1871. The south chapel contains several monuments to three local families all associated with the haunted manor house – the Knoyles, the Hutchings and the Medlycotts.

Ghosts seemed to fill the rooms and passageways of the old manor house during the Claridge era at Sandford Orcas. On the stairs leading to the Solar Room, where former ladies of the house

Sandford Orcas Manor House, photographed in the 1970s during the Claridge era. *(Photograph by Paul Adams)*

retired after meals, an old lady with snow-white hair wearing a red silk hand-painted dress was often seen. The Solar was particularly noted for phenomena. As well as being haunted by the figure of another elderly woman seen wearing a red shawl, there were also three 'child poltergeists' which would cause disruption after the Colonel and his wife had shown visitors with children over the room, overturning furniture and pulling pictures from the walls. This resulted ultimately in the room being permanently closed to the public.

Two women in black dresses, said to both be former housekeepers, were seen inside the house, one in the Great Hall and the other walking up and down the corridors leading to the front door. The Great Hall was also the haunt of a small, rough-haired fox terrier, a former family pet that Colonel Claridge also heard running around in the old nursery on the anniversary of its death in 1900.

Other phenomena experienced inside the building was far more sinister. At night, between 10 p.m. and 11 p.m., the Claridges reported the sound of a person passing into the staff wing from the gatehouse, accompanied by a dragging noise and the smell of decaying flesh. Apparently an employee from Georgian times – when he raped several maidservants – this ghost would only be seen by virgin women visitors and, according to Francis Claridge, had been caught on an infra-red photograph which had shown him to be a seven-foot-tall giant.

One wing of the house at one time contained a closed room with an observation slit mounted in the door. This cell was constructed to hold a murderer, a young naval man from Dartmouth College who killed another recruit and died at the age of twenty-seven; his troubled ghost was said to linger in the room, screaming as he had done in life, and was seen at least once by a visitor.

The Claridge's bedroom was also a haunted chamber, the Colonel and his wife, Josephine, claiming to have seen several ghosts there. As well as the arresting sight of six monks walking

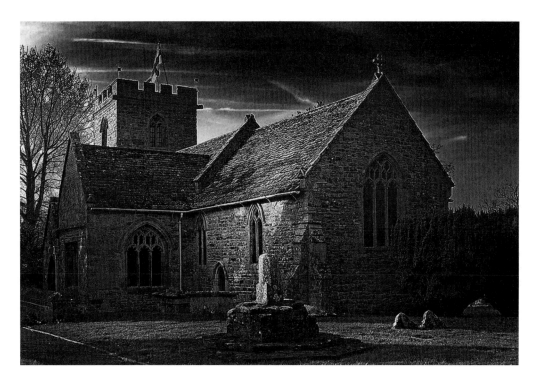

St Nicholas Church, with its close associations with the ghosts of Sandford Orcas Manor House. *(Photograph by Eddie Brazil)*

in procession, two murderous phantoms also put in an appearance – the apparition of a Moorish servant who strangled his former master with a cheese wire and the figure of a priest who killed a man by smothering him with his habit.

Many of the ghosts of Sandford Orcas and explanations for their appearances often relied on the sole testimony of the Claridges. However, the couple claimed to have received confirmation of previous experiences in correspondence with former members of staff and, in the mid-1960s, radical psychical researcher Benson Herbert reported favourably on the haunting after carrying out an on-site investigation. In interviews, Colonel Claridge described Sandford Orcas Manor as a 'strange house, very sad and unhappy'. He felt the haunting stemmed from a curse put on the house by a Saxon lord and pointed out Satanic symbols, which appear in one of the stained-glass windows, as an indication of past deeds which may have cast sinister shadows over the building through the years.

Colonel and Mrs Claridge were evicted in the late 1970s for failing to upkeep the building in accordance with their lease, although they continued to live in a cottage attached to the manor; the Colonel died in 1986 and his wife shortly afterwards. Between 1979 and 1981 the building was heavily renovated by the current owner Sir Mervyn Medlycott, who soon downplayed the now notorious haunted reputation. When Paul Adams visited in 1995 he poured cold water on the Colonel's claims, saying Claridge had made up 'a ghost a week'.

Despite this there is one phantom at Sandford Orcas for which good independent testimony does exist. This is the apparition of a former tenant farmer who has been observed several times in the garden and in the road outside St Nicholas Church. A suicide, he hanged himself from a pulley in the arch of the gatehouse which abuts the south-eastern corner of the churchyard. Wearing a white smock, the ghost was seen by a member of a BBC television crew in the 1960s and on another occasion by the wife of a visitor, who thought the solid, life-like figure sitting in the stables was a car park attendant.

A family snapshot taken by Colonel Claridge of his daughter in the garden outside the house seemingly showed an 'extra', which was identified as this particular phantom. A number of psychic investigators including Marc Alexander, Peter Underwood and Paul Adams, on a visit in 1977, have had the opportunity to view this particular photograph, in which the figure of a man wearing an old-fashioned cloth milking smock can be seen standing on the edge of the lawn and who was invisible to the enigmatic Colonel Claridge as he took his picture. Perhaps, as at Borley in Essex, a shift in emphasis from the haunted manor house to St Nicholas Church in years to come may result in a new series of paranormal phenomena being recorded by ghost hunters of the future.

 [Grid Ref: ST 622 211] Sandford Orcas is midway between two roads, the B3148 between Marston Magna and Sherborne and the B3145 between Sherborne and Charlton Horethorne; St Nicholas Church is 260 yards north of the centre of the village.

41. ST JAMES'S CHURCH, LUFFINCOTT, DEVON

In a remote corner of Devon, hidden in that no-man's land between Holsworthy and Launceston, deep in the pastoral landscape on the borders of Devon and Cornwall at Luffincott, stands the little church of St James. Nearby once stood the former rectory: both were haunted places. A hundred years ago the church was open and appeared to be in good condition, but, according to a letter in the *Western Morning News*, 'contained little of interest'. The rectory, a rambling and strange building, has more or less completely disappeared, with only a few stones to mark where it once stood.

The cause of the mysteries that engulfed both the church and the rectory seem to centre on the Revd Franke Parker, a bachelor who lived here alone, and many are the odd stories told about this strange and perhaps confused man who was rector from 1838 until his death in 1883. There is no doubt that he came to love the place and he repeatedly said that no successor would ever dispossess him of what he had come to regard as his and his alone.

He possessed an unusual collection of books on Satanism and the occult and, on occasions, thought of himself and acted like a dog or a toad. After Parker's death there were two very short incumbencies and a third, the Revd T.W. Browne, another bachelor, refused to live at the rectory and resided instead nearby at Clawton. He related that while at Luffincott Rectory, he saw the unmistakable ghost of Parker – and he left immediately and never entered the rectory again, leaving behind all his possessions. When the story spread, the rectory was pillaged and before long everything had disappeared. A few years later, either by accident or design, the house with its thatched roof caught fire and was burned down. Today hardly any traces of the house remain.

In recent years there have been many reports of a clerical figure appearing and disappearing in mysterious circumstances in the vicinity of the deserted church. One visitor approached the man and was astonished when, almost within touching distance, the seemingly solid form completely disappeared.

 [Grid Ref: SX 332 946] Luffincott is located one and a half miles north-west of Chapmans Well on the A388; the village with its church can be reached by narrow country lanes.

42. ST MARY'S CHURCH, OTTERY ST MARY, DEVON

Ottery, a town of very ancient foundations in the heart of rural Devon, is the birthplace of Samuel Taylor Coleridge (1772-1834) and was the setting for 'Fairoaks' in Thackeray's *Pendennis*. The town is associated with many peculiar activities, beliefs and practices. Here can be found references to Satan, pixies and suchlike and the town has long produced frolics particular to itself; especially around May Day, Midsummer and other pagan and pre-Christian anniversaries. Ottery's pixie-legend starts in the thirteenth century – or ever earlier – for the church with its twin towers, a copy of Exeter Cathedral on a small scale, was rebuilt in the fourteenth century by Bishop Grandison (who also worked on Exeter Cathedral), transforming it into a collegiate church, which status it held until the Reformation. It has been called the finest parish church in England. The pixies are blamed for the delay in the casting and delivery of the church bell named St Mary – anathema to the pixie realm. But eventually on Midsummer evening in 1454 the bell sounded for the first time over the Devon countryside.

Among the treasures of the church is a Norman font, a stone screen, an old season clock, a fine minstrels' gallery, and the quite remarkable statue tomb in the north aisle to Captain Coke, with died in 1632, supposedly murdered by his own brother to obtain an inheritance. The church also boasts a weathercock as old as the oldest stone in the whole edifice, which whistles in strong wind. The colourful and arresting statue of Captain Coke is said to come to life at midnight on certain nights of the year and to run around the interior of the church. It may be a legendary story whose origins are lost in the mists of time, but it is not difficult to find witnesses for this and other apparently paranormal activity inside this fine church.

Some twenty years ago, Peter Underwood was introduced to three independent witnesses with stories of unexplained happenings inside St Mary's. One, an elderly inhabitant who was born in the town, related how, in his youth, he had managed to spend several Midsummer nights inside the church, accompanied by church officials, and just once, all three including the informant swore they caught a brief glimpse of a brightly coloured figure disappearing behind a monument and the Coke memorial was devoid of its statue! Moments later everything had returned to normal. Both the other witnesses asserted that they had, comparatively recently, heard running footsteps inside the church, which had no apparent or visible origin. This is interesting in as much as it is known that certain ghostly manifestations 'run down' after a period of time, almost like a battery running out of power, and then visual aspects disappear while any aural attributes remain, until, with the passage of time, these aspects of a haunting also cease and, the haunting having apparently run its course, peace and quiet and tranquillity return to the locale of former ghostly activity.

 [Grid Ref: SY 098 955] Ottery St Mary's is south of the A30 between Honiton and Exeter. The parish church is on the B3177 road running through the centre of the town.

43. ST JOHN THE APOSTLE, TORQUAY, DEVON

The most well-known church haunting in the South West of England is arguably the case of the phantom organist at the church of St John the Apostle in the coastal resort of Torquay, south Devon. Accounts of strange and inexplicable phenomena, including the sighting of apparitions and the sound of the church organ playing by itself when the building has been locked and empty, date back over 125 years and surprisingly involve not one but two musical ghosts. A number of accounts of supernormal events were reported and set down by one of the church incumbents, who actively investigated the haunting, something of a rare event in itself as in the majority of cases, members of the clergy, for understandable reasons, often play down or dismiss stories of ghosts in and around their churches.

Compared with the majority of the churches included in this book, St John's is a relatively modern building. Dating from 1867, it was built on the site of a previous chapel and was designed by George Edmund Street (1824-1881), the noted ecclesiastical architect whose other commissions included churches in Eastbourne, Paddington and Southampton, as well at the Royal Courts of Justice in London; Street himself is buried in Westminster Abbey and St John's was actually completed by his son A.E. Street, working to his father's plans. The church, said by Pevsner to be 'one of the leading centres of nineteenth-century Anglo-Catholicism', consists of aisled nave with clerestory windows, chancel with south Lady Chapel and four-stage tower, and is noted for its paintings by English artist Sir Edward Burne-Jones (1833-1898) and its impressive total immersion font.

It seems that St John's became a haunted building before it was even two decades old, with reports of paranormal activity connected with the death of Henry Ditton-Newman, the resident organist, on 19 November 1883. Even before the young man had been laid to rest, it appears his ultimately unquiet spirit made its presence known to both the then incumbent and members of the congregation in equal measure. A parishioner holding a solitary vigil beside the organist's coffin on a bier inside the church reported the first alarming incident, that of the organ playing by itself with no one visible at the console and, shortly afterwards, after Ditton-Newman had been buried in Torquay cemetery, the Revd Harry Hitchcock, also alone inside St John's, heard the sound of an organ and on this occasion actually saw a figure he recognised as the late musician sitting in his former seat at the instrument.

Further incidents took place over the next forty years or so with, it would seem, enough regularity to enable a later rector, the Revd Robert J.E. Boggis, to make reference to the haunting in his *History of St John's, Torquay*, published in 1930, in which he mentions 'well-authenticated accounts' of the phantom organist being encountered inside the church.

The most active period of investigation and reporting into the haunting of St John's took place in the 1950s, during the brief incumbency of the Revd Anthony Thriscutt Rouse who, like Ernest Merryweather at Langenhoe and Alfred Henning at Borley, took an active interest in his church's resident ghost. Rouse was not only a man of the cloth but an active psychical researcher, President of the Torbay branch of the Churches Fellowship for Psychical Studies (later reorganised as the Churches Fellowship for Spiritual and Psychical Studies), an ideal investigator who was soon rewarded with incidents of phenomena involving not only the church but also the vicarage, known as Montpellier House, next door.

During a four-year period, beginning from the time he was inducted to the living of St John's in 1954, the Revd Rouse reported hearing footsteps while alone in the vicarage, particularly at the rear of the building, passing from the back stairs leading from the choir-well across the external yard and into the church. The rector also claimed to have heard the organ playing 'a heavy sort of music' by itself for several minutes on two occasions in the night; a lady helper reported seeing a shadowy apparition walking from the vicarage to the church during the Christmas period and a locum organist was so convinced of a presence sitting with him on the organ stool that he left the church and refused to return. Anthony Rouse ascertained that previous incumbents had also had similar experiences and took the happenings seriously enough to hold two services in the church in an attempt to quieten the ghost that he and his parishioners felt certain was the benign spirit of Henry Ditton-Newman, who simply felt a great attachment to the church and was unwilling to move on to another level of existence. However, this strange but pleasant atmosphere was ultimately not to last.

Prompted by a number of unsettling incidents, the Revd Rouse visited the College of Psychic Science in Queensberry Place, London (where at one time ghost hunter Harry Price had his headquarters) and consulted one of the resident mediums, giving examples of the apparent change in the nature of the haunting in recent months – a choir rehearsal abandoned due to an unpleasant atmosphere; the complaints of the full-time organist, who described feelings of being watched while seated at the instrument, and a paralysing feeling that took immense willpower to overcome. Rouse also described his own experience, that of an overwhelming feeling of depression which had began to permeate the top floor of Montpellier House itself. The medium, a Mrs Leith-Walker, advised the vicar that the church and the vicarage was haunted by the troubled spirit of a church organist who had committed suicide and was unable to rest due to not receiving what he considered to be a suitable funeral service at St John's after working there for some time. She suggested that a service held at the musician's graveside might alleviate the problem.

The Revd Rouse realised that this description did not fit that of Henry Ditton-Newman but on consulting with the current organist back at St John's came to the conclusion that a second ghost had taken up residence at the church, that of Francis Crute, a musician of some standing and a former organist who had committed suicide at the age of fifty by gassing himself six months before Rouse had been indicted to the living. He had lived on the top floor of the vicarage for a period in the winter of 1947, and at his funeral the coffin had been left in the hearse outside the church rather than being taken inside during the service.

On New Year's Day 1959, the Revd Rouse held a brief prayer ceremony in Torquay cemetery accompanied by Malcolm Russell, a counter-tenor from Exeter Cathedral who had known Crute personally, holy water was sprinkled on his grave and prayers were said by both men. On his return to St John's, Anthony Rouse noticed immediately that the uncomfortable atmosphere that had been present in both the church and the vicarage had gone and it remained that way for the rest of his time (a further year) at St John's.

Despite the comments of a subsequent rector during the 1970s, that sounds of the organ playing by itself were due to a semi-blind parish clerk who played the organ for pleasure and neglected to turn on the lights while doing so, the haunting of St John the Apostle in Torquay is one for which a substantial body of evidence exists from a number of responsible and seemingly reliable witnesses.

 [Grid Ref: SX 918 637] St John's overlooks the marina on Montpellier Road just off the B3199.

44. ST MARY'S CHURCH, SNETTISHAM, NORFOLK

Snettisham, nine and a half miles south-west of Kings Lynn, is a Norfolk Domesday village. The church of St Mary was built around the middle of the fourteenth century; its construction may have been associated with the granting of the Manor of Snettisham to John of Gaunt by Edward III but building work was delayed by the Black Death, which reached Norfolk in 1348 with the result that the church's famous stone spire, a noted landmark measuring 175 feet high, was not completed until 1390. At some time, during the late 1500s, the chancel was demolished by a local landowner, Sir Wymond Cayre; despite his disruption work there is a marble monument bearing his effigy inside the church. In 1856 renovations were carried out by Victorian architect Frederick Preedy. The marriage register for St Mary's dates from 1754 and the registers for burials and baptisms from 1760. A notable occurrence took place on 19 January 1915, when the church was damaged during a successful German Zeppelin raid on towns on the north Norfolk coast. A near miss by falling bombs blew in several windows on the south side of the building.

The interior of St Mary's contains several vaults and mausoleums, one of which is associated with a famous ghost story attached to the church. This is the tomb of Robert Cobb, who died on 15 May 1745 at the age of sixty-seven. In October 1893, a married woman from London, Mrs Goodeve, was visiting friends in the West Country. One night she awoke and was alarmed to discover a man standing close to her bedside; in a scene out of a melodrama the figure spoke and introduced himself as Henry Barnard, a former resident of Snettisham who now lay dead and buried in the churchyard of St Mary's Church. As if this wasn't enough, the apparition followed this announcement with an eerie request – that she should go to the church and wait beside the gravesite of a Robert Cobb, which she would find inside the building. If this was carried out, further instructions would be forthcoming. With that the figure faded away.

Mrs Goodeve was unfamiliar with the village of Snettisham and had not visited Norfolk before, but on her return to London she took the decision to follow the phantom's instructions. On arrival at Snettisham she made enquiries at the church and, after establishing that the tomb of Robert Cobb did exist, was directed to speak with one of the parish clerks, John Bishop, who eventually agreed to her bizarre request, the stipulations of which had been set down by the ghost of Henry Barnard, namely to be locked inside St Mary's Church for a period of half an hour at one o'clock the following morning. A few hours later, shortly after midnight, Bishop met Mrs Goodeve and accompanied her to the church. The stalwart lady went into the building alone and the clerk locked the door behind her.

What exactly happened in St Mary's Church during the half hour that Mrs Goodeve stayed inside is unclear, although the story asserts that she was again visited by the apparition of Henry Barnard who told her to convey specific information to Robert Cobb's surviving daughter, who resided at the nearby Cobb Hall. During the time he remained outside, John Bishop reported hearing voices in conversation despite the fact that Mrs Goodeve was alone inside the building. She is said to have later visited Robert Cobb's daughter and passed on Barnard's message, details of which neither of the two women would subsequently divulge.

Despite what initially appears to be a promising case of paranormal intervention, the haunting of St Mary's Church is difficult to authenticate. Despite records showing that a John Bishop was employed as a parish clerk at the time Mrs Goodeve is said to have visited Snettisham, the main stumbling block concerns the surviving daughter of Robert Cobb. Cobb was born around 1678 and married Katherine Rolfe at St Margaret's Church in Kings Lynn on 2 June 1698, when he was twenty years old. They had two daughters, Elizabeth, who died at the age of fifty in 1772 and is buried in the churchyard of St Mary's, and Anne, whose date of death is unclear but a surviving record shows that she was baptised on 4 August 1707 at the same church that her parents were married. Clearly she would have been long dead by the time the ghost of Henry Barnard made itself known to Mrs Goodeve.

As for Cobb Hall, if this is in fact Snettisham Old Hall, a Grade II listed building, formerly a late sixteenth-century manor house owned until recently by the Sue Ryder Cancer Trust and now being converted into apartments, then this building had a firm association with the Styleman

St Mary's Church, Snettisham, scene of a possibly notable psychic encounter during the 1890s. *(Photograph by Eddie Brazil)*

family and in the late 1870s was owned by a Victorian builder named Edward Green, who built Ken Hill, a large country house on the outskirts of Snettisham known in the past as Snettisham New Hall. As such, the ghost story of St Mary's must remain just that.

 [Grid Ref: TF 691 344] St Mary's Church is a landmark building. Take the B1440 to the centre of Snettisham village and then follow Old Church Road for 500 yards.

45. ST MICHAEL'S CHURCH, DIDLINGTON, NORFOLK

Many of the churches included in this book can boast haunted histories stretching back several decades. Ghostly incidents reported over the years include phantom organ music, strange lights, unearthly chanting, poltergeists, disembodied voices, apparitions, plus auditory and olfactory phenomena. Borley and Langenhoe, both in Essex, are good examples of locations with substantial paranormal pasts. There are others, however, such as St Michael's Church at Didlington, that have experienced only an occasional mystifying episode. This church can make a claim for being the site of genuine paranormal activity, but not enough to gain a place at the top table of England's most haunted. Nonetheless, such is the curious nature of the reported phenomena that the case deserves to be examined in detail.

St Michael's Church at Didlington, Norfolk, where Constable Williams heard phantom bell ringing. *(Photograph by Eddie Brazil)*

Didlington is a remote village located in the Breckland region of Norfolk, eight miles south-west of the town of Swaffham. The village is small, consisting of just a handful of farm buildings and a fourteenth-century church. It was the location of Didlington Hall, built in the sixteenth century and one of England's architectural treasures, that became the headquarters of General Miles Dempsey, Commander of the second British Army during the D-Day landings and was scandalously demolished in 1952 as it was 'surplice to requirements'. One of the owners of the hall during the nineteenth century, William Amherst Tyson, amassed a vast collection of antiquities ranging from rare books, tapestries and antique furniture to works of art and Egyptian artefacts. Tyson became patron of the young Howard Carter and the family were instrumental in Carter's entry into Egypt, providing him with the contacts and recommendations which proved valuable in his subsequent discovery of the tomb of Tutankhamun.

On a stormy November night in 1956, police constable Williams cycled round his beat patrolling the Didlington area and surrounding villages. It was bitterly cold with a harsh wind. At 10.50 p.m. the constable dismounted his cycle and, checking his watch, he calculated he would reach St Michael's Church at around eleven o'clock. From there he would cycle on to cover the final part of his beat before finishing for the night. Williams was about to set off when he heard the distant tolling of a bell. Puzzled, the policeman immediately assumed it was the bell of Didlington church and, mounting his bicycle, he pedalled quickly in the direction of the church.

On reaching the churchyard gate the ringing abruptly stopped. The constable walked up the church path, wondering what was going on. It seemed unlikely to be a prank or children playing as it was late and an unpleasant night. He took the key from its position under the mat and quietly opened the door. Entering, he shone his powerful torch around the interior, the beam picking out the bell-rope which was still swinging, giving the impression it had just been released by whoever had been ringing the bell – but the church was empty. PC Williams was disinclined to venture further into the building. His mouth went dry and he had the feeling that he was not alone. He hurriedly left the church and cycled back home without completing his beat. His wife, noticing his shocked state, said that he looked as if he had seen a ghost. 'Perhaps I have,' was his reply.

Some days later Williams met an elderly man who had once worked at Didlington Hall. Without mentioning his experience the constable asked him the date on which the previous owner of the Hall had died. 'It was on the fourteenth of November,' replied the old man, the same date as the policeman's frightening experience in St Michael's Church. Is it possible that PC Williams experienced a genuine paranormal incident? Writer Joan Forman, who interviewed the constable, found him to be a practical man who believed in what he actually saw rather than what he was told or heard by way of gossip.

It is unlikely that Williams invented the story for his own personal benefit and also doubtful his imagination got the better of him when he was alone in a church on a dark and stormy night. He was an experienced officer and accustomed to the many differing conditions of his duties. PC Williams had patrolled his country beat for over ten years and had never before experienced anything which could not be explained by factual or physical means. His experience at Didlington church, however, had certainly unnerved him enough to make him curtail his beat and flee to the sanctuary of his home. The incident remains unexplained and as far as we can ascertain no further paranormal happenings have been reported at Didlington since that time.

There is a curious footnote to this story which may have a bearing on what PC Williams experienced. As mentioned earlier, the Tyson family were instrumental in introducing Howard Carter to Egyptology. Carter's discovery in 1922 of the tomb of Tutankhamun was the great archaeological find of the century. As everyone knows, the opening of the Pharaoh's tomb is said to have unleashed a curse on all those who had despoiled the boy king's last resting place. Within a month, Lord Carnarvon, Carter's colleague and financier of the expedition, was dead. Back in England, the Lord's dog is said to have howled and whined before dropping dead at the exact moment of his master's demise.

Within thirteen years only two of the original team of excavators were alive, although Howard Carter lived to a ripe old age. The family and house which had inspired his love of Egypt did not fare so well. Didlington Hall had stood since the seventeenth century, but in 1944 it was taken over by the military as an army HQ, an event from which it never recovered. Ten years later the house was just a memory, its treasures sold off and its walls a pile of rubble. Had the curse of King Tut been finally brought to bear on the fortunes of the family who had inspired the chief desecrater of the Pharaoh's tomb? Perhaps what PC Williams heard on that cold night in 1956 was in fact a bell tolling for a house which had suffered the same fate as the last resting place of Tutankhamun.

 [Grid Ref: TL 779 969] Didlington village lies two and a half miles north-west of the small town of Mundford; closest main road is the A134.

46. THETFORD PRIORY, NEAR BURY ST EDMUNDS, NORFOLK

One of the most important East Anglian monasteries, the Cluniac Priory of Our Lady of Thetford, was founded in the early twelfth century by Roger Bigod, father of Hugh Bigod, created First Earl of Norfolk in 1141. Bigod laid the foundation stone in September 1107 but died the following week. The Priory owed much of its prosperity to a miraculous appearance of the Virgin Mary, whose statue here was discovered to conceal relics of saints and the place became a magnet for pilgrims. During its existence Thetford became one of the richest monastic establishments in England. In 1313, a rampaging mob broke into the presbytery and killed several monks at the high altar. The remaining brothers took sanctuary in the church next door as the priory was ransacked. Inevitably its wealth and treasures came to the notice of Henry VIII and in 1540, like the majority of English monastic establishments, it was dissolved. Although the Priory contained not only the last resting place of the Earls and Dukes of Norfolk but also that of Henry VIII's illegitimate son, Henry Fitzroy, its suppression could not be halted and the tombs were removed to Framlingham in Suffolk.

As the tombs were removed so too were the lay brothers. The Prior and thirteen monks signed a deed of surrender and two months later the Priory was purchased by the Duke of Norfolk, who sold off the valuable Caen stone. What was left of the fragmentary remains was plundered by locals, who no doubt used it to construct new buildings in Thetford. Only the Prior's lodgings continued in use, now as a private dwelling, but by the early nineteenth century this too was abandoned and fell into ruin.

Like many of England's monastic sites, Thetford Priory is not without its compliment of ghosts. A ghostly mass has been heard in the ruins, with singing in Latin followed by reading from a text. Monks have been seen walking within the grounds, and a nearby hotel, once formerly part of the Priory, has its own resident monkish ghost.

If one accepts that ghosts are a form of psychic recording, the so-called 'stone tape' theory in which the fabric of a building can somehow absorb human trauma and distress and then, at a later date, play back these emotions to a suitably sensitive person acting as a kind of psychic video player, then places such as Thetford Priory – and the majority of England's ecclesiastical ruins – would well suit such a hypothesis as an explanation for the supernormal phenomena reported in these places over the years. We can only imagine what heartache, grief and angst the monks endured as they were expelled from the Priory and then watched as their former home was dismantled. However, for the 'stone tape' theory to work, a haunted site must surely have just that: standing walls, doorways, rooms, roofs, columns; in short, buildings. At Thetford there survive but scant remains to remind us of its once former glory. Nonetheless, in August 1987, four students visiting the Priory witnessed an incident which would ultimately alter their views on the paranormal and subsequently lead one of their number to the science of parapsychology and a study into the nature of human consciousness.

The students, knowing nothing of the history of Thetford or having previously visited the ruins, decided to break their journey and take a look at the site. It was a pleasant early evening and on entering they were surprised to find the place empty, the Priory being in a built-up area of the town where they expected to find other people enjoying themselves in the late summer sunshine, yet all remarked the ruins seemed at that time a very lonely place. They decided to explore in two groups in order to inspect the remaining flint walls and take in the building's history and atmosphere. After a while all four gathered together again on the grass in front of the Prior's lodgings.

As they stood there, one of the students remarked that they were being observed by someone at one of the windows and, looking up, they all saw the figure at the window and then watched as it moved out of sight back into the room before becoming visible once more as it descended a flight of stairs which led down to the ground floor below. The students described the figure as being dressed in what appeared to be long, flowing black robes, somewhat similar to a monk's habit. On viewing the person, the young men thought it was in no way paranormal and assumed that somebody was playing a practical joke by pretending to be a ghost. As the figure continued to descend the stairs, two of the students thought they would try and apprehend the joker and rushed forward. As they did so the figure in black began to retreat back up the staircase.

The two men entered the former Prior's quarters and tried to run up the stairs; indeed both had the impression that they had gone a few steps up the flight. However, much to their astonishment, both found themselves pitching forward and hitting the flint wall before crashing down on to the gravel floor. Each was bleeding from the head and it took some seconds for them to realise that the staircase they had tried to run up was not there and neither was the figure in black. Unable to comprehend the situation, the students looked at each other in bewilderment before scrambling to their feet and fleeing the Priory in terror.

Sometime later, away from the ruins and in a calmer frame of mind, the young men independently wrote down accounts of what they had experienced. All agreed they had seen a figure in black watching them from the window and then descend the staircase. However, only two reported that it looked like a monk in a cowled habit. The third thought it was someone attired in what seemed to be eighteenth-century costume, while the fourth was of the opinion that the figure resembled a column of black smoke. As the students fled from the site each had the impression that the ruins seemed more 'alive', as if the Priory itself was coming back into existence. All agreed that the experience was frighteningly real and unnatural enough for them to question their sanity.

The students' encounter has the ring of truth about it and anyone viewing their retelling of the incident – which was featured as a contribution to broadcaster William Woollard's *Ghost Hunters* television series – cannot fail to be struck by the veracity and reasoning of their experience. If the sighting of the figure was an example of the 'stone tape' theory it still leaves one or two unanswered questions. What would have happened if the students had not tried to apprehend the figure? Would the apparition have continued down the stairs and completed the task as it had done whilst in life and which was now being played back into the present? What is also intriguing is that once the men had decided collectively to confront the figure, the black shape then began to retreat back up the stairs. It would seem logical to surmise that if it was a recording then any actions on the part of the students should not have affected the playback of the vision – one would not expect a recording of a Beethoven string quartet to change or start playing backwards just because the listener suddenly decided to rush at the record player.

Is it possible that the figure in black was indeed a 'flesh and blood' ghost, an 'apparition' which was fully aware of the viewers as much as they were of it and alarmed at the prospect of

Thetford Priory – the haunted Prior's house. *(Photograph by Eddie Brazil)*

The ruins of Thetford Priory, where four students encountered the timeslip apparition of a figure in black in 1987. *(Photograph by Eddie Brazil)*

being apprehended by four curious students? If it was the ghost of one of Thetford's past Priors then the chief candidate might well be Stephen of Savoy, a notorious and dissolute man who, in 1248, was stabbed to death during a quarrel with one of his monks whom he had refused permission to return to his home priory in France.

Undoubtedly to witness ghostly phenomena, certain conditions have to be in place, although what those conditions are we can only speculate. It is arguable that if the students had found the priory ruins full of other people enjoying the site on that day then they would not have seen the figure in black. It would appear that on that late summer evening in 1987, four young men experienced paranormal phenomena at Thetford Priory because, as is often and inexplicably the case, they were the right people in the right place at definitely the right time.

 [Grid Ref: TL 865 833] The Priory ruins are in Monksgate close to Thetford railway station.

47. DUNWICH VILLAGE, SUFFOLK

There is a beautiful melancholy to Dunwich. Those readers contemplating a visit to this remote coastal hamlet would be well advised to do so in the bleak seasonal months between November and February, as it is on grey, deserted days that one can fully savour the forlorn atmosphere and gain a sense of its lost past. Dunwich is a village haunted by the years; one which for centuries has been retreating from the sea. Stand on its lonely shore in the winter dusk or atop its crumbling cliffs in the cold glow of a moonlit night and it is easy to imagine a host of phantom villagers or hear the distant toll of bells from ancient churches lying forgotten out in the depths of the North Sea.

Ghost story writer M.R. James, who was raised close to this region, is said to have been influenced by the brooding, eerie East Anglian landscape, and at Dunwich it is easy to understand why. When Jonathan Miller adapted James' classic ghost story *Oh, Whistle, and I'll Come to You, My Lad* for television, he chose Dunwich as a location. Here are marshes, dark woods and an ominous silence broken only by the sound of the wind and crashing waves.

Today's village, a handful of cottages, a pub and sole Victorian church, huddle behind the cliffs, while up a lane outside the main centre stand the fragmentary ruins of thirteenth-century Grey Friars Priory. An encircling boundary wall, the remains of its refectory, and a mighty gatehouse hint at its once size and grandeur. Beyond the ruins, on top of the cliffs and among the wind-blown trees and undergrowth, lean solitary headstones, all that remains of the graveyard of Dunwich's last medieval church, which fell into the sea in 1919.

Yet it was not always so. As one looks out across the waves it is hard to imagine that a mile distant from the shore is where old Dunwich once stood, a town which rivalled in size most of the large East Anglia communities of the day. It once boasted fifty-two churches, a Bishop's palace, a Mayor's mansion with vast ancient bronze gates, and it was here, in the seventh century, that Sigebert was crowned King of East Anglia and where he built his palace.

However, the erosion of the coast had begun in Roman times. Then two great storms in 1286 and 1328 destroyed most of the town and Dunwich's fate was sealed. St Martin's went in 1340, St Katherine's in 1350, the church of St Nicholas in 1420, St John in 1530, St Peter in 1703 and finally All Saints, which succumbed in 1904, its tower hanging on until it collapsed the year after the First World War had ended. Nowhere in England has so much been reduced to so little.

Not surprisingly, Dunwich has its fair share of ghostly tales, the most popular being the echo of church bells, with fishermen returning at night reporting hearing chimes from beneath the waves. Of course, this is the stuff of legend; the oncoming tempest and the church's last days would have been foreseen. Valuables including the church plate, woodwork, monuments, relics and bells would have been removed. What went into the sea were the bare bones of the medieval building.

The lonely beach at Dunwich, where the sounds of lost church bells can still be heard. *(Photograph by Eddie Brazil)*

The ruins of Grey Friars Priory at Dunwich, where phantom lights have been seen as the sea mists roll in. *(Photograph by Eddie Brazil)*

Nonetheless, Dunwich fisherman stand by what they have heard while divers tend to avoid exploring the town's submerged ruins, which have a sinister reputation. Investigators have a feeling that they are not alone under the sea. Shrouded figures seen on the clifftops are rumoured to be the former inhabitants of Dunwich returning from their watery graves. Walkers on the beach late at night have reported hearing the disembodied laughter of children; youngsters still at play even in death.

Within the ruins of Grey Friars Priory, phantom lights have been seen glowing through the sea mist as it rolls in. The priory is also said to be the haunt of ghostly monks, who walk in ceaseless sorrow for the loss of their former spiritual home, while the woods adjacent to the priory have a reputation for being haunted by the tormented ghost of a young man, who eternally searches for the bride who jilted him for another lover. Dunwich also has its own phantom hound. In 1926, a large black dog was seen prowling the priory ruins – the animal was unknown to the villagers and all attempts to apprehend it failed.

The lost past is ever present at Dunwich. The history of this lonely place has no doubt furnished its many ghostly legends, and imagination and emotion often fuel what people want to see and hear, for none of the reported phenomena mentioned here can be substantiated with any certainty. Yet one instinctively feels that ghosts could roam this forgotten coastal community and may do so when Dunwich is no more. The crash of waves upon the shore is a constant reminder that each year the sea comes ever closer.

 [Grid Ref: TM 475 705] Dunwich is two and a quarter miles north-east of Westleton on the B1125; follow Dunwich Road into the village.

48. BORLEY CHURCH, BORLEY, ESSEX

The present church, dedication unknown, began life in the late twelfth century. A Saxon church once stood here and there is evidence of Saxon material in the present edifice; later alterations and additions took place in the fourteenth and sixteenth centuries. During the Reformation, the idolatrous and Popish symbols and apportions were replaced and the bare interior remained for some 300 years, until the nineteenth century saw a return to the Gothic style and the church resumed some of its medieval appearance that can still be seen today. The existing Register of Baptisms dates from 1652, burials from 1656 and marriages from 1709.

There have been suggestions that following the destruction of haunted Borley Rectory, long known as 'the most haunted house in England', that stood almost directly opposite the church, the ghostly manifestations, including the famous Borley nun, transferred their activities to the nearby church. Be that as it may, a wealth of curious happenings in and around Borley Church have been reported for well over sixty years.

In 1947, John May heard apparently inexplicable sounds in the churchyard at night, including the click of the churchyard gate and footsteps on the path to the church, followed by the sound of a key turning in the lock, the creak of door hinges and the sound of a door opening, succeeded by the soft notes of organ music. The whole area outside the church was plainly visible – and apparently deserted – while the church itself was closed and locked. Later, May, a religious man from Bury St Edmunds, learned that the sound of organ music had been reported by several people in the village when the church was locked at night.

A former rector, the Revd Alfred Henning (1888-1953), in his *Haunted Borley* (1949), is only one of the responsible people to report the sound of music from the empty church; in fact there are a number of such instances extending right up to the present time.

In 1947 Steuart Kiernander, an experienced investigator of haunted houses, saw a 'mysterious figure or white shape' pass the church porch. A couple of years later, again while sitting in the church porch, he suddenly heard heavy footsteps hurriedly approaching. As he stood up to

Borley Church in 1972; the anomaly in the foreground on the left corresponds to reports of a nun-like figure seen in the immediate area over many years. *(Photograph by Eddie Brazil)*

The Tudor porch at Borley Church, were John May and Steuart Kiernander both experienced phenomena in the 1940s. *(Photograph by Eddie Brazil)*

greet whoever might be approaching, the sounds abruptly ceased and, going out of the porch, he was astonished to see no sign of anyone and nothing to account for the footsteps he heard. He resumed his seat in the porch and about half an hour later he again heard footfalls exactly as before. When he judged the perpetrator to be no more than a yard or two from the porch, he rushed out: there was immediate and complete silence and no sign of anyone or anything that could have been responsible for the sounds he had heard. Unexplained footsteps is one of the most commonly reported activity at Borley Church.

Two years later Kiernander again visited Borley Church and this time, while again sitting in the church's Tudor porch, he heard a considerable number of taps and clicks that appeared to originate from the church door near him, but again he could find no explanation. During discussion on the matter, Kiernander added that he had sat in Borley Church porch many times both before and after this occasion but he had never heard anything like these noises.

In 1949, Dr Margaret Abernethy saw the stooping figure of a nun standing beside a hedge between the rectory site and the churchyard. When she stopped and reversed the car, there was no sign of the seemingly solid figure she had seen, whose age she put at about forty. She and the then rector made extensive enquiries but could find no evidence of a real nun being in the vicinity.

In the same year, the Revd Stanley C. Kipling, visiting Borley to read the lesson at the funeral of a friend, saw from the church porch the figure of a 'veiled girl' in the churchyard; she passed swiftly between some shrubs to disappear behind a bush. He investigated immediately but found nothing to explain the appearance and disappearance of the distinct and seemingly solid figure. Previously sceptical of the Borley haunting, this personal experience gave him considerable cause for thought on the subject.

Terrance Bacon, who lived with his sister, parents and grandparents at the old Rectory Cottage (directly opposite the church) for some twenty years from 1951, claimed to have seen the Borley ghost nun on three occasions, twice in the churchyard. Additionally in 1949 the then rector, Alfred Henning, and his wife Annette were giving a talk on confirmation to a group of children inside the church when three loud and resonant blows were heard close to the massive Waldegrave tomb that somewhat dominates the church interior. (The Waldegrave family were Lords of the Manor at Borley for some 300 years.) All the children glanced towards the monument, everyone present hearing the loud knocks, but no explanation was ever discovered.

Over the following years a number of unexplained sounds have been reported from the vicinity of the Waldegrave tomb and from the interior of the church,

The Revd Alfred Henning and family; Henning was rector during much of the Harry Price era at Borley. *(Peter Underwood Collection)*

The Waldegrave
monument in
Borley Church.
*(Peter Underwood
Collection)*

including the sound of bell ringing, organ music, rhythmic thumping noises, movement of objects, strange smells and odours, the smashing of an altar lamp, footsteps, raps and taps, creaking – as of a door opening and closing, the sound of earth falling, unaccountable bright lights, a strange snapping sound, stone throwing, the sound of voices – whispering and singing, the chancel window lighting up; in fact a wealth of mysterious happenings have been reported from Borley Church and its immediate vicinity.

A visit from BBC executive Charles Chilton MBE, accompanied by a friend, encountered inside the church the unmistakable sounds of a storm with howling wind that seemed to be raging outside. When they left the church, individually, they were astonished to find all was quiet outside and they could find nothing to account for the loud and prolonged sounds, which both found quite frightening. After a few moments conversation together in their car, Charles returned but found everything silent and peaceful inside the church, where moments before there had been the overwhelming noise of a violent storm.

But it is mysterious footsteps that predominate. Poet and author of distinction James Turner heard 'something or somebody with a lame leg and a swishing skirt' approaching along the church path; Denny Densham, a film executive, heard and recorded footsteps and other sounds; Michael Bentine's psychic father, Adam, experienced an all-enveloping coldness and an impression of evil; Mr D. Wright of Chingford, together with four friends, all heard footsteps;

Borley Church, one of the most well known haunted churches in England. *(Photograph by Eddie Brazil)*

and Mr Charles Hunter of Haverill, Suffolk, is among many people who have provided us with convincing evidence of unexplained footfalls at Borley. Adrian Dening (son of the late Revd John Dening) and his partner Tone have both 'felt uncomfortable there' and Tone described it as 'a dishonest church'.

Furthermore, a number of curious photographs have been taken in Borley churchyard, perhaps the most puzzling being one taken by Eddie Brazil in 1972 and reproduced on page 110 of the present volume, which shows a figure corresponding to the nun-like apparition reported in and around the old rectory grounds over many years.

A variety of vaguely human forms have alleged to have been seen hereabouts and several people, local and visiting, have reported being conscious of a shadowy shape or an invisible 'presence' inside the church, including the celebrated clairvoyant Tom Corbett, who told us he was convinced that the church 'held within its walls the sad and lost spirit of a clever and youthful nun' who 'continued to serve there...'.

All three of the present authors have spent many hours at Borley over the years and all have experienced strange happenings at this enchanting place.

 [Grid Ref: TL 847 431] Borley is two miles north-west of Sudbury. From the B1064 Borley Road take the Lower Road and turn off after crossing the River Stour bridge; the village and church is three-quarters of a mile further on at the top of the hill.

49. ST MARY THE VIRGIN, GREAT LEIGHS, ESSEX

The Scrapfaggot Green Poltergeist was a bizarre psychic event which enlivened English newspaper headlines during the closing months of the Second World War and caught the attention of no less a ghost hunter than Harry Price, a high-profile researcher during the previous two decades noted for his involvement in the famous Borley case. The disturbances were centred on the Essex village of Great Leighs, four miles south-west of Braintree, home to the St Anne's Castle Inn, said to be the oldest (*c*.1170) in England, and lasted in all for a number of weeks. They were, as Price later commented, 'partly genuine, partly the work of a practical joker, and partly due to mass-hysteria,' and the main focus appeared to be the twelfth-century church of St Mary the Virgin.

As at Borley fifteen years earlier, Price was alerted to the manifestations at Great Leighs by the newsdesk of a national newspaper, in this case the *Sunday Pictorial*, who had a staff reporter in the village sending back astonishing copy. Through the *Pictorial* editor, Price learnt that almost everyone in the village was describing strange and disturbing events. They included the apparent dematerialisation of animals – chickens had escaped from locked enclosures and sheep were found strayed through unbroken hedges; the displacement and movement of objects – haystacks were wrecked and scaffolding poles thrown around, while a decorator's paint pots and brushes had been moved and hidden under a bed. More disturbing were the sudden and violent deaths of both village and farm animals – thirty sheep and two horses were discovered lying dead in a field apparently poisoned and a number of chickens were found drowned in water-butts. Several cows in calf also gave birth prematurely and the village hens were so disturbed that they stopped laying.

Together with a friend, Harry Price visited Great Leighs on 11 October 1944, by which time the 'phenomena' had been taking place for some time. As well as several houses and buildings he was shown around St Mary's Church, noted for its circular flint and rubble tower, where a number of curious manifestations had been reported. The church clock had lost an hour each day since the start of the disturbances and had taken to striking midnight at 2.30 a.m.; the tenor bell tolled by itself in the early hours of the morning while the bell ropes had been found to play reversed chimes when rung for the previous Sunday service.

Not surprisingly the Great Leighs locals were keen to introduce the famous psychic expert to their own particular experiences of the disturbances. William Reynolds, landlord of the Dog and Gun Inn, showed Price a large boulder of unknown origin, weighing nearly 200lbs, which had allegedly been apported outside his front door, while the publican of the St Anne's Castle, Arthur Sykes, opened up a locked bedroom where the contents were thrown about and scattered over the floor night after night. It was this poltergeist aspect of the disturbances that seemed to interest Price more than anything and which he considered to be the most convincing paranormally. Interestingly enough, the current owners of the St Anne's Castle consider the inn to be haunted by a generous quota of ghosts, including a lady in a wedding dress, the apparition of a young girl carrying a mixing bowl, several monks, and the figure of a man smoking a pipe.

It was the consensus of opinion amongst the villagers that what Price later collectively described as a poltergeist infestation began after a bulldozer, driven by an American G.I., had widened part of the main road through the centre of the village in order to facilitate the passage of military traffic in the area. At a point on the Scrapfaggot Green crossroads a large stone weighing over two tonnes – which purported to be the gravestone of a seventeenth-century witch (a 'scratch-fagot' being an old Sussex euphemism for an old hag or witch) buried with a stake through her chest – had been knocked over. At Price's suggestion the stone was ceremoniously reinstated at midnight on 11/12 October in a scene reminiscent of the Brocken Experiment in the Harz Mountains, which, under Price's supervision, had captivated newspapermen back in 1932, and the Scrapfaggot Poltergeist was heard from no more.

 [Grid Ref: TL 738 156] The church of St Mary the Virgin is located one and a quarter miles south-east of the centre of Great Leighs village; from the crossroads by the St Anne's Castle Inn follow Boreham Road for a mile and a half and the church is on the left directly opposite Lyons Hall.

50. LANGENHOE CHURCH, ESSEX

Langenhoe is a forgotten haunting. The fourteenth-century parish church of St Mary was closed for worship in 1959 and, after standing abandoned and neglected for three years, it was demolished in 1962. The principle witness to the haunting and its chief chronicler, the Revd Ernest Merryweather, who for some twenty-two years kept a diary of the strange incidents he witnessed, passed away in 1965, and today all that remains to remind the curious traveller that a house of God once occupied this lonely corner of Essex is a weed-strewn graveyard reminiscent of a discarded Hammer Horror movie set. And yet this remote marshland village can claim to have once been the site of seemingly the most haunted church in England.

In 1937, the Revd Merryweather, originally from the north, was inducted as rector. Soon after taking up his post he began to experience paranormal activity within the church. Incidents ranged from poltergeist phenomena, such as the great west door being violently slammed shut on a still, windless day and objects disappearing only to be found elsewhere, to footsteps, thuds, knocks, bangs and disembodied chanting being heard within the building. The rector also reported seeing apparitions inside St Mary's while officiating during the Sunday service. He described the figures as dressed in medieval or Elizabethan clothing. On another occasion, whilst alone in the church practising at the organ, Merryweather turned from his seat to view a woman in a modern cream dress staring at him, upon which the figure immediately vanished.

For many years the villagers of Langenhoe considered the area to be haunted. Local legends tell of a 'Lady in Black' who walks around the church at night, and there is an account of two sisters in 1908 who reported seeing the figure of a woman dressed in 'old fashion nun-like garb', which moved slowly along the path before disappearing into the north wall towards the west end of the church.

Curiously, the Revd Merryweather was to discover that Langenhoe and the village of Borley, twenty miles to the north and site of the famous haunted rectory, were historically connected. In 1583, Nicholas Waldegrave, Lord of the Manor of Borley and son of Sir Edward Waldegrave, acquired the Manor of Langenhoe when he married Catherine Brown, who had inherited the Langenhoe estate in the same year. Not only are there historical connections between the two

Langenhoe Church. *(Peter Underwood Collection)*

villages but, strangely, the paranormal phenomena which was alleged to have occurred at Borley seems to have been repeated, in a mirror-like fashion, at Langenhoe.

In 1958, several séances were held at Langenhoe church in an attempt to establish a cause for the haunting. The communicating entities allegedly contacted included the Lord of the Manor during the reign of King James I, the tyrannical Sir Robert Attford, who had supposedly murdered his lover, a serving girl named Mary Felicity, in the church in the early 1600s. A similar tale tells of a past rector who had also done away with his illicit sweetheart within St Mary's.

One would certainly expect the 'stone tape' theory we have already encountered – if there is any truth to the idea – to apply to Langenhoe. Perhaps the church itself, which had stood through all the troubled times of the area, became the focal point for the various forms of psychic activity? Yet some of the strange events at Langenhoe might possibly be explained away as nothing more than the effects of seismic activity. In 1884, St Mary's was extensively damged during a freak earthquake which shook this part of Essex. The geophysical theory of poltergeist phenomena became popular in the 1950s, and a number of parapsychologists today suggest there is a link between seismic activity and the experiencing of paranormal phenomena.

Although many people experienced the curious happenings at Langenhoe, the chief witness to the phenomena was the Revd Merryweather, his diary entries record many strange and unusual happenings and it is his testimony we must ultimately accept or reject. Peter Underwood has described him as a shrewd man who would not be easily fooled or carried away by his imagination and was as puzzled, critical and sceptical of the events he experienced during his incumbency as anyone else; in short, he was a good witness. We can possibly attribute the sounds of knocks, bangs, creaks and falling masonry in the church to the fragile condition of the fabric of St Mary's, but the incidences of footsteps, voices, spectral singing and the sighting of apparitions ultimately fall outside this kind of explanation.

Scattered gravestones, all that remain to indicate the site of the much haunted Langenhoe church. *(Photograph by Eddie Brazil)*

With the church's demolition in 1962 and the death of Ernest Merryweather three years later, the strange events which occurred at Langenhoe over the years have now all but faded from living memory. Today's visitor will find the the site occupied by a few modern farm buildings but, hidden behind a surounding hedge and tall trees, the graveyard remains. The few surviving headstones lean in the tall grass and weeds and one acutely feels that even though Langenhoe church has long gone, its restless phantoms still linger here.

 [Grid Ref: TM 007 187] Langenhoe is located on the B1025 between Colchester and West Mersey. The site of the church is at the end of Langenhoe Hall Lane off the B1025. Nearest railway station is Colchester on the Great Eastern Line.

51. ST OSYTH PRIORY, NEAR CLACTON-ON-SEA, ESSEX

The village of St Osyth near Clacton suffered acutely from the ravages of the self-styled Witch Finder General, Matthew Hopkins. A large number of the village women were victims of the witch hunt hereabouts and some 300 years later, in 1921, a grisly souvenir of those terrible days was uncovered in a garden: the skeleton of a woman was discovered whose bones had been firmly riveted together. This was a practice at the time designed to prevent the body leaving the grave and finding and haunting, and perhaps attacking, those responsible for her death.

Other reports state that a man digging in the village unearthed the skeletons of two women, buried with their heads to the north – indicating they were executed witches – with their joints at elbow, wrist, knee and ankle riveted. Thought to be 300 years old, they may well have been two of Matthew Hopkins' victims. Oddly enough, the house of the man who made this discovery was burned to the ground shortly afterwards and everyone in the village was certain that this was his punishment for disturbing the graves.

The twelfth-century Priory here is attractively situated between a tide mill on a creek of the River Colne and is approached through the massive and renovated late fifteenth-century flint gatehouse. Some years ago, the late Andrew Green told us he had traced recent reports of a phantom monk long reputed to haunt the area; conspicuous in a white robe or habit and sporting a black scapula, his face 'furrowed with anxiety'. Apparently, in 1969 and again in 1970, reliable witnesses saw such a figure, described as 'resembling a monk carrying a candle'. The phantom was clearly seen in the vicinity of what had once been a monks' graveyard to the east of the chapel and the place where, in fact, the monks of old gathered before attending church for the evening service.

We learn from Graham McEwan that the Priory was founded in 1121 by the then Bishop of London, Richard de Belmeis, and that the bones of St Osyth, an abbess killed by the Danes in 653, were housed there. The Priory was dissolved in 1539 and passed through several hands before being acquired in 1924 by Brigadier-General Kincaid-Smith, who entertained Queen Mary and other members of the Royal Family and various notables there. In 1948 it was bought by the Quakers' Society of Friends, who established a convalescent home in Rochford House, north of the Abbey Church. In 1954 the whole estate was purchased by Somerset de Chair, a prolific novelist, biographer and writer on military history and an MP for eleven years. The convalescent home was closed in the 1980s.

Among the prevalent ghosts at St Osyth, apart from the monk in white, there is a tradition that St Osyth herself haunts the area. Eric Maple told us he had traced several accounts of the ghost seen standing in front of the parish church on the anniversary of her execution carrying what looks like her severed head! There are also reports of the ghost of St Osyth wandering about the estate at night carrying a lighted candle. There is also apparently a ghost monk in Rochford House and also an unidentified female form, glimpsed briefly near the site of the Abbey Church.

The gatehouse at haunted St Osyth Priory. (*Photograph by Eddie Brazil*)

Mrs Joyce Bennett, who lived locally and was for a time a nurse at the convalescent home, told many a strange story of the ghost of former owner Brigadier-General Kincaid-Smith being seen around the place and of strange happenings involving the unexplained movement of objects, including a carpet; once a cleaner was thrown by some invisible force against a wall – she left and never returned. There were also unexplained crashing sounds, doors banging by themselves and icy cold patches.

On one occasion Mrs Bennett had received a new batch of patients and she found them all gathered at an upstairs window of Rochford House where they said they had watched a group of monks below walking side by side through an archway. When they were told there were no longer any monks at St Osyth they were amazed and insisted that they had all seen them. The area where the monks were seen was very near the graveyard mentioned previously and at a time when they would have been collecting there to attend a service.

Once, Mrs Bennett encountered the ghostly form of a woman when she walked into the laundry room. Knowing she was the only nurse on duty at the time, she was really puzzled and before confronting the mysterious individual – seemingly using a machine – Mrs Bennett placed the linen she was carrying in a corner and turned to ask the woman how she had gained entrance and whether she had permission to use the machine. Imagine her surprise when she found no sign of the woman she had so clearly seen! When she walked over to the washer she had seen being used, she found she had walked into a patch of icy-cold air, which was constricted to the immediate vicinity of the machine. Later, mentioning the incident to the lady who supervised the weekly wash for the home, the latter just nodded and said, 'Don't worry, it happens all the time'. Mrs Bennett added that in addition to seeing this 'woman' she had also seen a monk, who came and went through the wall by the washing machine.

The late Betty Puttick, who wrote extensively on the ghosts of East Anglia, many of her accounts based on personal experience and investigation, revealed that a passing driver apparently picked up a ghostly passenger at St Osyth. He was driving past the Priory gatehouse early one morning when he found, glancing in his mirror, that he had acquired an unknown middle-aged lady sitting on the back seat. She said nothing but he noticed she was dressed in clothes of an old-fashioned style and wore a hat with a posy of small flowers on one side. When he stopped and went to look in the back seat there was no sign of the mysterious passenger, but he immediately noticed a strong smell of violets and he then recalled ,with something of a shock, that the flowers in the vanishing woman's hat were violets!

Jessie Payne in her *Ghost Hunter's Guide to Essex* (1987) says that Osyth, the daughter of Frithwald, the first Christian King of the East Angles, was betrothed to Sighere, King of Essex, but took advantage of an opportunity during the feast to flee to a nunnery, where she took the veil. When Danish pirates arrived 653 she refused to worship their gods, so they struck off her head. She rose up at once, picked up her head and walked with it to the church, where she knocked on the door before falling down dead. Where her head fell a stream of water gushed forth and the stream in Nun's Wood runs to this day. Here, once a year, St Osyth is said to return, bearing her head in her hands. The late Roy Christian, college lecturer, writer and broadcaster, tells a similar story.

The haunting of St Osyth's Priory may lie more in the realm of folklore and fantasy than in the arena of modern ghost sighting, but still there are the occasional stories of true ghostly encounters there. During the course of a Ghost Club visit, two individual members of the party asserted they had seen a human form which disappeared in inexplicable circumstances.

 [Grid Ref: TM 122 156] St Osyth is on the B1027 road to Great Clacton; the entrance to the Priory is off The Bury to the west of the village centre.

52. ST MARY'S OLD CHURCH, CLOPHILL, BEDFORDSHIRE

One of England's most notorious ruined buildings, the so-called 'Black Magic' church of St Mary's, stands isolated on a windswept hillside overlooking the small rural village of Clophill, midway between Luton and the county town of Bedford. In 1961, London-born petty criminal James Hanratty brought the locale from anonymity firmly into the public consciousness through the brutal and far-reaching 'A6 Murder' at nearby Deadman's Hill, and less than two years later Clophill's reputation as a centre for the macabre was sealed when graves were desecrated and a skeleton removed from an eighteenth-century brick vault as part of what appeared to be some form of occult or necromantic ritual. In the years which followed, the old church has gained an additional, and for the inhabitants of the nearby village, unwelcome notoriety as a hotbed of strange paranormal activity, including overwhelming sensations of evil and the sighting of apparitions, the result being that the ruins continue to act as a magnet for visitors from all over the world.

The origins of the old church building, the structure of which dates from the fifteenth century, are steeped in legend which befit its modern supernatural image. A well-known explanation for the church being just under half a mile from the nearest building in Clophill is that at some time in the dim and distant past a pestilence caused the villagers to abandon the original hilltop settlement in favour of a new location free from disease lower down in the valley of the River Flit. Unfortunately, however plausible as it may sound, there is no real evidence to support this and a similar story that the church occupies the site of a former leper.

Probably the most famous tale associated with St Mary's is that the church was built, either by accident or design, facing the wrong way, the idea being that facing the Devil rather than God created the correct conditions for all manner of strange things to take place, including paranormal activity and the suitability of the site for devil worship and witchcraft. For the record, a quick glance at the layout of the church and its relationship to the compass shows that this can be easily dismissed. Most English parish churches are orientated so that the altar is at the east end of the building, i.e. the side nearest to Jerusalem. At Clophill we have a west tower, a central nave with a south-facing door and, before it was demolished in the mid-1800s, a chancel on the east side with the altar located on the far east wall – nothing out of place and a clear example of the way urban legends can arise and be made to fit into the history of a building or location which later obtains a notorious reputation.

For 350 years, St Mary's served its parish well. However, by the early 1800s an increase in numbers in the Clophill congregation put pressure on the church authorities to either enlarge the existing church or construct a new building closer to the village itself. Several proposals were made at various times which stalled due to problems with funding, and it was not until 1847 that a new rector, the Revd John Mendham, was able to create enough interest, which included

The hilltop church at Clophill around 1910, several years before it acquired a sinister reputation. *(Bedfordshire and Luton Archives Service)*

the patronage of local politician Thomas de Gray, 2nd Earl de Gray of nearby Wrest Park, to see through to completion the building of a brand new church in Clophill village, which was consecrated by the Bishop of Ely on 10 July 1849.

Due to the decision to keep the new churchyard of St Mary's open for burials, the old hilltop church was immediately adapted for use as a mortuary chapel. The timber galleries, built in 1814, were removed and the chancel pulled down, and for the next hundred years the only services which took place were those for funerals and a single yearly village congregation, which was normally held on an August evening. By the early 1950s these had come to an end and the old building, now tired and neglected, was fast becoming a target for vandalism and theft. In 1956 most of the lead sheet was stolen from the roof and, unable to re-roof the building or even maintain it as a safe building, it was abandoned by the Parochial Church Council and left to the mercy of the elements and the whim of occasional visitors.

Just a mere eighteen months after the rampage of James Hanratty, Clophill village, in the words of historian Mary Philips, 'still not quite recovered from the publicity thrust upon it by the ghastly events of Deadman's Hill, found itself once more in the limelight.' In March 1963 two Luton schoolboys, playing in the deserted churchyard, came across a grisly sight inside the derelict church – a human skull skewered on a spike in front of the old altar slab, on which lay more remains; arm and leg bones together with parts of a pelvis and sternum. All had been arranged in a curious pattern and the immediate area was scattered with cockerel feathers, clear evidence that some form of ritual involving an animal sacrifice had taken place.

The bones were those of Jenny Humberstone, the wife of a former Clophill apothecary, who had died in 1770 at the age of twenty-two. The ritualistic nature of the desecration quickly gave rise to much speculation both locally and nationally that a Black Mass had taken place inside the ruined church. Although this is debateable, what is certain is that this was not an act

Old St Mary's,
Clophill, Bedfordshire
– 'black magic
church' and
churchyard.
*(Photograph by Paul
Adams / Eddie Brazil)*

of senseless vandalism – it took four policemen to replace the slab over the opened grave, clear proof that a sizeable group of determined people were involved. With churchyard desecrations and pseudo-occult ceremonies gaining publicity throughout the 1960s, the Clophill incident made newspaper headlines around the world and brought scores of visitors to the small village, eager to see the site of a modern Satanic ceremony.

During April 1963, Peter Underwood visited Clophill in the company of fellow psychical researcher Tom Brown (see also Minsden Chapel). They were able to see the site of the desecration at first hand and interview several of the locals, including the mother of one of the schoolboys who had found the opened grave the previous month. Other later incidents also made headlines – on Midsummer's Eve 1969, another grave was disturbed with an attempt to dig up the body inside and six years later, in 1975, robed figures were seen inside the church ruins while the following morning a burnt-out vault was discovered in the churchyard.

Not surprisingly, stories of ghost sightings were soon to follow in the wake of such macabre and dramatic events. In 1972, Luton-born ghost hunter Tony Broughall investigated St Mary's, accompanied by his wife Georgina, a natural medium, and subsequently published a photograph taken during a visit that contained what the researcher described as a figure in white, possibly that of a cleric attired in his vestments, silhouetted in one of the gaping and glassless windows. Despite the image receiving limited circulation, it has been cited and at times misinterpreted by later ghost hunters who have erroneously described the apparition as being that of a White Lady or a spectral monk without seeing the original photograph or knowing its history. Tony Broughall himself was told by one Clophill resident during a later visit that many locals regarded the old church as being haunted and went so far as to name the phantom as being 'Sophie's ghost'. A recent study by Paul Adams and film-maker Kevin Gates suggests that the photograph has in reality a natural explanation, created by patches of light and shade and the position of tree branches between the camera and the church.

Hertfordshire-based ghost hunter and writer Damien O'Dell has collected several accounts of alleged paranormal experiences at Clophill. They include encounters with a hooded monk, a spectral horse, the figure of a First World War airman, as well as the apparition of a mysterious motorcyclist, said to be the victim of a road accident which took place at an unspecified time near to the village. None of these experiences can be substantiated with any degree of certainty. O'Dell himself carried out his own investigation in the church building when he was convinced that he and his colleagues encountered a genuine 'presence of evil' in the old ruins. How much this and other reported paranormal experiences are the result of suggestion due to the locale's unenviable reputation as a centre for the dark and disturbing side of human nature remains to be seen.

 [Grid Ref: TL 092 388] From the junction with the A6 follow Clophill High Street for approximately three quarters of a mile, then turn into a narrow single track roadway on the left; after 600 yards there is a small parking area by the church.

53. ST MARGARET'S CHURCH, STREATLEY, NEAR LUTON, BEDFORDSHIRE

Streatley is a small village on the eastern wing of the Chiltern Hills, a mile and a half from the northern suburbs of Luton and close to the impressive chalk escarpment known as the Sharpenhoe Clappers, itself reputed to be a haunted location. The church of St Margaret's dates from the early thirteenth century and up until the Dissolution of the Monasteries was in the possession of Markyate Priory; the windows and the four-stage tower are from a later period, all dating from the 1600s. The original chancel was demolished in 1898 and rebuilt the same year.

Local legend has it that at the beginning of the twentieth century the church was abandoned by its congregation due to a disagreement with the then incumbent, the Revd Cecil Mundy, who, to the villagers dislike, introduced high church practices to the service. Whatever the reason, St Margaret's was allowed to fall into disrepair and for a period of twenty years up until 1937 was in a derelict and almost ruinous state, with the nave open to the sky and the north wall shored up to prevent total collapse. Following a two year period of restoration, the church was reopened in October 1938 by the Bishop of St Albans, Dr Michael Furse.

The haunting at St Margaret's concerns a former vicar, the Revd James Hadow, whose apparition is said to walk in the churchyard from time to time, although dates of sightings or details of witnesses are decidedly lacking. Hadow, originally from St Andrews in Scotland, was vicar between 1781 and 1840 and is interred in the burial ground, to which his ghost allegedly returns. A graduate of St Andrews University and Balliol College, Oxford, he is reputed to have eloped with his wife, Sarah Wye, who subsequently bore him eight children and now lies beside him. The only other point of interest here is another Streatley vicar, the Revd John Gibson, who

The haunted churchyard of St Margaret's Church at Streatley, near Luton. *(Photograph by Paul Adams / Eddie Brazil)*

officiated at St Margaret's between 1943 and 1949, was the brother of the famous Dambusters airman, Wing Commander Guy Gibson.

 [Grid Ref: TL 070 286] Streatley lies on the A6 trunk road close to the Barton-le-Clay cutting. The entrance to St Margaret's churchyard is adjacent to The Chequers public house.

54. ALL SAINTS' CHURCH, GREAT FARINGDON, OXFORDSHIRE

The noted historian Sir Nikolaus Pevsner called All Saints at Faringdon 'one of the richest churches in Berkshire' and this remained true until the mid-1970s, when changes in the county boundaries moved it into Oxfordshire in the newly created parish of Great Faringdon. The church, comprising an aisled nave, transepts, chancel and a north-east chapel, dates from the twelfth century and has seen several periods of alteration and adaptation, namely in the 1400s and again with Victorian restoration work in 1853. During the Civil War, Faringdon's position on the road to Radcot Bridge, an important crossing point on the River Thames, made it a key strategic objective and during a skirmish in 1645 a cannon round damaged the upper section of the tower, which was later reconstructed at a lower height.

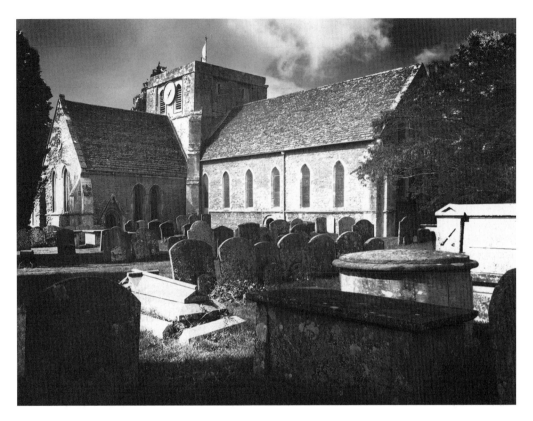

All Saints' Church, Great Faringdon, Oxfordshire, haunted by a headless phantom. *(Photograph by Eddie Brazil)*

The haunting of All Saints' Church features a heraldic wall monument located on the west wall of the Unton family chapel and dedicated to Sir Edward Unton (1534-1582), a Knight of the Bath at the Coronation of Queen Elizabeth in 1559 and later Sheriff and Member of Parliament for Berkshire. Whether it is actually Sir Edward's ghost that is involved is unclear, but ghost hunter and author Marc Alexander has recorded an incident involving a Miss Letitia Rawdon who, at an unspecified point in the past, visited All Saints' Church and, while surveying the memorial to Sir Edward Unton, had what amounted to a horrifying experience.

Alone in the church, which had been opened especially for her to view the interior, she saw a dark and seemingly cloaked figure moving down the centre of the nave, which quickly vanished into the growing darkness, it being dusk by this time. Due to the failing light, Miss Rawdon concluded her tour of the church but, on leaving, again saw the figure walking in the churchyard which, as she came up to it, seemed to be a solid black apparition without a head. Terrified she ran across to the vicarage, where she was told by the then incumbent that the ghost was that of one of the Unton family, who, despite several attempts at exorcism, still returned to haunt the church. Alexander notes that the figure has been seen 'on several occasions' since that time but whether the headless phantom still returns today is unclear.

 [Grid Ref: SU 288 957] Faringdon is midway between Oxford and Swindon on the A420; the church lies on the A4095 on the north side of the town.

55. ST NICHOLAS CHURCH, EMMINGTON, OXFORDSHIRE

Emmington is a solitary place. Situated at the end of a narrow lane off the main road between Thame and Chinnor, it consists of an abandoned church, an old rectory, a farm and two or three cottages. Visitors are rare and a melancholy air hangs over this seemingly forgotten hamlet, especially during the bleak winter months. The church of St Nicholas dates mainly from a rebuilding in 1873-4, although the tower is fourteenth century. There is evidence that a Norman church once stood here, for a priest is mentioned at Emmington in 1190. The most notable family connected with the village are the Hampdens – Sir John Hampden was a cousin of Oliver Cromwell. He was mortally wounded at the Battle of Chalgrove in 1643 during the English Civil War.

The church of St Nicholas is unique among the buildings detailed in this survey in that it is privately owned and was sold off in 2003, when it became redundant. At the time of writing its future use is unclear and sadly it would seem that the church will never again resound to the sound of hymns or the toll of bells on a Sunday morning. The doors are locked, the windows barred and the church's only occupants are rats and mice; a place one would expect to find ghosts and, indeed, accounts of phantom figures seen within the churchyard have been reported over the years. The main apparition is that of a woman attired in a long grey Victorian dress. She wears no bonnet or hat and her hair is said to look as if it is damp and matted across her face. She is reported as walking or gliding silently through the churchyard but her spectre has never been seen inside the church. Curiously, many of the reported sightings seem to have occurred during foggy or misty weather or else on damp and drizzly days, when such conditions can lead one to imagine all manner of figures and shapes. If one is susceptible to Emmington's lonely atmosphere then phantoms may be seen at every turn.

In 1987, one definite sighting of the Lady in Grey was reported by a photographer, who had journeyed to Emmington to take some pictures of the church. The weather, being misty, was not good for exterior shots of the building but the young man was hopeful that the church would be open and he could get some photos of the interior. Parking his car in the lane, he proceeded along the narrow path which runs alongside the old rectory to the lych gate. The churchyard was quiet and deserted but, just as he was about to pass through the gate, the photographer saw another person ahead of him on the path that runs through the yard and skirts the church. Presuming it was a local resident on a church errand, he watched the figure move slowly along the path and then fade from view when it was roughly parallel to the north side of the chancel. Thinking no more of it, the photographer proceeded to walk around the west end of the church by the tower. On reaching the south side of the building he pulled up sharply, realising that the woman he had seen was wearing what appeared to be a long Victorian-type dress and that her uncovered head strangely seemed to be soaking wet.

Puzzled, he made his way back around to the path but it was deserted. The young man explored the whole of the churchyard but there was no sign of the woman. He reasoned that she could have made her way into the garden of the rectory and entered the old house from the rear, but found this was impossible as a thick high hedge barred the way to the back of the building. Slightly unnerved, he thought about going inside the church but, on trying the door, found it locked. Feeling that he had outstayed his welcome at Emmington, he quickly made his way towards the lych gate. However, on reaching the exit, he turned to look back down the path and was shocked to see the woman in the Victorian dress standing motionless and just visible within the mist. What unnerved the photographer most was the silent stare she gave him, which sent a shiver down his back. Such was his fear that the thought of raising his camera and taking a picture of the figure didn't enter his head. As he watched, the woman melted slowly into the increasing gloom and disappeared, at which point he took to his heels. The young photographer was in no doubt that had witnessed an apparition on that bleak day – but who was Lady in Grey?

The isolated church at Emmington, where the figure of a woman in grey has been seen. *(Photograph by Eddie Brazil)*

Some think she is the restless spirit of Sarah Thorne, who lies buried in this very churchyard. Said to be governess to the children of a titled family in London during the late nineteenth century, she became hopelessly infatuated with the twenty-six-year-old elder stepson of the head of the family when he returned from serving with the army in India. Her employer, the young man's stepfather, was an intolerant brute of a man who had designs on young Sarah himself. When he discovered their secret liaison he banished his stepson from the house and forbade the couple from seeing each other again. Sarah and her lover ignored the ruling and continued to meet in secret but their clandestine meetings were betrayed and Sarah was held prisoner in the house, her employer refusing her wish to leave until he had, by his influence in the Government and the army, conspired to have his stepson, whom he despised, re-posted overseas. The soldier was sent to Lucknow, where he was tragically killed in a drunken brawl with a fellow officer, and his gloating stepfather wasted no time in bringing the devastating news to the distraught Sarah, who rejected his advances and was dismissed and sent packing back to her home town of Thame.

Despite her grief, the young woman was determined to exact revenge. Whilst her callous employer was attending a regimental dinner, she stole into the family nursery and, under cover of night, made off with Lord's two-year-old child, whom she took with her back to Oxfordshire. Half crazy with grief and hatred, she is said to have thrown herself and the child into the River Thame. Another version has it that soon after taking the child she felt remorse and left the infant on a bench on the Thames embankment, hoping it would soon be discovered. The child was never seen again and, some days later, Sarah's body was retrieved from the river and laid to rest at Emmington. Does she walk the churchyard in perpetual grief for her lost love or the death of an innocent child?

 [Grid Ref: SP 743 024] Emmington is on the B4445 between Thame and Chinner.

56. CHURCH OF ST MICHAEL, RYCOTE, OXFORDSHIRE

Rycote lies three miles south-west of the town of Thame in south Oxfordshire. Visitors might be excused if they find it a little difficult to locate for today the former village has gone. Rycote House and church stand together in an intimate hollow surrounded by trees and approached by a track which turns off the main Thame to Oxford road. The setting, which was once a grand landscaped park, is very picturesque, with the red brick gables of the house glimpsed through the trees, expansive lawns around the church and a great yew tree, which is said to have been planted in the year of the Coronation of King Stephen in 1135.

St Michael's Church, Rycote, Oxfordshire. *(Photograph by Eddie Brazil)*

St Michael's is not a parish church but was built in 1449 by Sir Richard Quartremayne as a chantry chapel. After Edward VI dissolved the chantries in 1547, the building became the private chapel of a succession of families occupying the house. Henry VIII, Elisabeth I and Charles I all visited here. Today it is justifiably famous for its unrestored interior and furnishings, which date from the fifteenth to the seventeenth century. To enter Rycote chapel is to step back in time 500 years.

Its historical attractions apart, Rycote is also the site of reported paranormal activity and, in keeping with its royal associations, one of the apparitions said to have been sighted is that of Lord Chancellor, Sir Thomas More, executed for refusing to recognise Henry VIII as the head of the Church of England. The ghost of Robert Dudley, Earl of Leicester, has also been reported within the chapel. It is said his spirit wanders in eternal penance for the murder in 1560 of his wife, Amy Robsart, whose ghost was thought to haunt the rectory of St Mary's Church at Syderstone in Norfolk.

As with many of England's historic houses and ancient religious establishments, ghost stories and haunting tales seem to be a required and traditional accompaniment. Rycote is no exception

Robert Dudley, Earl of Leicester, whose ghost is said to haunt Rycote church.

for here there are also tales of phantom monks, ghostly milkmaids and grey ladies. The most persistant presence seems to be the ghost of Arabella, who is said to haunt the chapel on moonlit nights. Her true identity is unclear but we have a very detailed account of a sighting of her apparition by the chapel custodian of the time.

This took place late on a winter's afternoon in December 1968. The figure was reported to be seen standing by the ancient yew tree adjacent to the west door of the chapel. At first the custodian thought it must be someone in fancy dress, as her costume was in the Tudor style with a square neck, tight waist, full skirt and voluminous sleeves.The lady was tall and slim but her face was turned away and obscured by the flowing veil of her head-dress. As the custodian walked towards her she disappeared from view behind the yew tree and, by the time he had reached the spot, she was nowhere to be seen. However, looking around he suddenly saw her once more, this time moving across the grass at the east end of the chapel. The custodian continued to follow her and describes how she glided rather than walked along the north side of the building. As he watched, the figure paused and then moved quickly in the direction of Rycote Park, following the route used in former days from the chapel to the house. The apparition passed by a chestnut tree, down a slope, and, on reaching the level grass at the bottom, simply just disappeared. The custodian became instantly conscious of an icy feeling and found himself trembling uncontrollably.

 [Grid Ref: SP 667 046] Rycote can be found three miles south west of Thame on the A329. Nearest station is Haddenham and Thame Parkway on the Chiltern line.

57. ST MARY MAGDALENE, SHERBORNE, GLOUCESTERSHIRE

Sherborne is a picturesque village five miles west of the town of Burford on the Oxfordshire-Gloucestershire border. It lies amid beautiful open countryside close to the River Windrush. A chapel was built on this site by monks from Winchcombe Abbey in AD 811 and a monastery was founded at a later date. Thomas Dutton acquired the lands in 1551 and made Sherborne his home, where he entertained Queen Elizabeth I.

The parish church of St Mary Magdalene, which stands next to Sherborne House, was founded in the twelfth century but has been much altered, restored and rebuilt over the centuries. John Dutton had the house re-faced in 1651-5 and James Dutton, 1st Baron Sherborne, had alterations made to the church between 1743 and 1776. In the mid-nineteenth century John Dutton, 2nd Baron Sherborne, had the medieval nave and aisle of the church demolished to allow more light into Sherborne House, and a new nave and sanctuary was built further north. Yet it is the numerous ornate monuments to members of the Dutton family for which the church is justly celebrated. On the south-east wall of the church stands the grand memorial to James Lennox Dutton by Westmacott. Erected in 1791, it is an exceptional, if somewhat macabre, piece of sculpture, depicting a triumphant angel trampling on a prostrate skeleton (representing Death) as it emerges from the base of the plinth. Both figures are remarkably life-like and demonstrate the eighteenth-century fascination with memento mori.

The haunting of St Mary Magdalene is unusual in that reports of phenomena have only occurred within the past twenty years, the building seemingly having no history of a ghostly nature before this time. In this respect it is similar to the singular incidents reported at places such as St Michael's Church at Didlington in Norfolk and also Thetford Priory. As well as the unusual lighting up of one of the chancel windows, which has been noted to occur on occasions when the church was locked and for all intents and purposes empty – although it must be considered that this may well have a perfectly natural explanation such as an out of hours cleaner – the most persistently reported occurrence has been the appearance of a man dressed in black who has been glimpsed on occasions inside the church.

In 1989, two female tourists from Boston, Massachusetts, on a touring holiday of the Cotswolds, spent part of a weekday afternoon at Sherborne. While one of the women went to fetch a camera from the back of their car her friend remained inside and, while standing looking at the Dutton memorial, she noticed what she later described as an elderly man wearing a black coat with matching trousers standing with his back towards her, close to the altar rail. The figure was in view for approximately five to ten seconds; she looked away for a moment while moving her position in front of the memorial and on turning back saw that the figure had disappeared. The lady walked around the inside of the church but there was no sign of the man, and her friend, who arrived soon afterwards with her camera, was adamant that no one had either gone into the church or come out during the time that her companion had been waiting inside. The day was dull and overcast, making it more difficult to explain away the experience as the result of the moving or sudden appearance of a shadow or patch of sunlight.

The Dutton monument in St Mary Magdalene Church at Sherborne, Gloucestershire. *(Photograph by Eddie Brazil)*

Perhaps it should be mentioned that the reporting of ghostly phenomena at St Mary Magdalene's, where to our knowledge no previous paranormal experiences have taken place, does coincide with the general increase in the public awareness of ghost hunting in the past few years, due in no small way to paranormal-related reality programmes on satellite and cable television. Whether sightings of the unidentified figure in this particular English church is due to suggestion as a result of this modern media exploitation remains to be proved. The two other reports of the figure, despite a lack of firm detail, did not involve paranormal groups, so there is a possibility that a careful and discrete investigation may result in better and substantiating evidence of what at present may be a haunting waiting to happen.

 [Grid Ref: SP 169 147] Sherborne lies on the A40 between Northleach and Burford. The church is half a mile west of the centre of the village; Sherborne House is now a school.

58. ST PETER'S CHURCH, HEREFORD, HEREFORDSHIRE

As well as its Cathedral, the city of Hereford has two parish churches dating from medieval times, of which St Peter's is the oldest. The main body of the church comprising chancel and nave with a south aisle is late thirteenth century as is the tower although the ribbed spire dates from the early 1400s as does the tower bell thought to be the 'common bell' used to sound warnings of impending danger or invasion to the populace.

St Peter's was founded by the Norman baron Walter de Lacy around 1085 and he was to meet an untimely death on the site. While inspecting the last stages of construction work on the church tower he fell from a ladder and was killed outright; he is buried in the Chapter House of Gloucester Cathedral. However, this was not from the tower of the present building but the first church to occupy the site of which nothing now remains. St Peter's is noted for its fifteenth-century choir stalls which were salvaged from the nearby Benedictine priory of St Guthlac's in 1539 at the time of the Dissolution and for carvings displaying the Royal Arms of William III and Queen Mary. As with many parish churches the building saw restoration during Victorian times, in this instance in the mid-1880s.

The haunting that concerns us here is a cyclical one most often recorded during the month of December when the apparition of a monk, cowled and wearing black robes, has been seen both inside the building but most often in the precincts outside. A notable sighting took place in 1926 when two policemen walking the night beat around St Peter's Square noticed a person moving around outside the building. Entering the churchyard with the intention of questioning what they considered was a potential housebreaker, the officers followed the figure up the church path but were totally unprepared for what was to happen as they drew close. On approaching, the monk-like figure, seemingly unaware of their presence, passed straight through the closed wrought-iron gates fronting the church porch and quickly vanished by the locked oak doors into the empty and silent building.

In 1934 the hooded apparition, thought to be a medieval monk killed centuries earlier by Welsh invaders, was again seen in the churchyard and there are also reports of encounters that pre-date the experience of the two policemen including an account by the father of a former church organist who claimed to have seen the figure vanish into the floor in front of the altar. More recent sightings of this particular phantom seem to be lacking, a deficit which may be made up if the ghost hunters of today and tomorrow keep a note in their diaries to visit St Peter's during the run up to Christmas in the next few years.

 [Grid Ref: SO 512 400] St Peter's fronts onto St Peter's Square at the junction of Union Street and St Owen Street close to the A438 dual-carriageway through the centre of Hereford.

59. ETTINGTON PARK CHURCH, WARWICKSHIRE

In 1963, a Hollywood movie was released in cinemas across Britain. *The Haunting* was one of the first films to treat the subject of paranormal phenomena seriously. Based on the novel *The Haunting of Hill House* by American novelist Shirley Jackson, it tells the story of four psychical researchers as they investigate the ghostly happenings at fictitious Hill House, situated in a remote part of New England. When it came to finding appropriate locations for the building, the producers decided to scour England rather than the US for suitable properties, for, as director Robert Wise pointed out, 'In the States haunted houses are few and far between, yet in Britain they are ten a penny.' Wise and his crew found just what they wanted some six miles outside Stratford-upon-Avon. Ettington Park in Warwickshire became haunted Hill House in Massachusetts, and the house became the central character of this film.

The house, now a hotel, was the ancestral seat of the Shirley family, whose line can be traced back to before the Domesday Book. There has been a building on this site since Saxon times, although the structure we see today is a rebuilding of a Tudor house in the Victorian neo-Gothic style, complete with romantic towers and turrets.

The church at Ettington Park, Warwickshire, said to be haunted by a woman in grey. *(Photograph by Eddie Brazil)*

Ironically, and perhaps unknown to the producers and cast of the film at the time, Ettington Park House is itself haunted. A lady in grey is said to walk the main staircase, having allegedly been pushed to her death by a disgruntled maid while in the games room; the clack, clack of a ghostly game of billiards has been heard yet no players are seen. What concerns us here is that the haunting at Ettington is said to extend to the ruins of the twelfth-century church of the Holy Trinity, which stands adjacent to the house.

From a gallery built into the west tower the ghostly form of a woman has been seen looking down into the roofless nave. The spectral figures of two children have also been observed playing in the ruined church. They are thought to be members of the Shirley family who tragically drowned whilst swimming in the River Stour during the nineteenth century. A guest staying at the hotel was awoken one night by the sound of a child sobbing. Looking out of her bedroom window into the moonlit grounds, she saw the figure of a young girl standing motionless and looking pensively towards the river.

Of all the haunted churches included in this book, the church of the Holy Trinity is one of the most atmospheric. Its remaining weather-beaten west tower, south wall, and nave columns readily conjure up a sense of mystery. On stormy nights or fog shrouded winter afternoons it is all too easy for the impressionable visitor to imagine all kinds of ghostly happenings. Such is the creepy nature of the ruins, that the producers of the 1981 children's movie *The Watcher in the Woods* chose the church as a setting.

For disbelievers of the paranormal, locations such as Ettington church with its accompanying ghostly ambience only goes to prove that the atmosphere of the archetypal spooky setting, coupled with an obligatory myth or legend, is enough to produce suitable apparitions in the minds of the gullible or those who simply see what they want to see. Alternatively, those who are more open-minded in accepting the reality of psychic phenomena could argue that the 'eerie' atmosphere of allegedly haunted sites is an actual product of genuine paranormal activity. Moreover they would add that a place which is psychically active doesn't necessarily need to be teaming with apparitions or violent poltergeist manifestations to be deemed 'haunted'. Many hauntings over the years appear to gradually lose energy until the building, be it a house or church, eventually becomes a place where only an unpleasant or sad feeling, or a melancholy, eerie atmosphere, remains – an environment which is often encountered and experienced by sensitive or psychic people. Perhaps one site included in this book which demonstrates this view better than most is at Langenhoe in Essex, where, although the church was demolished many years ago, its remaining weed-strewn graveyard still retains a sinister nature.

The haunting of Ettington church has never been thoroughly investigated. In 2008, television presenter Carol Vorderman conducted a ghost hunting video diary during a solo all-night vigil within Ettington Park House. She was to learn that the apparition of the lady in grey had been seen walking the corridors and that a guest, on opening his bedroom door late one night, was confronted by the frightening vision of a screaming, wailing woman. It would appear that paranormal phenomena continues to be active at Ettington and from that we may reasonably conclude that this also includes Holy Trinity church.

 [Grid Ref: SP 248 474] Ettington Park is five and a quarter miles south-east of Stratford-Upon-Avon on the A3400 between Newbold-on-Stour and Alderminster.

60. ST NICHOLAS AND ST PETER AD VINCULA, CURDWORTH, WARWICKSHIRE

In several instances in the present work we have seen the harrowing results of the long and bloody Civil War, which in some cases seems to have left its mark not only physically but also in the unseen psychic fabric of England. The church of St Nicholas and St Peter at Curdworth (from

Credeworde or 'Creda's Settlement') in Warwickshire is a notable case in point. Here, in August 1642, Roundhead and Royalist forces met for the first time in the fields south of the village when Cromwellian troops attempted to intercept a Royalist brigade travelling from Kenilworth Castle to Tamworth, in what became known as the Battle of Curdworth Bridge. The skirmish saw twenty Parliamentarians killed and the marks of a stray musket round can be seen today in one of the windows of the church, which by that time was already 500 years old. The fighting also seems to have left behind, if reports can be believed, other more inexplicable and intangible impressions.

The church at Curdworth dates from around the middle of the twelfth century and initially comprised a simple arrangement of nave and chancel. In the fifteenth century the nave was extended and a four-stage west tower together with a south porch added. During the eighteenth century the building fell into disrepair and the first of two restorations took place in 1800. This was followed by a late Victorian restoration nearly a hundred years later, when, in 1895, an unusual font bowl was found buried under the floor and subsequently restored for use. All the registers for this particular church date from 1685.

For the ghost hunter prepared to make the journey to this particular site, the locale of which is much changed from Civil War days by the advancing suburbs of Birmingham and the construction of the M6 motorway, it is the churchyard which is of particular interest as it is here that at least two phantoms are said to manifest. Both these ghosts are associated with the aftermath of the Battle of Curdworth Bridge, as it is thought that a mass grave was dug here in which the bodies of Cromwell's soldiers were buried. The apparition of an unknown lady dressed in green is said to appear in the churchyard, apparently a relative of a Royalist officer who was also killed in the skirmish and interred in the grave along with the rest of the dead. Details of witnesses and dates of sightings are lacking, as is similar information concerning the second ghost, this time a headless figure said to guard a hoard of treasure which was concealed on the body of one of the Parliamentarians and buried with him.

 [Grid Ref: SP 177 928] On the A4097 close to the M6 Toll and M40 motorways; take Coleshill Road and turn off into Church Lane.

61. ST JOHN THE BAPTIST, BOUGHTON, NORTHAMPTONSHIRE

The case of Boughton church is an advisory tale that could well apply to many of the locations included in this book. Boughton (from Bucca or 'he-goat') is a small village to the north of Kingsthorpe in Northamptonshire and was once home to Boughton Green Fayre, said to be the largest in the country which was held here from the middle of the fourteenth century through until the middle years of the First World War. The area is rich in history and noted archaeologically for both Saxon and Roman remains, and an ancient turf maze existed on the Green until it was obliterated by military exercises in 1914. Charles I played bowls here in 1647 and the Scottish novelist and poet George Whyte-Melville (1821-78), remembered for his *Songs and Verses* (1869), was a resident for a time and after whom one of the villages' pubs is named. Nearby Boughton Park is noted for its collection of follies built in the eighteenth century by the Earl of Strafford.

In 1978, New Zealand-born writer Marc Alexander made mention of Boughton Green (incorrectly naming it Broughton Green) in his book *Haunted Churches and Abbeys of Britain* in connection with the ruined church of St John the Baptist, which lies isolated and surrounded by a small cemetery on the edge of Boughton, half a mile distant from the replacement fifteenth-century church of the same name that currently serves the village and which plays no part in the events that follow. The old church, comprising nave, chancel, north chapel and a three-stage west tower, was derelict by the middle of the eighteenth century to the point that the tower and spire collapsed in 1786 and, unsurprisingly, like other churches of note included in this survey, such as St Mary's at Clophill and All Saints at Thundridge, the ruins quickly developed a haunted reputation which survives to this day.

One historical figure that has become connected with alleged hauntings at St John's is George Catherall, a highwayman who went by the name of 'Captain Slash'. Arrested while carrying out a robbery at Boughton Fayre, he was subsequently hanged before a large audience in Northampton on 21 July 1826, kicking off his shoes into the crowd before falling through the drop. Catherall's apprehension at Boughton has resulted in colourful but unsubstantiated stories of his ghost returning to the area at Christmas time, where he is said to moan eerily in the deserted ruins of St John's. A version of this legend is reported by Marc Alexander, who describes Catherall as a horse thief who was executed and then buried in the churchyard.

Another ghost story reported in local newspapers in recent years (*Northampton Chronicle & Echo* in 2002) concerning St John's is again a seasonal tale, this time involving a doomed couple and dating back to the end of the eighteenth century. Here a young man and his red-haired bride were married but their union was to last less than a day, as the groom dropped dead a few hours after the wedding and the grief-stricken young woman later committed suicide at his graveside. It appears to be her vengeful ghost who materialises each Christmas Eve to waylay male travellers passing by the ruined church at night. Anyone foolish enough to kiss the ghost on the lips will die within a month, as did a man named William Parker, who is said to have had an encounter with the flame-haired spectre during the winter of 1875.

When Paul Adams made enquiries into the history of the church building through the parish council, he was told in no uncertain terms by the present vicar that the ruins of St John the Baptist are not haunted and rumours of ghosts (as at Clophill) cause continual problems at the site (which remains consecrated ground in use for burials), including disturbances and damage to graves. Rather than omit reference to this particular 'haunting' it is included as an indication of the need for responsibility in carrying out serious paranormal research, both in terms of field work and data gathering from historical sources.

 [Grid Ref: SP 764 657] Boughton is on the A508, one and a half miles north of Kingsthorpe. The church ruins are half a mile to the east of the village in Moulton Lane.

62. ST LAWRENCE'S CHURCH, LUDLOW, SHROPSHIRE

St Lawrence's is an ancient church whose foundations date back to the eleventh century. Known as the 'Cathedral of the Marches' it has undergone much rebuilding and alteration work over the centuries, the most extensive being in the fifteenth century when the tower, nave and chancel were altered into the Perpendicular style. The ashes of A.E. Housman, the author of the famous poem anthology *A Shropshire Lad* (1896), are interred in the churchyard and it is the church grounds which are of interest here as they have long been associated with the apparition of a woman, most often seen on warm summer evenings walking between the rectory and the church door, where she quickly fades away.

The story of the churchyard ghost was given much support in the late 1930s when Sir Ernest Bennett, author of *Apparitions and Haunted Houses: A Survey of the Evidence* (1939), wrote to the then incumbent, the Revd F.G. Shepherd, asking for details of the haunting. Shepherd, who moved into Ludlow Rectory in 1930, was able to confirm several personal experiences which linked in with sightings of the ghostly lady. The most prevalent of these was the sound of shuffling feet (as opposed to the most often recorded sound of footsteps or footfalls) moving along the first floor passages of the house during the night.

However, one evening in 1935, around a quarter to eleven, the Revd Shepherd had an encounter with an apparition as he was about to retire to bed. In a letter to Sir Ernest Bennett dated 23 July 1937 he recalled the incident:

It was a woman; she came down [the stairs] slowly but did not seem to notice me. I was standing in the hall. She was tall and slim with grey hair and wearing a light blue-grey dressing gown; she passed into our drawing-room, which was in darkness. I followed her and without switching on the light closed the door behind me. I saw her pass into the drawing-room and was then four or five yards behind her, but when I reached the room she had vanished. My object in closing the door was to have the experience of being in a room with a 'ghost' but she made no re-appearance.

Subsequent writers on the Ludlow haunting, including Antony Hippisley Coxe, have concluded that the rectory and churchyard apparitions are one and the same, although more recent sightings which may or may not confirm this appear to be lacking.

 [Grid Ref: SO 512 746] St Lawrence's is located in College Street close to its junction with King Street and the B4361.

63. ST ANDREW'S CHURCH, STOKE DRY, NEAR UPPINGHAM, RUTLAND

The pleasant rural atmosphere of the small village of Stoke Dry, two miles south-west of Uppingham in the county of Rutland in the East Midlands belies one of the most chilling paranormal experiences included in this book. The fabric of the parish church of St Andrew's dates from the thirteenth and fourteenth centuries but the foundations are older and go back to the 1100s. The church is known for its wall paintings, which show St Andrew and the Madonna as well as St Christopher and the Martydom of St Edmund. The main body of the church has no electricity, evening services being lit by long candle holders fixed to the ends of the pews, and rudimentary heating is provided by an open fire grating set in the floor of the nave. Immediately to the south of Stoke Dry is the Eyebrook Reservoir, where aerial practice for the Dambuster air raids on the Ruhr Valley took place in May 1943.

Both the village and the church have a strong association with Sir Everard Digby, who was executed on 30 January 1606 in the churchyard of Old St Paul's Cathedral for his involvement in the failed Gunpowder Plot of the previous year. There are monuments to Kenelm Digby in the chancel, Jacqueta Digby in the south aisle and Everard himself in the south chapel. The Manor of Stoke Dry was part of the Digby estate and this has given rise to a local tradition that Everard, together with several fellow conspirators including Robert Catesby, Thomas Percy and Guy Fawkes, met in a small room over the church entrance, where they plotted the assassination of King James I and the destruction of the House of Lords during the 1605 State Opening of Parliament. This same parvis chamber, accessed by a narrow stairway off the front porch, is where another account states that a former vicar kept a woman parishioner imprisoned during the local witch purges of the seventeenth century – her screams and cries were ignored for several days as she was brutally starved to death.

Despite the apparition of a monk being at times connected with Stoke Dry church, the principal haunting of St Andrew's is ghostly female laughter, clear and dramatic first-hand evidence of which was provided to Paul Adams by medium and psychic researcher Rita Goold of Leicester. In 1988, Rita, together with fellow ghost hunter John Barden, visited Stoke Dry with the intention of carrying out a preliminary inspection in preparation for holding an all-night vigil inside the church. Barden, despite being an experienced UFO investigator, was relatively new to psychical research and was keen to have hands-on experience of investigating allegedly haunted buildings. At the time of their experience, both were unaware of the actual nature of the haunting but had been encouraged to carry out a visit by another ghost hunting colleague, Stan Willet from Southampton, who had read about the witchcraft connection at Stoke Dry in Antony Hippisley Coxe's 1973 book *Haunted Britain*.

On arrival at the church, Goold and Barden found that another party, a husband and wife together with their grown-up children, were already inside looking around the building. Not wanting to draw attention to what they were doing, John Barden suggested that they wait in their car, which was parked overlooking the church entrance, until the family had left. Shortly afterwards pandemonium seemed to break out – the ghost hunters saw one of the family run out through the churchyard and desperately knock for help on the door of a nearby house. Several people were summoned including the local churchwarden, and after a short time an ambulance crew arrived and went inside the church.

Somewhat alarmed, Rita Goold and John Barden left their car and on approaching the main door were prevented from going inside by the St Andrew's churchwarden, who revealed that the husband of the party had collapsed and died while standing next to the church altar. As they stood talking in hushed tones all three heard the clear sound of a harsh female voice laugh out and echo round the inside of the building. The churchwarden's face went pale and he visibly sagged in the doorway. The two investigators looked at each other, each thinking that the wife had become hysterical, but it was not the case, as the churchwarden later told them.

After the ambulance crew had taken the man's body out of the church and the building became empty he spoke with them again, asking for confirmation of what they thought they had heard. He then confessed that the same sound of laughter had been heard inside St Andrew's on a number of occasions, most often when a funeral service was taking place. The spot where the unfortunate visitor had fallen was the grave of an eleven year-old girl, whose curious epitaph strangely states that she is 'Waiting for her Love'.

Was she the person who heartlessly laughed out, seemingly from beyond the grave; or is this curious and somewhat disturbing haunting connected with another tragic figure from Stoke Dry's past, namely the starving and screaming 'witch' whose untimely end may well be more

St Andrew's Church
at Stoke Dry,
Rutland, haunted
by ghostly laughter.
*(Photograph by
Eddie Brazil)*

real than most people would give credence to? We may never know. The experience certainly shocked Rita Goold's companion – to the extent that he felt unable to go through with the planned vigil inside St Andrew's and the investigation was subsequently abandoned. For the present, the church of Stoke Dry continues to keep its ghostly secrets to itself.

 [Grid Ref: SP 855 968] Stoke Dry lies on the A6003 midway between Caldecott and Uppingham. Follow Main Street into the village and St Andrew's Church is on the left.

64. ALL SAINTS' CHURCH, ASHOVER, DERBYSHIRE

The aftermath of a brutal Victorian murder gave the pleasant picture postcard church of All Saints in the Domesday village of Ashover, midway between Matlock and Chesterfield on the fringe of England's Peak District, a sinister and haunted reputation. Parts of All Saints dates from the late thirteenth century but most of the building is from the fifteenth, comprising an aisled nave with clerestory windows, south porch, chancel and an embattled west tower surrounding a stone spire.

In 1841 tragedy struck the village when a local tradesman, John Towndrow, a maltster, attacked his wife with a hammer and bludgeoned her to death. Afterwards Towndrow carried out a grotesque mutilation, severing the corpse's head, which was found by villagers close to the body; they also discovered John Towndrow, who had died by his own hand. Ghost hunter and writer Marc Alexander records that in the decades following this gruesome event the apparition of a headless woman was seen in the churchyard of All Saints' Church with some regularity and, not surprisingly, was thought to be the restless ghost of this unlucky woman, although dated sightings containing details of witnesses appear to be lacking.

Nothing seems to have been seen of this particular phantom for over a hundred years now but ghost hunters who visit Ashover today may like to try to find out the truth behind a local legend concerning an empty stone coffin, which can be found in the churchyard. According to tradition, if one walks around the sarcophagus three times before sitting in it, it is possible to hear the sounds of the unquiet dead in their graves.

 [Grid Ref: SK 348 632] The B6036 leads into Ashover; All Saints' Church is in Church Street next to the Black Swan public house.

65. LINCOLN CATHEDRAL, LINCOLNSHIRE

Lovely Lincoln, Lindos (marsh or pool) to the ancient Britons and Lindum to the Romans when they made it the first permanent fortress of the IXth Legion. Newport Arch, the most northern gate to the Roman colony, is the only Roman archway in the British Isles. It still spans the Roman Ermine street used by modern traffic.

Lincoln Cathedral is built in the highest part of the city and the central tower is one of the tallest in England (blown down in 1547 but rebuilt); in it hangs 'Great Tom', a bell weighing over five tons. The ground plan of the first church was laid out by Bishop Remigius (who is interred on the north side of the presbytery) in 1086. The Cathedral contains the earliest purely Gothic work extant. Begun in 1255 and completed during the following century, the English Gothic Angel Choir takes its name from the thirty angelic figures in the spandrels of the arches.

Above the easternmost pier on the north side is the tiny but celebrated Lincoln Imp. Legend tells of the mighty Wind carrying the imp into the structure to marvel at the splendour of the building work being carried out. He settled on the top of a pillar to admire it more fully, but, seizing their opportunity, the surrounding angels turned him into stone for all eternity; although it is said the supernatural Wind still haunts the area awaiting his return.

The peak on the northernmost spire is mounted by a figure blowing a trumpet, often known as 'the swineherd' and possibly representing the second bishop of the cathedral, Robert Bloet; occasionally sounds attributed to the paranormal blowing of this horn have been heard within the Cathedral precincts. In 1976 the local newspaper carried an account of a man who claimed to have witnessed a human head rolling down the hill from the Cathedral – a story that resulted in a number of similar reports in the same area.

The cloisters in particular are said to be haunted by ghostly monks, walking in silent procession; there are also stories of candles crumbling inexplicably and of the Pyx falling and spilling its holy contents, while long-past suicides from the many spires and turrets have been witnessed in replay; and there is the occasional ghostly wind suddenly wafting through the Cathedral and most often through the Angel Choir.

Nor are the buildings in the Close immune from ghostly activity. Antony Hippisley Coxe had a friend who lived there and one day she looked up and thought she saw her sister, who was a nun. She quickly realised that this was impossible since her sister was dead and that she could in fact see clean through the figure! .

 [Grid Ref: SK 978 718] Lincoln Cathedral is a landmark building in the centre of the city; from the A15 Lindum Road, Pottergate leads into Minster Yard, which runs around the south and west side of the Cathedral.

66. EPWORTH RECTORY, LINCOLNSHIRE

Epworth Rectory, a Grade I listed building within a stone's throw of the church, is famously known as the eighteenth-century home of John and Charles Wesley, the founders of Methodism. The Wesley's sought reform by way of a return to the Gospel within the Church of England. While at Oxford, where John Wesley was a professor, they set up a Holy Club, which met weekly, and systematically set about living a holy life. The term Methodist was originally derogatory as fellow students derided the Wesleys for the methodical way they ordered their lives; the brothers, however, took the mockery and turned it into a title of honour. The movement spread and soon many significant Anglican clergy became known as Methodists. Today it is estimated that there are twenty million Methodists worldwide.

Given the Wesleys stature within the Church in England, their reforming zeal and legacy to the Anglican faith worldwide, it would be no exaggeration to classify the series of events which occurred at their Lincolnshire home in 1716 as extraordinary, for between December of that year and the following January of 1717, Epworth Rectory was invaded by a violent poltergeist.

On 1 December 1716, the Wesleys' servant, Robert Brown, and a housemaid heard eerie groans and mysterious knockings emanating from the dining room. On investigation they found the room to be empty. Soon afterwards, the children too insisted that they could hear footsteps ascending and descending the stairs at all hours of the night, but when they looked out into the hallway there was no one to be seen. On one occasion Brown saw a hand mill move on its own at the top of the stairs. The heavy tread of a man in leather boots was heard throughout the house, but no explanation for the noises was forthcoming.

The initial disturbances continued for a week and were witnessed by all the family, except the Revd Samuel Wesley. The Wesley children nicknamed the spirit 'Old Jeffrey' and during the following weeks the disturbances gained in frequency and energy. As well as crashing glass, moving furniture, clanking chains and loud banging sounds there was the terrifying spectacle of a levitating bed, which was occupied at the time by one of the Wesley children.

Sometime later Samuel Wesley experience the poltergeist for himself. One night he was awakened by nine loud knocks, with a pause for every third stroke. The sounds seemed to be coming from the next room but when he looked into the chamber it was empty. The Reverend still thought it could be someone playing a practical joke and sent in his dog, a stout Mastiff, to rid them of the nuisance, but the dog, which had at first barked loudly at the sounds, refused to enter the room and seemed more terrified than the children.

The Wesleys began to believe that Samuel, the eldest son who was not at home, had died and that it was his spirit which was trying to contact the family. One night, after several deep groans had been heard, the Reverend tried to communicate with the entity. 'Thou deaf and dumb devil,' he shouted, 'Why dost thou frighten these children? Come to me, come to my study... I am a man!' The clergyman's request was met with a few knocks, but then silence. The following night, as Samuel Wesley opened his study door, it was flung back and shut with a powerful force. Sometime later, the Revd Wesley and his wife heard that their son, also called Samuel, was safe and well and thereafter the strange disturbances became a matter of curiosity rather than alarm.

By now the children had overcome their initial fear of the invisible being and had come to accept its antics as a welcome relief from the boredom of village life. Curiously, it achieved the status of a pet among the Wesley family and it was soon observed that the entity was quite sensitive in nature. If any visitor slighted Old Jeffrey by claiming that the rappings were due to natural causes such as rats, birds, or wind, the haunting phenomena quickly intensified so that the doubter stood instantly corrected. Even more remarkable is the fact that witnesses invited into the rectory to view the phenomena reported watching a bed levitate to a considerable height while a number of the Wesley children squealed and laughed from on top of the floating mattress.

As the haunting continued apparitions began to be observed. The ghost of a man in a long, white robe that dragged on the floor was seen by the children, while other family members claimed to see an animal similar in appearance to a badger scurrying out from under their beds. The servants swore that they had seen the head of a rodent-like creature peering out at them from a crack near the kitchen fireplace. The disturbances continued into January 1717 and then, just as mysteriously as it had started, the phenomena abruptly ended, never to return.

The Epworth Rectory haunting is indeed a curious case. Poltergeist activity would seem to be a phenomenon of the modern world with its origins in the trials and frustrations of contemporary urban existence; certainly not the kind of thing to invade the respectable household of a devoted Christian family in a leafy English village. Is Poltergeist phenomena the manifestation of repressed pubescent anger, or is it, as veteran paranormal researcher, Guy Lyon Playfair suggests, the violent mischievous actions of spirit entity, thriving on the fear of its victims and determined to wreck havoc and cause dread where it chooses? It is curious to note that once the Wesley family became used to their invisible intruder and were no longer scared of it, the disturbances at Epworth abruptly ceased.

Whatever the real explanation, the Wesley Poltergeist is an exceptionally well reported account. Noted investigator Harry Price, writing in the mid-1940s, went as far as to say that 'this case has become a classic – perhaps *the* [Price's italics] classic of the early cases – amongst the best-authenticated ghost stories.'

 [Grid Ref: SE 785 035] Epworth is eight and a half miles north of Gainsborough on the A161.

67. ST MARY'S IN THE BAUM, ROCHDALE, LANCASHIRE

The annals of English ghost lore contain many reports of phantom animals witnessed over the years throughout the country. As well as spectral dogs, horses, cats and birds, there are several strange and unusual species, such as the mysterious insect said to have buzzed a visitor in the grounds of Borley Rectory in Essex, and the long-snouted white creature seen during accounts of haunting phenomena associated with Willington Mill on North Tyneside. One of the two reported ghosts on the site of St Mary's in the Baum, an interesting red-brick church at Rochdale in Lancashire, brings shades of Lewis Carroll's famous 1865 work *Alice in Wonderland* to our survey of haunted churches as, during the 1870s, a phantom white rabbit was often seen 'cavorting' in the churchyard with such regularity that a local poet composed a poem castigating the creature for the trouble and fright it caused local people passing by the church at night. The rabbit's paranormal nature was seemingly confirmed at the time by its imperviousness to buckshot, as a number of travellers reported taking pot shots at the creature, but it should be no surprise to learn that the animal has not been reported from the area now for over a century.

St Mary's is not in fact the first church to occupy this particular location in Rochdale. An original building and the one outside of which the spectral rabbit was reported was a chapel-of-ease, built in 1742 and dedicated to St Chad. This building was allowed to fall into disrepair, to the point that at the beginning of the twentieth century, with costs estimated to be in the region of £8,000 to carry out repairs, it was decided to demolish the church and build a new one. Scottish architect Sir John Ninian Comper designed the new building and its was consecrated in February 1911 by the Bishop of Manchester. The church's unusual name comes from the original field where the chapel of St Chad's was first built, where a medicinal herb or balm, pronounced locally as 'baum', grew in some profusion. The church is known variously as St Mary's in the Baum or the Baum Chapel.

During the period that the new church was constructed changes were made to the boundary line on the south side of the churchyard, with the result that several graves had to be disinterred and relocated in another part of the church grounds. Several bodies, including those belonging to a number of children, were removed. Due to the high water table from the nearby Lordburn stream, the coffins were very well preserved and were reburied in three large trenches.

The second ghost from this Lancashire location is that of a male apparition, which was reported with some regularity up until the early 1970s. The figure was often seen drifting out of the churchyard and through into a neighbouring market place, where it vanished in a particular corner. Lancashire writer Kathleen Eyre reported that on a number of occasions police were called to reports of a man seen moving around the deserted market stalls at night, but they were unable to either locate or intercept the figure. The area around St Mary's in the Baum has been drastically altered over the past few years, including the construction of the large Rochdale

Exchange Shopping Centre to the south, and, as such, it would seem that this unknown male ghost may have faded away into obscurity forever.

 [Grid Ref: SD 896 139] St Mary's in the Baum is located on the A58 St Mary's Gate dual-carriageway road in the centre of Rochdale, 350 yards south-west of its junction with the B6266.

68. ST MARY'S AND ST BENEDICT'S CHURCH, BAMBER BRIDGE, PRESTON, LANCASHIRE

Here there have been several examples of the psychic phenomenon known as a timeslip or timewarp. This is when an incident that seems to be set in the past is experienced by one or more people usually at a particular place. An obvious example is the famous experience of the Misses Moberly and Jourdain, scholarly ladies of high integrity, who seemingly walked through the gardens of the Palace of Versailles as they were a hundred or more years earlier. There are plenty of other examples of timeslips at Versailles and elsewhere.

Ghost hunter and television presenter Jason Karl describes a particularly interesting example of a timeslip in his *Preston's Haunted Heritage* (2007) when two local friends walk into a never-to-be-forgotten experience at St Mary's Church, Bamber Bridge. 'The day felt strange', they decided – a peculiarity often noticed by those who come into contact with timeslips, including the two ladies at Versailles. Everything seemed somehow unreal, the colours of the trees, the sunlight, the whole environment: it all seemed so different and unsubstantial but the friends walked around the quiet churchyard, deserted except for themselves, and then headed for the church. After a while spent looking at the architecture and the monuments, they were leaving the church by the main door when a group of a dozen or so people walked in, pushing silently past them. Our two local visitors idly watched the party as they went into the building and were somewhat surprised to see that they went straight through a doorway which was clearly marked 'Bell Ringers Only' and disappeared from view up a spiral staircase.

Discussing the matter between them the visitors agreed that they had both been aware of the complete silence as the party had approached them and as they had passed them within the church and they then realised that everyone they had seen seemed to be wearing clothing of the 1970s or thereabouts and this was the year 2000 and a beautiful summer day – or it was when they started out. They now agreed that nothing had seemed right, not the people, the churchyard, the inside of the church, even the weather; and together they walked back into the church, determined to set their minds at rest.

Inside they found everything changed and different. The atmosphere was normal, not unnaturally quiet as it had been before; and when they looked for the doorway the group had passed through, they found it alright but on opening the door they discovered a brick wall facing them, covered in dust – obviously no one had passed that way recently. They then examined the exterior wall and found no evidence of a spiral staircase, yet they had both clearly seen one. More than a little confused and at a loss to know what had happened, they left the church and returned home.

It all remained a mystery they never solved but several years later they remembered the experience when they revisited St Mary's. By then the whole area had been renovated and they could find no trace of the bricked-up door, the staircase or the sign over the doorway. In 2005, having heard firsthand of the experience, Jason Karl visited the church one bright autumn day and he too found no staircase, no doorway, no silent visitors and no explanation. What might have happened, he wondered, if the two friends had followed the group up the staircase?

 [Grid Ref: SD 561 263] St Mary's and St Benedict's Church is located on the B5257 Brownedge Lane, 600 yards from the A6 London Way junction.

69. HOLY TRINITY CHURCH, MICKLEGATE, YORK, NORTH YORKSHIRE

This must count among the churches with unusual paranormal activity and it has been reputedly haunted for many years. The Revd Sabine Baring-Gould (1834-1924), himself no stranger to ghosts and the author not only of such works as the *Book of Were-Wolves* and *Curious Myths of the Middle Ages* but also the words to the hymn 'Onward, Christian Soldiers', chronicled eye-witness accounts of supernormal activity here in his *Yorkshire Oddities and Incidents*, published in 1874. Very recently, if not today, visitors have their attention drawn to its ghostly reputation by a notice on its information board.

The church is unusual in having at least three recognised ghosts: a former abbess, a woman, and a child. Both the latter are said to be victims of the plague, the burial site of which is outside the east window. Holy Trinity stands on the site of a much earlier church which was donated by Ralph Pagnel to the Benedictine Abbey of Marmontier in France in 1110, and it remained under monastic control until the Dissolution. When the soldiers of Henry VIII arrived to take possession in 1539, the abbess endeavoured to defend the establishment and was murdered, but before expiring she gasped out that her spirit would return to haunt the scene of her death until the authority of the Pope was again recognised. Be that as it may, the ghost of an abbess has been repeatedly seen hereabouts.

Baring-Gould reproduced in his book on Yorkshire a letter from 1874 describing a first-hand experience of another ghost. The structure of the church has since been altered but at the time there were two east windows and through these were seen, moving gracefully outside the windows, the figure of a girl of perhaps eighteen or twenty, her face covered with a white lace veil. The figure passed, her veil flowing back as she moved, and a few seconds later she returned, gliding back the way she had come – and then she vanished.

A later witness described exactly the same double appearance but then a third, accompanied by a young child, before finally vanishing. It was verified that the figure or figures were seen only from inside the church, outside nothing was seen. This haunting is said to have been witnessed for literally hundred of years, most frequently on Trinity Sunday and often on dull, rainy days but also occasionally in bright sunshine. In 1957 two historians, knowing nothing of the haunted reputation of the church, were talking at the spot where the 1874 informant had been seated when it was noticed that the whole atmosphere changed to what was described as 'earthy and cold, a very charnel house atmosphere of death and decay'. It was not until seven years later that they learned of the tradition of haunting at that very spot. They made a point of revisiting the church but this time all was well and the atmosphere free of any unpleasantness.

The churchyard is said to be haunted by the ghost of Thomas Percy, Duke of Northumberland, who led an uprising during the reign of Elizabeth I. He was captured and beheaded and his head buried in the churchyard. Is his the headless phantom that wanders at midnight, on occasions, searching for his head, removed from Micklegate Bar where it had been placed as a warning to others?

 [Grid Ref: SE 598 515] Micklegate is close to the A1036 and York mainline railway station.

70. YORK MINSTER, NORTH YORKSHIRE

This cathedral is known as the Minster although at no time was it attached to a monastery. The area of Minster gateway has long been reputed to be haunted. York Minster was founded by King Edwin or Edwine (*c*.585-632) King of Northumbria, who was baptised here in the Norman crypt by Paulinus, first Archbishop of York in 627. He was killed by Cadwallon of Wales at Hatfield. The haunting consisted in the main of a disembodied voice, seemingly calling out.

The choir stalls of the Minster are reputedly haunted by the figure of a man seen occupying a seat in the Dean's pew. This figure is generally thought to be the ghost of Dean Gayle, who died in 1702 and was buried inside the Minster in a fine tomb. Shortly after his death a local preacher sought to deliver a sermon from the pulpit, but the usually eloquent minister became dumbstruck and shakily pronounced that he saw the dead Dean Gayle occupying his usual seat. Ever since, the ghost of the devoted Dean has been seen in the same seat from time to time.

One witness stated that she thought the figure seemed strangely unmoving and, wondering whether the man, who otherwise appeared to be quite normal, was unwell, she quietly approached him and was about to ask after his health when suddenly, when she was literally inches from it, she found the figure no longer there and no possible explanation for its appearance or disappearance.

A visitor to the Minster a few years ago said she was somewhat surprised to be approached by a workman as she was admiring the carvings on the West Door. He appeared to be a stonemason and wore a long apron and carried a stonemason's tools. He came and stood close to her and, after a moment, asked quietly whether she liked the carvings. As she smiled and said, 'Yes, I like them very much,' the figure replied, very quietly, 'That is good, I carved them.' When the visitor turned to continue the conversation, she discovered that the man who had seemed completely solid and life-like in every way, had disappeared and she was entirely alone.

York, of course, is full of ghosts and hauntings; indeed it revels in the title of 'Britain's most haunted town'. It must also be one of Britain's most historic towns. King Charles I set up his printing press here in 1642; a stone's throw from the Minster; Guy Fawkes was reputedly born in Petergate; the real Robinson Crusoe was born near Skeddergate; Shelley and his bride stayed at The Black Swan in 1811; Henry VIII and Katherine Howard visited the city in 1541 when the streets were swept, sanded and gravelled for the first time ever; and Dick Turpin lived at York and was executed here in 1739.

An interesting superphysical incident apparently occurred in York Minster and was reported in a popular periodical of the time. A young man, accompanied by a young lady, were members

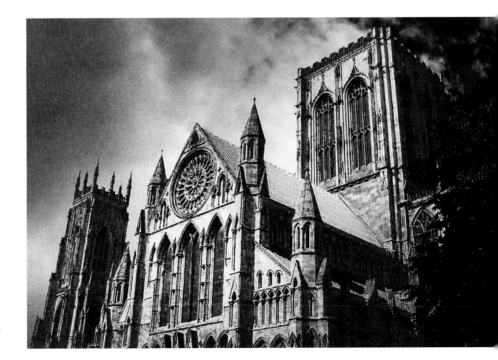

York Minster –
full of ghosts.
*(Photograph by
Eddie Brazil)*

of a party visiting the Minster from London, when they noticed that a young naval officer was approaching them. He seemed about to speak when the young couple were struck by the pallor of his complexion; he appeared to be much agitated and to be labouring under some strong emotion. As he drew nearer the girl became agitated and she caught hold of her companion's arm, all the time gazing at the officer with something approaching terror and amazement.

The naval officer looked intently at the girl and then passed, saying quietly but distinctly, 'There is a future life'. He passed the couple and soon disappeared. The girl then spoke to her companion and said he was her brother. She said they had often discussed the question of life after death and they had made a contract between them that whoever died first would, if it were possible, appear to the other. When she saw the figure in naval uniform, she knew at once that it was her brother, come to let her know that there was life beyond the grave, and that she knew she would shortly hear of his death. Within a few days she was notified that her brother had died, as far as she could judge, at just about the time she saw his ghost; a classic crisis apparition.

Is there something about York Minster that is conducive to ghosts?

 [Grid Ref: SE 603 523] York Minster is a landmark building on the north bank of the River Ouse close to the A1036.

71. WHITBY ABBEY, NORTH YORKSHIRE

In the closing years of the nineteenth century, the Stage Manager of the Lyceum Theatre in London sought a brief respite from the heavy demands of actors and the biting invective of newspaper critics in regular visits to the small fishing village of Whitby, 300 miles away from the bustling Victorian metropolis among the jagged cliffs of the North Yorkshire coast. Here he was able to use the unique atmosphere and landscape as added inspiration for a growing body of manuscript that, on publication in 1897, changed forever the developing phenomenon of modern supernatural fiction. Perhaps then it should be of no surprise that the stark yet beautiful – and haunted – ruins of such an imposing building as Whitby Abbey should overlook the arrival in England of Irishman Bram Stoker's astonishing literary creation – the dangerous vampire lord Count Dracula. Immortalised when the fictional ship *The Demeter*, carrying Transylvania's most famous son, is shipwrecked close to this imposing site, the origins of Whitby's now famous and iconic Abbey ruins date back over 1,500 years.

Whitby Abbey was founded over thirteen centuries ago in a remote location known as Streonaeshalch or the 'haven of the watch-tower', a reference to a Roman coastal signal-station which most historians agree occupied the site as a protection against invasion from the sea during the last years of the Roman occupation of Britain. In 655, King Oswy of Northumbria fought and defeated the heathen Penda, King of Mercia, at the Battle of Winwaed and, in the years immediately following, founded twelve monasteries, of which Whitby was one; it was established in 657 and presided over by St Hilda, formerly Abbess of Hartlepool, who took Oswy's daughter Elfled into her care.

Whitby was a double monastery of men and women and became noted for its piety and ecclesiastical training. Hilda died in 680 and was succeeded as Abbess by Elfled. For 200 years there was peace, until 867, when a powerful army of heathen Danes crossed the Humber and invaded south as far as York, which was sacked. The Danes stormed Whitby, the Abbey was destroyed and for another two centuries the site was laid to waste.

Towards the end of the eleventh century, a group of monks from abbeys in the south, on a pilgrimage to visit holy sites in the north of England, brought about the eventual re-founding of Whitby Abbey. This was ultimately affected by Reinfrid, an unlettered monk who settled in Whitby around 1078; later his brother Serlo de Percy became Abbot and they built the first stone church here, although only parts of the foundations of this structure now survive. Over the next 200 years a vast Benedictine abbey was raised on the site comprising nave with crossing, presbytery and north and south transepts.

Like the previous community at Whitby the monks flourished and, at one time the Abbey was third in value of the Benedictine houses in Yorkshire after those of St Mary's at York and Selby, but the Dissolution saw not only the end of monastic life but the beginning of the end for the inspiring Abbey building which, as the decades passed, was allowed to fall into decay and ruin. On 14 December 1539, the last Abbot of Whitby, Henry Davell, surrendered the Abbey to Henry VIII's Commissioners and it passed into private hands. These later years were a sad tale of neglect and destruction. In 1762 the nave collapsed, succeeded the following year by the south transept. Just over twenty years later the colossal west front fell and on 25 June 1830 the central tower over the crossing was reduced to rubble. A final ignominy took place on 16 December 1914, when German warships launched a salvo of shells, which destroyed part of the west end of the ruins.

Today the east front and northern walls of the nave and presbytery, together with the north transept, survive as, in Stoker's words, 'a most noble ruin, of immense size', where it seems the shadows of Whitby Abbey's turbulent past may still linger.

Whitby Abbey on the North Yorkshire coast – the shrouded form of the first Abbess, St Hilda, is said to look out from the highest window. *(Photograph by Eddie Brazil)*

The oldest ghost here must be that of the White Lady, said to be the shade of the first Abbess, St Hilda, whose shrouded form has been seen on occasions silhouetted in the highest of the empty and gaping windows. The ruins also appear to have its own cyclical haunting in the presence of a phantom choir, which is said to sing in the ruins at dawn each 6 January, which would be Christmas Day in the old Julian calendar. Another literary link that these eerie ruins share with Bram Stoker is in the writings of Sir Walter Scott, whose epic poem *Marmion*, first published in 1808, is said to have been inspired by the story of Constance de Beverly, a nun at Whitby who was walled up alive in the dungeons of the Abbey for an affair with a knight of the same name; her weeping ghost is said to haunt the ruins, particularly at the top of the steps which lead down to the twelfth-century passage located on the site of the now ruined south transept. For good measure, the Abbey also has its own death coach in the form of a carriage drawn by headless horses, which has been reported driving through the ruins before plunging over the nearby East Cliff, only to disappear before hitting the stormy waves beneath.

However one views these kind of accounts, the ruins of Whitby Abbey will not disappoint the determined ghost hunter who endures the climb of the 199 steps up from the harbour below to savour its unique atmosphere and historic architecture.

 [Grid Ref: NZ 904 115] The main road into Whitby is the A171 from Scarborough. The Abbey ruins overlook the town on the East Cliff.

72. ST ANDREW'S CHURCH, NEWCASTLE, TYNE AND WEAR

Built on the site of what may have been a former chapel, the twelfth-century church of St Andrew's incorporates Roman masonry in areas of its construction and is considered to be the oldest church in Newcastle. It occupies a position close to the former New Gate entrance, one of seven gateways through the medieval town wall constructed during the thirteenth and fourteenth centuries to ward off the threat of Scottish invasion. This section of the defensive structure was heavily fortified and from the early 1400s was used as the town prison; the route that convicted felons took from the gaol to the gallows on the Town Moor survives in the road name Gallowgate, which runs east to west immediately north of the old church. The New Gate Gaol eventually became surplus to requirements and was demolished in 1823.

Architecturally St Andrew's is noted for the Gothic arch separating the nave from the chancel and, as with other English churches such as the Church of the Blessed Virgin Mary at Clapham on the South Downs also included in our survey of hauntings, the walls of the chancel have been constructed on a different line to those of the nave, an effect designed to create an impression of the angle of Christ's head on the Cross. The chancel in fact has two of the oldest gravestones in the city, one possibly being that of Thomas Leighton, the fifteenth-century Sheriff of Newcastle. The church was severely damaged during the siege of Newcastle by the Scots in 1644, when a cannon was mounted in the tower, but it was subsequently rebuilt; the entrance porch was reconstructed in 1792 and a south transept added in 1844.

The churchyard of St Andrew's is the area of interest to psychic investigators as, to our knowledge, no phenomena has been reported inside the church itself. The figure of a young woman dressed in a long flowing gown has been reported on occasions to run through the burial ground; the apparition is fleeting and vanishes almost as soon as she is observed. The origins of the haunting are somewhat anecdotal and have been put down to the tragic outcome of a doomed love affair between an anonymous local trainee priest and the equally un-named daughter of a wealthy landowner. Having arranged a secret meeting in the grounds of St Andrew's Church, the young man arrived at the appointed time to see his beloved wandering around between the gravestones in a dazed manner, apparently unaware of his presence. As he

St Andrew's Church, considered to be the oldest in Newcastle. *(Photograph by Darren Ritson)*

The churchyard of St Andrew's; the apparition of a woman in a flowing gown has been seen on occasions running between the gravestones. *(Photograph by Darren Ritson)*

approached, she turned and faded away in front of his eyes. The following day the novice learnt that, stricken with a malady, the young girl had in fact died the previous evening.

It was not long after this that reports began to circulate of the appearance in the vicinity of St Andrew's Church of a spectral figure matching the unfortunate girl's description. When the last appearance of the ghost took place is unclear. Future investigations in this interesting and historic spot by the ghost hunters of today and tomorrow may in fact obtain the much needed evidence to support this colourful tale of the supernatural.

 [Grid Ref: NZ 245 645] St Andrew's Street with its church is off the B1307 Gallowgate, close to St James' Park football ground in the west end centre of Newcastle.

73. THE CATHEDRAL CHURCH OF ST NICHOLAS, NEWCASTLE, TYNE AND WEAR

A number of English churches owe their haunted reputations to strange and, at times, convincing 'extras', which appear spontaneously on camera films and photographs taken during visits when the subject of ghosts and the paranormal is far from the minds of the people involved. For the serious psychic researcher this can make a subsequent investigation all that more problematic when the location concerned has no previous history of a haunting or reported experiences of a paranormal nature. Several of the churches included in our survey fall into this category.

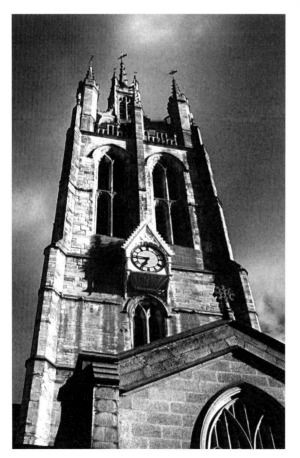

An alternative scenario is when a paranormal photograph appears to confirm aspects of an already established haunted status and it has been suggested that the Cathedral Church of St Nicholas in the centre of Newcastle is one such building.

The first parish church on this particular site was built towards the end of the eleventh century. This was a wooden structure which was replaced after a hundred years by a stone church with a dedication (around 1194) to St Nicholas. This building was to see much alteration and extension work over the next few centuries; a fire in 1216 caused extensive damage but the church was later rebuilt and enlarged; increased height to the external walls, clerestory windows and a tower with an unusual lantern spire were all additions carried out during the fifteenth century. The church interior suffered

The Cathedral Church of St Nicholas, Newcastle. *(Photograph by Darren Ritson)*

A thirteenth-century effigy of an un-named knight, focus of paranormal activity in the Cathedral Church of St Nicholas, Newcastle. *(Photograph by Darren Ritson)*

much damage from Scottish soldiers during their occupation of Newcastle in 1640 and during the English Civil War the complete destruction of the church was only prevented when Scottish prisoners were used as a 'human shield' inside the tower to ward off the threat of attack by long-range cannons. During less turbulent times, in May 1882, the creation of the Diocese of Newcastle, the most northerly Anglican bishopric in England, paved the way for the Church of St Nicholas to become a cathedral. Much of the stained glass seen in the building today dates from Victorian renovations and a hall, library and vestry were added in the mid-1920s.

The oldest memorial in the Cathedral Church of St Nicholas dates from the thirteenth century and appears to be the focal point for instances of paranormal activity reported inside the building. This is an effigy of an un-named knight, possibly a member of the household of Edward I, known as Edward the Longshanks, who was King of England between 1272 and 1307, which occupies an alcove in the west wall, and it is the form of a knight in full armour which has been seen on occasion in this part of the building. Possibly connected with the appearance of this apparition are metallic sounds which could be interpreted as the footsteps or movement of such a figure that have been heard echoing around the vast interior of the building. More information is required from forthcoming investigators able to carry out controlled vigils inside the cathedral, for this is a case for which good authenticated evidence is wanting. A photograph reportedly taken inside the cathedral and which is said to contain what has been described as an image resembling the figure of a knight in armour has yet to be located by researchers.

 [Grid Ref: NZ 250 642] The Cathedral Church of St Nicholas is a landmark building located a quarter of a mile north-west of the Tyne Bridge at the junction of Mosley Street and St Nicholas Street.

74. FORMER CHURCH OF ST MARY, WOODHORN, NORTHUMBERLAND

The haunting of the church of St Mary at Woodhorn, fourteen miles north of Newcastle, is an interesting case but one which cannot be substantiated by hard evidence. The village may be the Wudecestre ('Woodchester') granted to the Lindisfarne community by Ceolwulf in 737 and St Mary's is an ancient building whose nave and west tower may pre-date the Norman Conquest. It was heavily restored with some sections being practically rebuilt in 1843 in a pastiche Norman style. The church became redundant in 1973 and is currently used as the Woodhorn Church Museum.

Local tradition has it that the lane outside the churchyard is haunted by the ghost of a skeletal cyclist, who passes unsuspecting pedestrians before vanishing into the night. Needless to say there appear to be no documented reports giving dates of encounters or details of witnesses. However, the most persistent story concerning paranormal phenomena at St Mary's involves a crisis apparition which was allegedly seen in the churchyard during the First World War.

At some time during the 1914-18 conflict, an assistant sexton named George Charlton was digging a fresh grave when he noticed a young man walking through the churchyard towards him and recognised him to be Tom Chalkley, whom he knew through a friendship with the youth's parents. Charlton was surprised to see him as he knew that Chalkley was serving in the navy, but assumed he was home on leave. As the young man approached he noticed that he was holding his side and looked pale and ill and, strangely, didn't respond when Charlton called out to him. The sexton carried on with his work but thought enough of the incident to mention it to one of Tom Chalkley's cousins when he saw him on his return to his lodgings in nearby Newbiggin in the evening of the same day. It was then that George Charlton learnt that Chalkley's parents had received a telegram that very day announcing that their son had been killed in action; he was later buried in the family grave at Woodhorn and, according to researcher Marc Alexander, his apparition was seen subsequently at least three times walking in the churchyard.

What appears to be a classic crisis case unfortunately doesn't stand up to close scrutiny, as we have been unable to find reference to a Thomas Chalkley being a casualty in the First World War in the records kept by the Commonwealth War Graves Commission. Of the two servicemen named Chalkley with Thomas as part of their Christian names who died during the First World War, neither served in the navy and both were buried in France; in fact there are no servicemen buried at Woodhorn who died in the conflict. Unless the surname of the unfortunate man has become corrupted in the retelling of the story, this is one haunting which not only lacks credible witnesses but also a firm basis in fact.

 [Grid Ref: NZ 302 888] Woodhorn and St Mary's Church lies on the A197 road into Newbiggin-by-the-Sea.

75. THURSBY CHURCH, BETWEEN WIGTON AND CARLISLE, CUMBRIA

It was Vivienne Rae-Ellis, the Tasmanian-born writer, who first told Peter Underwood about the legendary Grey Lady of Thursby church; an account she includes in her book *True Ghost Stories of Our Time* (1990), a copy of which she presented to Peter Underwood inscribed 'From the novice to the master'. Since then several other reports of the Grey Lady have come to light.

Legend has it that the original Grey Lady at Thursby was the mistress of wealthy William Brisco, a family man who lived a few miles away at Crofton Hall, between Wigton and Carlisle, in the eighteenth century. To all appearances Brisco lived contentedly enough with his wife and family at the home of his forebears but in fact he kept a mistress, housed in a lodge not far from Thursby church and when she died Brisco wished her body to be interred in the family vault, but the family were outraged by the suggestion and in the face of united opposition Brisco compromised and she was buried near the church door, in a grave surmounted by black railings.

But Brisco's mistress did not rest in peace and there were many reports of her wandering about the churchyard. Eventually, it is said, the churchwardens and local people disinterred the body and hammered a stake through the heart, on the principle that if such an action could quieten a vampire it should be able to placate a wandering spirit.

A local inhabitant informed Vivienne Rae-Ellis in the 1980s that 'an evergreen tree grows out of the grave' obscuring Brisco's inscription on the headstone, and a curse will be activated on anyone who interferes with the branches of the evergreen. This informant, who was married in Thursby church, maintains that the Grey Lady still haunts both church and churchyard. A former vicar and his wife used to tell of being visited by 'a lady ghost dressed in a grey dress and bonnet'. Once, when they were discussing the haunting as they sat on a wooden cupboard inside the church together with a friend, all three of them felt a draught and heard a loud rustling sound, as though someone invisible but wearing a long skirt had passed close to them. And they all noticed a strong smell of lavender. The vicar's wife, it seemed, was quite used to visits from the phantom and she quietly commented, 'Yes, she just went past us then, leaving her usual smell of lavender perfume behind her.'

Other reports of a shape suggesting a Grey Lady has come from visitors and local people, from both inside the church and in the churchyard.

 [Grid Ref: NY 324 503] Thursby is on the A595 between Wigton and Carlisle.

Map of England, showing the locations of the churches featured in the Appendix.

APPENDIX

ADDITIONAL CHURCH HAUNTINGS IN BRIEF

The following is a concise but not exhaustive list of a further forty English church buildings, priories and abbeys with haunted reputations that, due to limitations of space and the anecdotal nature of some of the reported phenomena, we have not included as full-length accounts. A number of these hauntings are in fact well known and more detailed commentaries will be found in the volumes included in the Bibliography. These churches are listed in the regional order used for the entries in the main part of this book.

LONDON AND SUBURBS

A1. St Paul's Cathedral, City of London
For several years the Kitchener Memorial Chapel was haunted by the whistling ghost of a former cathedral official, although it has not been reported now for several decades. [Grid Ref: TQ 320 812]

A2. St Bartholomew's Church, City of London
Haunted by Rahere, a courtier to Henry I, his apparition has been seen on a number of occasions. A monk has also appeared during a pageant held in the church and Elliott O'Donnell reported a crisis apparition of the daughter of a church official appearing to him one morning while the officer was alone inside the building. [Grid Ref: TQ 319 817]

A3. St Sepulchre's Church, Holborn Viaduct, City of London
Haunted by the ghost of a tall, pale-faced clergyman whose apparition was seen on several occasions in the years immediately following the Second World War. [Grid Ref: TQ 317 815]

A4. St Botolph's Church, Aldgate High Street, City of London
An impressive ghost photograph was taken here in 1982 by photographer Chris Brackley while visiting the church with his wife. On developing his negatives, Brackley found the unmistakable figure of a woman had appeared in the shot, looking down the nave towards the altar; the apparition was standing in a high balcony on the far edge of the picture but the couple were adamant that they were alone in the building at the time. Some time later, Brackley was contacted by a building contractor, who had disturbed several coffins while carrying out restoration work in the church crypt. The face of one of the bodies was apparently in a highly preserved state and is said to have borne a likeness to the figure in the photograph. [Grid Ref: TQ 337 817]

Chris Brackley's noted photograph of the interior of St Botolph's Church, City of London – the figure in the high gallery was only noticed after the photograph was developed. *(Photograph by Chris Brackley)*

SOUTH-EAST

A5. Canterbury Cathedral, Kent
Haunted by the ghost of Simon of Sudbury, who may also walk St Gregory's Church in Sudbury. According to Graham McEwan, a vision of the still alive Terry Waite, Assistant for Anglican Communion Affairs to Dr Robert Runcie, who was being held forcibly in the Lebanon, was reportedly seen inside the cathedral in September 1987. There is also here the ghost of a twelfth-century knight. [Grid Ref: TR 152 579]

A6. St Mary's Church, Reculver, Kent
A ruined twelfth-century coastal church said to be haunted by the eerie sound of a crying baby. Excavation work carried out during the 1960s uncovered several infant skeletons, which seem to support previous local legends of the ghosts of screaming children associated with the site. [Grid Ref: TR 227 694]

A7. Church of the Holy Cross, Basildon, Essex
According to local tradition, an apparition dressed in a red robe was seen inside the church on a number of occasions is a former pre-Reformation rector. [Grid Ref: TQ 714 898]

A8. Michelham Priory, near Eastbourne, East Sussex
A well-known haunted Augustinian priory established in 1229. There are a number of ghosts including a Grey Lady, the apparition of a woman in a Tudor dress, the figure of a monk and an unidentified phantom wearing a black cloak. [Grid Ref: TQ 558 094]

A9. Hitchin Priory, Hitchin, Hertfordshire
Occupied by White Friars before the Dissolution, the building has been used as a technical college and is now a conference facility. There are two ghosts, a Grey Lady seen in the grounds as recently as 1973 and the apparition of a Royalist officer named Goring, whose headless ghost is said to ride to the Priory on the night of 15 June each year. [Grid Ref: TL 184 287]

A10. St Nicholas Church, Arundel, West Sussex
This fourteenth-century church is well known for a photograph said to have been taken by a local solicitor in 1940 that seemingly shows a prominent ghostly figure standing near the altar. In 1984 the image was examined and debunked by Dr Stephen Gull and Tim Newton using a computer enhancement programme, who concluded that the photograph was in fact a single long exposure that had accidentally captured multiple images of a woman walking up the altar steps to light the candles, unaware that a photograph was being taken at the time. [Grid Ref: TQ 013 072]

SOUTH WEST

A11. St Nectan's Church, Hartland, Devon
Haunted by the ghost of a monk in a black habit; the apparition was seen at least once during the 1970s by the vicar, the Revd Harold Lockyer. [Grid Ref: SS 263 244]

A12. St Peter's Church, Combe Martin, Devon
A church whose alleged haunting dates from the 1930s, when the ghostly re-enactment of the church's dedication ceremony involving a spectral bishop and an accompanying procession of figures was seen to enter the church and pass along the aisle towards the altar before disappearing. [Grid Ref: SS 586 464]

A13. Church of the Blessed Virgin Mary, Oare, Somerset
The ghost of a former rector is said to return on the occasion of the induction of a new clergyman and ring the church bell; the ghost was seen at least once during the first half of the twentieth century. [Grid Ref: SS 802 474]

A14. Church of St Clement, Bishop and Martyr, Powderham, Devon
The roadway opposite the church is haunted by the figure of a woman wearing a long cloak; at least two sightings took place in the late 1930s. [Grid Ref: SX 973 845]

A15. St Bartholomew's Church, Yealmpton, Devon

A phantom hole seemingly appeared in the ground in the churchyard here and was seen by the Revd Dr Byles in the late 1940s. Despite being championed by Graham McEwan as 'unique in the annals of paranormal phenomena', Peter Underwood later interviewed the Revd Byles and felt the incident was almost certainly the result of a natural phenomenon. [Grid Ref: SX 577 517]

A16. Methodist Chapel, Bossiney, Cornwall

A phantom light was seen in the window of the closed and locked chapel one night in 1965 by publisher Michael Williams and a group of friends; Graham McEwan has collected the account. [Grid Ref: SX 065 887]

A17. Church of St Gluvia, Penryn, Cornwall

Local tradition has it that a former bell-ringer returns on occasions to toll the bell he loved so much in life; Graham McEwan notes that a crisis apparition case involving the church was related to a meeting of the Ghost Club in the 1950s. [Grid Ref: SW 787 346]

A18. Church of St Mary Magdalene, Launceston, Cornwall

A supernatural ghoulish creature, known as a 'kergrim' in old Cornish, is said to haunt the churchyard; when and how it manifests does not seem to have been recorded. [Grid Ref: SX 333 846]

A19. St Neot's Church, Poundstock, Cornwall

Haunted by two ghosts – a murdered fourteenth-century priest often seen near the altar rail and the apparition of an unidentified Bishop, which was seen standing outside the church by a mourner before a funeral in 1971. [Grid Ref: SX 203 995]

EASTERN

A20. All Saints' Church, Elm, Cambridgeshire

A ghost monk is said to ring a bell in the former vicarage announcing the death of someone living in the village; reports of the haunting have been collected by Peter Underwood. [Grid Ref: TF 470 069]

A21. St Mary's Church, Syderstone, Norfolk

The rectory adjacent to St Mary's Church was at one time the focus of poltergeist activity thought to be due to the ghost of Amy Robsart, wife of Robert Dudley, the Earl of Leicester. [Grid Ref: TF 833 326]

A22. St Gregory's Church, Sudbury, Suffolk

Traditionally the haunt of Simon of Sudbury, Archbishop of Canterbury and Lord Chancellor (executed 1391), whose severed head is preserved in the vestry. [Grid Ref: TL 874 414]

MIDLANDS

A23. Priory Methodist Church, Bedford, Bedfordshire

A small church built in the 1950s. Ghost hunter Tony Broughall reports that the apparition of a smart-looking man in a tweed coat and black trousers was seen by a lady member of the congregation during a Christmas day service in the late 1960s. [Grid Ref: TL 066 499]

A24. Priory Church of St Peter, Dunstable, Bedfordshire

Twelfth-century priory founded by Henry I and haunted by two ghosts – Sally the Witch whose troublesome spirit was caught in a bottle and buried in the churchyard and the apparition of Cuthbert, the second prior, whose ghost is said to visit the choir stalls at night. [Grid Ref: TL 022 218]

A25. Burford Priory, near Witney, Oxfordshire

A former Augustinian Priory later used as a nunnery after the Second World War. Several sightings of apparitions have taken place here including a monk and a figure thought to be a former gardener or gamekeeper. [Grid Ref: SP 250 124]

A26. Christ Church Cathedral, Oxford, Oxfordshire

The apparently supernormal image of the former cathedral Dean, John Liddel, who died in 1898, appeared on an internal wall of the building in 1923; it may still survive, concealed behind an altar that was constructed in front in the 1930s. [Grid Ref: SP 515 060]

A27. St Mary's Church, Dallington, Northamptonshire

Haunted by a spectral congregation which has been seen at least once since the early 1900s. [Grid Ref: SP 737 618]

A28. St Mary's Church, Woodford, near Kettering, Northamptonshire

Known for its ghost photograph taken by Gordon Carroll in June 1964, which seems to show a kneeling apparition in the act of praying before the church altar. A later attempt during the 1980s to debunk the photograph as the image of a cleaning lady captured on a long exposure was strenuously denied by the photographer. [Grid Ref: SP 969 767]

The kneeling ghost of St Mary's Church, Woodford, photographed by a visitor in 1964; the figure was not visible when the picture was taken. *(Photograph by Gordon Carroll)*

A29. St Mary the Virgin, Fotheringhay, Northamptonshire

The church contains the gravesite of Edward, Duke of York, killed at the Battle of Agincourt in 1415; paranormal medieval music has been heard here on a number of occasions. [Grid Ref: TL 060 932]

A30. All Saints' Church, Hollybush, near Ledbury, Worcestershire

An interesting photograph involving apparitional 'extras' was taken here in 1928 by a Mrs Wickstead, who was on a car tour of the area with friends. While stopping off briefly at All Saints' Church, Mrs Wickstead photographed one of her companions, Mrs Laurie, in the churchyard. When the negative was developed some six weeks later it showed the clear figures of an embracing couple standing on the path against the background of a yew tree – a spot known to be deserted at the time. Mrs Wickstead corresponded with Sir Oliver Lodge concerning the photograph, which, despite being later examined by the Society for Psychical Research, remains a mystery to this day. [Grid Ref: SO 768 367]

A31. Hereford Cathedral, Herefordshire

The road outside the cathedral, and particularly the immediate vicinity of the Lady Chapel, is said to be haunted by the apparition of a ghostly monk, believed to be a murder victim dating from the 1100s. It was seen collectively by several people during a festival at the cathedral in the 1950s. [Grid Ref: SO 510 397]

A32. St Mary's Church, Ilmington, Warwickshire

An apparition of a former church clerk who died in the 1790s was reported with some regularity inside the building during the latter part of the nineteenth century. [Grid Ref: SP 209 435]

A33. St Lawrence Church, Measham, Leicestershire

Medium and psychic investigator Rita Goold reports that some years ago a photograph taken of the church interior showed the clear figure of a deceased parishioner sitting in her old pew at the front of the nave near the altar. The image was of sufficient detail to show a hat pin and the woman's features, but its whereabouts today are unknown. [Grid Ref: SK 335 123]

A34. St Mary's Church, Rostherne, Cheshire

More of a superstition than a haunting – the lych-gate was at one time said to bring bad luck to newly wedded couples passing through it after a service in the church. [Grid Ref: SJ 743 837]

A35. St Peter and St Paul, Caistor, Lincolnshire

Another English church where the organ is said to play by itself. At one time an audio tape existed of the ghostly music recorded here in the late 1960s; its whereabouts today are unknown. [Grid Ref: TA 116 014]

A36. St Margaret of Antioch's Church, Marton, Lincolnshire

The ghost of an Edwardian parishioner was seen here by the Revd Alan Taylor during the 1960s. Other people have reported hearing footsteps inside the church. [Grid Ref: SK 840 817]

NORTH

A37. St Peter's Church, Burnley, Lancashire

Another English church with a tradition of being haunted by a phantom dog. Here the apparition is said to appear in the church rather than in the churchyard. [Grid Ref: SD 844 329]

A38. Bolton Priory, near Skipton, North Yorkshire

A ghost monk in black robes haunts the area. Masonry from the ruined Priory was used in the construction of the adjacent Bolton Hall and rectory, where the Marquis of Hartington saw the ghost during a stay there in 1912; Lord Halifax published the account in 1936. [Grid Ref: SE 074 543]

A39. Church of Christ the Consoler, Skelton-cum-Newby, North Yorkshire

An iconic ghost photograph of a cowled, monk-like figure standing on the altar steps was taken here in 1954 by the Revd K.F. Lord. Despite the apparition looking like a staged double-exposure, the rector maintained his photograph was genuine and it remained unpublished for several years until finally appearing in a national newspaper in the 1960s. If the possibility that the Revd Lord was the victim of a practical joke achieved by his camera being used without his knowledge is ruled out then the genuine appearance of a medieval monk in this church is problematic, as it is in fact a Victorian building constructed in the grounds of Newby Hall in 1871 as a memorial to the murdered son of Lady Mary Vyner, and there is no history of a haunting occurring previously at this site. At this distance of time it seems unlikely that an explanation either way will be forthcoming and as such the Newby ghost remains an enigma. [Grid Ref: SE 347 675]

The ghostly monk of Christ the Consoler at Skelton-cum-Newby, taken during the mid-1950s. *(Photograph by Kenneth F. Lord)*

A40. St Nicholas Church, Guisborough, North Yorkshire

An apparition of a shrouded figure was said to have been seen in the churchyard in the opening years of the twentieth century; its origins and any later appearances have not been recorded. [Grid Ref: NZ 616 159]

SELECT BIBLIOGRAPHY

Adams, Paul, Brazil, Eddie and Underwood, Peter (2009) *The Borley Rectory Companion*. Stroud: The History Press

Alexander, Marc (1978) *Haunted Churches and Abbeys of Britain*. London: Arthur Barker

Alexander, Marc (1982) *Haunted Houses You May Visit*. London: Sphere Books Ltd

Andrews, Ross (2010) *Paranormal Oxford*. Stroud: Amberley Publishing

Baldwin, Gay (2004) *Most Haunted Island*. Newport: Baldwin

Bennett, Sir Ernest (1939) *Apparitions and Haunted Houses: A Survey of the Evidence*. London: Faber & Faber

Broughall, Tony and Adams, Paul (2010) *Two Haunted Counties*. Luton: The Limbury Press

Dening, John C. (2000) *The Restless Spirits of Langenhoe*. Brandon, Suffolk: John Dening

Farrant, David (1997) *Beyond the Highgate Vampire*. London: British Psychic and Occult Society

Farrant, David (2005) *Dark Journey*. London: British Psychic and Occult Society

Foreman, Joan (1978) *The Haunted South*. London: Robert Hale

Hippisley Coxe, Antony D. (1973) *Haunted Britain*. London: Hutchinson & Co. (Publishers) Ltd

Karl, Jason and Yeomans, Adele (2007) *Preston's Haunted Heritage*. London: Palatine Books

Lindley, Charles (1936) *Lord Halifax's Ghost Book*. London: Geoffrey Bles Ltd

Manchester, Sean (1991) *The Highgate Vampire*. London: Gothic Press

Matthew, Rupert (2005) *The Haunted Places of Nottinghamshire*. London: Countryside

McEwan, Graham J. (1989) *Haunted Churches of England*. London: Robert Hale

Newton, Toyne (1987) *The Demonic Connection*. Poole: Blandford Press

O'Dell, Damien (2008) *Paranormal Bedfordshire*. Stroud: Amberley Publishing

O'Donnell, Elliott (1939) *Haunted Churches*. London: Quality Press

Price, Harry (1945) *Poltergeist Over England*. London: Country Life Ltd

Rae-Ellis, Vivienne (1990) *True Ghost Stories of Our Time*. London: Faber & Faber

Underwood, Peter (1973) *Haunted London*. London: George G. Harrap & Co. Ltd

Underwood, Peter (1977) *Hauntings*. London: J.M. Dent & Sons Ltd

Underwood, Peter (1983) *Ghosts of Hampshire & Isle of Wight*. Farnborough: St Michael's Abbey Press

Underwood, Peter (1986) *The Ghost Hunters' Guide*. Poole: The Blandford Press

Underwood, Peter (1994) *Ghosts and How to See Them*. London: Anaya Publishing

To wish Emily a
very happy 6th Birthday
with love from

Alexander & Imogen
xx

THE LORD OF THE
RUSHIE RIVER

THE LORD OF THE
RUSHIE RIVER

Written and illustrated by

CICELY MARY BARKER

BLACKIE

To
Dear Miss Edith

With Love

First published in 1938 by
Blackie and Son Ltd, 7 Leicester Place, London WC2H 7BP
This edition first published in 1988

British Library Cataloguing in Publication Data
Barker, Cicely Mary
    The lord of the rushie river.
    I. Title
    823'9'1 [J]

ISBN 0-216-92419-7

Designed by Malcolm Smythe

Typeset in Bembo family *by* Dorchester Typesetting Group Limited

Printed in Italy

CONTENTS

The attentive swans.

CHAPTER 1
LEFT BEHIND

"Good-bye, my darling," said the Sailor, kissing his little girl and setting her down on the footpath by the river. "You must go back now, and be a good child. Dame Dinnage loves you as though you were her own, and I have left money with her to pay for all you need. Then, some day, you will see me coming back, with a bag of gold, I hope; and I will never go away from you again."

Then he went his way, down the river path that led to the great ships and the sea; and little Susan walked slowly back to the village of Rushiebanks, turning often to wave her hand, until she could see her Daddy no more.

Susan could not help crying; but happening to look up, she smiled to see a family of swans who were swimming close by—the Cob and Pen, as Mr and Mrs Swan are called, and all their fluffy cygnets. "The baby swan is quite well now," she said to herself, remembering the day when her father had rescued one of them from a cruel boy who had tied a string to its leg and was teasing it. It was nearly dead; but the Sailor had put the leg, which was broken, into a splint, and tended the poor little cygnet until it could swim again.

"The baby swan is quite well now," she said.

He did not see what a wicked woman Dame Dinnage was. He had hired her to take care of his house and his little daughter, and he would have been angry indeed if he had known what happened as soon as his back was turned. The Dame's love for Susan had been all pretence. She fed Susan on the poorest scraps, and on milk that was watered until it was scarcely milk at all. Susan's clothes were not outgrown (for who could grow with no good food?) but in time they wore out; and as the Dame did not trouble to mend them, and bought no new ones, Susan patched them herself as best she could. "Daddy wouldn't like to see me all ragged when he comes home," she said.

And every week the Dame's old stocking, hidden in her locked box, grew heavier with money that had been meant for Susan's care.

Day by day, Susan watched from her little window, or wandered down the river path, talking to the swans. She saved bits of her scanty bread for them, and felt sure that they loved her and understood what she said.

"My Daddy will come home some day, up this path," she used to tell them. "I shall run out and meet him here. You will see!"

And the swans bent their necks and listened.

The young ones grew up; gradually their brown feathers were replaced by lovely white plumage. They

Susan patched her clothes as best she could.

were now over a year old, and the largest and loveliest of them all was the one whose leg had been broken. He was indeed a splendid swan; and as he sailed along, with his brothers and sisters (and even his father and mother) following behind, he seemed to be saying: "See me! I am the Lord of the Rushie River!" But though he was proud and stately, he was gentle with Susan, and would feed from her hand. So the months passed, while she waited hopefully. "It takes a long time to get a bagful of gold," she told the swans.

"Swan, swan, take me to Rushiebanks!"

CHAPTER 2
THE CITY

All of a sudden, Dame Dinnage announced that they were going away from Rushiebanks. In vain Susan cried and pleaded; everything was packed into a wagon, Susan was pushed inside among the baggage where she could see nothing, and for a night and a day they jolted along country roads, up hill and down dale. By the second night they reached a city, and Susan found that her new home was an attic at the top of a tall rickety old house in a maze of narrow streets. This was where Dame Dinnage thought to hide herself with her ill-gotten gains.

Now Susan was really unhappy. She thought of her father coming home, and finding no little daughter waiting for him, and no one to tell him where she was. She gave up trying to mend her frock. She had not even the swans to talk to; and the Dame threatened to beat her if she spoke to the other people in the house.

But one day, as she leaned out of the attic window, she heard the sound of a great bird's wings; and there, to her delight, was a beautiful swan flying slowly over the house-tops, with its neck stretched out, looking from side to side.

"Oh, can it be one of my swans looking for me?" thought Susan; but it did not see her, and sailed away out of sight.

The next day she saw it again. But again it passed by, though poor little Susan stretched out her arms and cried: "Swan, Swan, take me to Rushiebanks!"

"Hey, what's that?" said the Dame from inside the room, jerking her away from the window by her ragged

old frock. "It's no good talking about Rushiebanks; you're not going *there* any more."

Susan made no answer; she did not even cry; but that night, when the Dame was asleep and the house was still, she tied a little old shawl over her head and shoulders, and crept very, very quietly downstairs. Very, very gently she drew the bolt of the street door, pulled it just a little way open, and slipped out.

"It *was* my swan," she was saying to herself; "if he can't find me, I must find him."

The only way Susan knew through the narrow streets and alleys was the way to the market-place, but she did not go there. She thought she knew which way the swan had gone, so she turned down one street, and another, and another, looking up at the stars, and trying always to face the same direction. The houses were silent and dark; no one looked out of a window or heard her feet pattering over the cobble-stones.

On she went; and by and by the houses were fewer and further apart, there were trees and hedges, and she saw that she was coming to the country. It was still the dark night; but in one house a dim light burned in an upstairs window. It gave her a feeling of company; it might be the night-light of a little girl like herself. She crept into a corner of the creeper-covered porch, and rested there.

In the early, early morning, when the first streak of light was in the sky, and before the earliest farm-boy was about, Susan started off again. Her feet were sore and dusty; and there was no river like the Rushie, where her Swan might be.

Presently, however, she saw a pond a little way from the road, and thought she would wash her feet in it. She pushed through some bushes, and there, on the grass of the opposite bank, was a large and beautiful swan preening his feathers.

He saw Susan; he flapped his great wings, launched quickly into the water, and swam across to her. "Oh, my Swan!" she cried with joy; and as he stepped up the

16

She threw her arms around his neck.

bank she fell on her knees and threw her arms round his neck. It was so white and strong, and yet so soft and feathery, she thought she had never felt anything so lovely in her life.

"Did you come to look for me?" she asked, and he bent his head and gently caressed her hair with his beak.

"Are you going to take me to Rushiebanks?" was her next question; and at that the Swan nodded gravely and said: "Yes! If you are not afraid, I will take you on my back."

Somehow Susan forgot to be surprised that she understood the Swan's speech, as he had long understood hers. He crouched low on the ground, and spread out his wings. Full of trust, Susan laid herself down on the white feathers, put her cheek against the back of his neck, and clasped her arms tightly around it. The great wings on either side of her were lifted, and the noble swan with his burden soared into the air—so large a bird, and so small a girl! She nestled there quite safely, and soon was fast asleep.

Stretching one wing protectingly around her.

When Susan awoke, she was lying on a great pile of rushes, and she could see nothing but rushes, rushes, and water, all around her. She sat up and stretched, and then saw a swan watching her.

"She is awake!" said the swan; and at that a number of other swans appeared through the rushes.

Last came her friend. He stepped up on the rushpile beside her (it was a swan's nest, now disused) and with a gracious air he laid half a loaf in her lap. Stretching one wing protectingly around her, he said:

"Your father saved my life, and you fed me when you had little enough for yourself. Now I will take care of you until your father comes home. Have no fear; am I not the Lord of the Rushie River?"

"Oh, my Lord Swan," said Susan, "how can I thank you?" Then, being very hungry, she began to eat the bread, while the swans looked on approvingly. Presently she asked:

"How did you know where to look for me, my Lord Swan?"

"Ah," said he, "I asked all the birds for news of you. The seagulls, who come up the river, knew nothing; but an owl had seen the flitting, and the swallows went about seeking tidings. At last one of them found a housemartin who knew a sparrow, far off in the city; and *he* told of a child who leaned from a window,

"A swallow found a
        house-martin
                who knew a sparrow—"

weeping for Rushiebanks. So I came there; but the roofs and chimneys confused me, and I could not see you. But I should have tried again, had you not come to me. Shall the Lord of the River be baffled when he has a debt to pay?"

He said this proudly, looking around in his most majestic manner.

"The seagulls have promised," he went on, "to bring the news as soon as your father's ship reaches port. They will tell us when he lands, and is nearing Rushiebanks. Until then you must lie hidden with us. This is the backwater of the river, where no one comes; it belongs to us and to the other water birds. We will bring you food; and you may swim in the early mornings, but not in the day, when the landfolk are about. Will you be good, and do as we say?"

And Susan was only too glad to answer, "Yes."

Where the wild ducks had their homes.

CHAPTER 3
DAILY BREAD

The summer days went by, and Susan lived with the swans in great content.

She spent long hours on a tiny island, covered with willows, and hidden by beds of reeds and tall bulrushes. Sometimes she crept through the secret channels among the rushes, where the wild duck, the mallards, had their homes. If anyone else had intruded there, they would have flown up with clamour and alarm; but the Lord of the River had given his orders, and not a duck betrayed her. Soon they forgot to be shy, and she had friendly chats with them, and with the coot and moor-hens too.

When she lay resting on the old swan's nest, the water-rat would climb up beside her, and let her stroke his soft fur. When it was wet or cold, she sheltered under a slanting willow, curling up like a little animal on a bed of dry leaves and swans' feathers, until the wind or rain was over.

Every day the Lord of the River brought food for Susan. He was well-known, and had regular calling-places.

He made so many journeys to and fro, between village and backwater, with each bit he collected, that

Susan said: "I must make him a basket." She tried, this way and that, with rushes and willow-withies, until she found out how to do it.

She made a handle, by which the Swan could carry it in his beak, and he swam forth with it, highly pleased.

Sometimes he visited the water-mill, where the miller's wife always spared him something; or the riverside garden where the Squire's children would

The baker's little daughter.

come running to him. Or he would stop at the bridge, and catch in the basket the best of the crusts and bits of biscuit the people threw down. He let the small pieces fall in the water for the ducks.

Most days he called at the baker's backyard. The baker's little daughter would sit on the low wall, looking out for him. In her lap were buns or scones, rolls or broken cakes, from yesterday's baking; and she little guessed that they would be eaten by a child like herself! The Swan kept his secret; bowing his head courteously in thanks, he would swim on.

Wherever he went, he always returned proudly, with the basket filled.

Bread, cakes, pieces of pie—with these, and her open-air life, Susan became taller and plumper, browner, happier, and prettier, every day. Often, too, as summer drew towards autumn, she would swim in the early mornings to a place where the trees of an orchard overhung the river, and rosy windfall apples went bobbing down the stream. She helped herself to these, and to ripe blackberries and hazel nuts from the tangled thickets that bordered the backwater.

Sometimes she ventured to scramble up the bank, and run in the dewy grass of the meadows; but not when the careful swans were looking—they would have scolded her for rashness.

26

Only one thing troubled Susan. Where could she get a dress to put on, when the time came to meet her Daddy? She could clothe herself in her tatters well enough for conversations with ducks or kingfishers, who, though beautifully dressed themselves, had not much idea of what was proper for a human child. But she thought her father would be ashamed to take her into the village like that.

At last she told her difficulty to good Madam Pen, the mother swan.

Madam Pen considered.

"It seems to me so odd, and so unfortunate," she said, "that you human children cannot grow your own clothes, as mine do. I suppose you can't help it; but I'm

She told her difficulty to good Madam Pen.

sure I don't know what to advise. I'll ask my son—he'll think of something."

She swam away, to where the Lord of the River was enjoying a meal of water-weed, and Susan saw the two swans in consultation. Soon Madam Pen came back with a look of triumph.

"My son says it is quite easy," she announced. "Every Monday the baker's wife hangs out her washing in her backyard; and next time he sees one of the little girl's frocks there, he will fly up, remove the pegs, and bring the frock to you. The child is just your size. Now, isn't that a clever plan? Isn't it just what you want?"

But Susan was quite distressed.

"Oh, please, Madam Pen," she said. "It is ever so kind of him, but he mustn't do that! That would be stealing!"

This was a new idea to Madam Pen. It was natural for her to be brave and patient and kind, and wise in her own affairs; but she never worried her head about right and wrong, as humans have to do. Susan had to explain what is meant by stealing.

When this was clear to the swan, she swam off again to tell her son. "No doubt the human child is right," she said. "Just think how I should feel if some strange bird came and plucked the down off a cygnet of mine, to line her own nest!"

But the Lord of the River was loth to give up his plan.

"The baker's child has many frocks; it would not hurt her to lose one."

"No, my son," replied Madam Pen; "right is right and wrong is wrong. Susan explained it all to me. Maybe, before her father comes, we may find a frock for her somewhere, or the wind may blow one into the river; if not, she must be content without."

So the Lord of the River allowed his mother to persuade him. No more was said, and Susan thought the swans had forgotten the matter. But the son kept his little black eyes open on windy washing days, lest by good luck a frock should come blowing through the air from the village clothes-lines.

CHAPTER 4
THE SEAGULL MESSENGER

Now the mornings began to be misty, and the nights cold for Susan, who had no covering but her little old shawl.

Autumn had come, and with it the seagulls. They flew up the river and joined the mallards and coot on the backwater at night; during the daytime they followed the plough over the brown fields.

There were so many of them, that Susan felt anxious.

"They promised to look out for my Daddy's ship, but they have all come away from the sea," she said to the Lord of the River one day.

"There are plenty there yet," he replied. "They never leave the coast without sentries; they will keep their word, depend upon it."

It was but a few days after this, that a big herring-gull came flying at full speed from the sea, crying "News! News!"

Susan and the swans gathered eagerly to hear.

He told how he had been keeping watch on the cliffs that morning early, when he saw a sail on the horizon. He flew out to see what ship it belonged to, and found her to be a merchant vessel making for port, slowly, for the wind was against her.

The gull had perched on the rigging and listened to the talk of the sailors, as they spoke of their homes and their wives and children. One of them said: "My Sue will be a big girl by now. I'm going straight off to her, when we've landed the cargo." This sailor, said the gull, was a tall man with thick grey hair and dark eyes. There might be other sailors with daughters called Sue; but the gull felt sure he was the right one.

"Yes, my Daddy has thick grey hair and dark eyes. Did he speak of Rushiebanks?" asked Susan.

"No, the sailors had no more talk then. So I flew straightway to tell you. The ship should be in port tonight; or maybe not till to-morrow. I shall have some lunch, and then go back, ready to bring you news again."

Susan could hardly believe that her Daddy was so near. She wanted to dance and shout and sing, but the swans said she must be quiet and good a little while longer.

If only she had a dress to put on! She began to think

The seagull messenger.

how she could tidy herself without one.

The Lord of the River was thinking of something else.

"I am going to see for myself that this is the right man," he said, suddenly; and he spread his wings and rose in the air. With his long neck stretched out, he went flying steadily away towards the sea.

CHAPTER 5
A WONDERFUL DRESS

In the lovely sunset light the vessel lay at anchor outside the harbour. The wind had dropped, and the tide was running out; the ship could not enter until the morning. The cargo was all ready to be unloaded next day, and now the sailors had some leisure. A group of them were leaning over the side, watching a large swan who had come flying from the land, and was now swimming slowly round the ship, looking up at the men.

"It's queer for a swan to come out to sea. What does he want, I wonder?" said one of them.

"I threw him a bit of bread," said another, "but that wasn't what he wanted."

Another sailor joined the group, a tall man with thick grey hair and dark eyes.

"Hullo, John Swan!" he called; "have you come all the way from Rushiebanks to welcome me home? If you have, tell my little Susan I'm coming!"

The Swan raised himself to his full height, and flapped his great wings. The men laughed.

"Looks as though he understood you, Jim!"

Then they turned to the sorting and packing of the treasures they were taking home.

The grey-haired man shook out a beautifully embroidered garment which he had brought on deck; it was creased from having lain folded in his locker for many months.

"What's that, Jim? My word, it looks like a present for a princess!" said one of his mates.

"It *was* made for a princess," replied the Sailor. "So I was told by the woman who sold it to me. The queen of that land, it seems, is a dame who takes a different whimsy every day; and though she had ordered this dress for her daughter, when it was finished it didn't please her. So the poor woman, who had spent months of work on it, took it to market, to get what she could for it. I gave a good price, more than I ought to have spared, maybe, but I was sorry for the poor body. It is for my little girl. She was a tiny thing when I left her, but I reckon she will be about the size for this by now. I'm going to hang it up, to air it, and take the creases out."

He hung it over a rail, and stood admiring it. "She should look bonny in it!" he said.

And indeed it was a wonderful sight, as the setting sun lit up its glowing colours. Around the hem was embroidered a border of leaves and flowers of every lovely hue. All over the dress, butterflies and little birds and falling blossoms were worked with delicate skill; except where, on the breast, was a great golden sun, with long rays that went glinting down between the birds and flowers. At the neck and wrists, on a narrow edging of deep blue, were tiny silver stars.

The oldest sailor, a little wrinkled man, looked closely at the dress.

"That's fairy stitchery," he said. "You mark my words, Jim, it will bring you luck. She was a fairy body, and no mortal woman, who sold you this."

Suddenly, as he spoke, there was a loud swish, swish of wings. The Swan had risen from the sea, and was circling above the ship. At the same moment, a breeze sprang up, caught the wonderful dress, and

The swan seized it and bore it away.

wafted it into the air. The men sprang after it, but the Swan was quicker; he swooped down, seized it, and bore it away.

What could a swan want with such a thing? Yet there he went, as though bent on urgent business, flying shorewards with his fluttering prize.

He grew smaller and smaller in the distance, and the Sailor could only stand gazing helplessly. Then he turned with a sigh to his bundle.

"There are some other little things—slippers, and beads, and what-not; but she *would* have looked bonny in the dress."

CHAPTER 6
TRAVELLER'S JOY

Not the next day, but the day after, sunset time had come again. Seagull messengers had been busy, and now Susan knew that her father was near.

All day she had waited in a little thicket of willows and alders, on the river bank, where the wild clematis, covered with its fluffy "Old Man's Beard" made a secret arbour for her to hide in.

The Lord of the River kept watch near by, and the blackbirds had promised to warn her of any prying person who might invade the thicket. No one came; and the hours, as they passed, were not dull—she had so much to think of, and she had her dress to look at.

Early, before anyone was about, she had swum there (she was far too big, now, for the Lord of the River to carry her) and it was there that he had given her the dress. He had put it in a hollow tree for safety, and had guarded it these two nights.

He would not say where it came from; and Susan was so charmed that she took it without question. After all, he was a wonderful bird, so why should he not give a wonderful gift?

She was all ready; her old shawl, tied up by the corners, and full of something soft and light, lay beside her. She had said good-bye, the day before, to her shy friends in the backwater; but not to the swans, for they were all near, gathered in a group with their eyes on the bank.

A traveller, tramping towards Rushiebanks, saw and wondered at them; also at the seagulls who seemed to be going with him, dashing ahead every now and then, crying and calling, then returning and wheeling around him.

"What's the excitement?" he asked them. "If you think there's fish in my bundle, you're mistaken!"

Thinking of his bundle, he sighed. He had hoped to bring back a bag full of gold; and so he had, but it was a very small one. He blamed himself for having wasted so much on a frock for his little girl; a foolishly splendid frock, now, alas, lost beyond recall. Then once more his thoughts were busy about his Sue.

Would she be looking out of her little window for him, or be wandering on the path where he had left her? Or would she have grown into a big girl with other

She stood in the path, shading her eyes from the setting sun.

friends and pleasures, and have forgotten all about her old Dad?

The Sailor's eyes roved from the familiar country-side to the fluffy Old Man's Beard that hung on the bushes by his path.

"That's called Traveller's Joy, when it is in flower," he said to himself; "will there be traveller's joy for me, I wonder?" He began to hum a song he used to know:

"Traveller, traveller, tramping home
From foreign places beyond the foam——"

and was ending, *"Luck be with you, and Traveller's Joy!"* when, from a little thicket in front of him, a girl ran out. She stood in the path, shading her eyes from the setting sun. Her hair was bound with a wreath of Old Man's Beard; and the warm light that shone full on her rosy face and bare brown hands and feet, shone too on her dress, and showed all its marvel of fairy colours and gold-embroidered sun.

The next moment she darted forward, and with a glad cry she was in her father's arms.

The seagulls ceased their screaming, and the swans—all but one—glided silently away.

There was so much to tell of the past, and plan for the future, that when the stars came out Susan and her father were still lingering on the river bank.

The birds had told her that other people were living

in their old cottage, so the Sailor said they would spend that night at the inn.

"Come," he said at last, "it is time for supper and bed," but as they turned to go, she gave a last look at the river, and saw her faithful friend waiting near, on the dark water.

"Oh, Daddy," she said, "here is the Lord of the Rushie River! We never said good night to him!"

The Sailor took off his cap.

"My Lord," he said, "I am a plain man, and John Swan was the name I gave you when we met before, not knowing your title. But whatever I call you, I thank you, sir, with all my heart, for your care of my little girl."

Well satisfied, the Lord of the River bowed his head, then sailed majestically home.

CHAPTER 7
THE END OF THE STORY

Great was the Sailor's wrath against Dame Dinnage. He wanted a search made for her, to bring her to justice; but as Susan could not tell the name of the city where she had been hidden, there seemed little chance of success. And Susan begged her father to do nothing, for she hoped never to see or hear of the Dame any more.

He did not go to sea again.

Luckily for him, at that very time the old ferryman gave up his job and came to live in the village, so the Sailor stepped into his shoes. The little cottage by the ferry, a mile down the Rushie, just suited him and Susan. The Lord of the River visited her every day; and when spring came, and he took a wife, they chose a spot within sight of the ferry for their nest. It was a proud day when first he brought a trail of fluffy cygnets with him to show Susan.

Each night, when she went to bed, she laid her head

on a little pillow made out of the lovely soft swans'-down and moulted feathers which she had brought away as a keepsake from her friends.

She wore her gorgeous dress on summer Sundays, and on holidays when there was dancing on the green; and strange to say, it was never out-grown, but seemed to grow with her. It must indeed have been a fairy dress.

She still loved to swim in the river, and soon learned to take a turn with the ferry boat. Thus the time went by; until one evening, as she and her father sat by the fire, there came a tap on the door, and who should be there but Dame Dinnage!

Thanks to John Swan.

Such a changed Dame Dinnage! Susan could not be afraid of her now, for she was weeping and trembling, and had brought back all the money she had stolen.

She had not had a moment's pleasure out of her hoarded wealth. She had lived in fear of being found out, and could not rest for wondering what had become of Susan. At last she journeyed back to Rushiebanks; and great was her relief to find, on inquiry, that the Sailor had returned, Susan was safe, and it was not too late to make amends for her wickedness.

The kind-hearted Ferryman was so sorry for her, that he would not keep the money, but, instead, bought a tiny cottage for the Dame.

This was undeserved and unexpected kindness! She could not do enough to show her gratitude. She would scrub, cook, or sew for the Ferryman and Susan, and bring presents of home-baked cakes, honey from her hive, or pears from her tree. In time she became feeble, and then, the bad old days forgotten, Susan went to help *her*.

Jim the Ferryman never tired of telling how all his happiness was due to John Swan, the Lord of the Rushie River; and John Swan, looking on at all these things with his wise little eyes, was proud of his share in the story.